PROUST

A COLLECTION OF CRITICAL ESSAYS

Edited by
René Girard

GREENWOOD PRESS, PUBLISHERS
WESTPORT, CONNECTICUT

Library of Congress Cataloging in Publication D. a

Girard, René, 1923-   ed.
Proust.

Reprint of the 1962 ed. published by Prentice-Hall,
Engelwood Cliffs, N. J.; which was issued in series:
Twentieth century views.
    Bibliography: p.
    1. Proust, Marcel, 1871-1922--Criticism and interpretation--Addresses, essays, lectures.
[PQ2631.R63Z6135 1977]   843'.9'12   77-9577
ISBN 0-8371-9710-4

© 1962

BY PRENTICE-HALL, INC.

All rights reserved. No part of this book may be reproduced in any form, by mimeograph or any other means, without permission in writing from the publishers.

Originally published in 1962 by Prentice-Hall, Inc., Englewood Cliffs, N.J.

Reprinted with the permission of Prentice-Hall, Inc.

Reprinted in 1977 by Greenwood Press, Inc.

Library of Congress catalog card number   77-9577

ISBN 0-8371-9710-4

Printed in the United States of America

Table of Contents

INTRODUCTION—*René Girard*	1
CREATIVE AGONY—*Robert Vigneron*	13
THE LEGACY OF PROUST—*Henri Peyre*	28
ANALYTIC TRADITION—*Jacques Rivière*	42
FACES OF PROUST—*Albert Thibaudet*	47
CRITICISM AND CREATION—*Walter A. Strauss*	53
THE INHUMAN WORLD OF PLEASURE—*Germaine Brée*	69
IMAGES AS INSTRUMENTS—*Georges Cattaui*	88
RELIGIOUS IMAGERY—*Elliott Coleman*	92
INTUITION AND PHILOLOGY—*Leo Spitzer*	97
ARCHITECTURE OF TIME: DIALECTICS AND STRUCTURE—*Richard Macksey*	104
PROUST, BERGSON AND OTHER PHILOSOPHERS—*Robert Champigny*	122
THE PROFUNDITY OF PROUST—*Charles Du Bos*	132
IN SEARCH OF THE SELF—*Ramon Fernandez*	136
PROUST AND HUMAN TIME—*Georges Poulet*	150
TO THE READER—*Marcel Proust*	179
Chronology of Important Dates	181
Notes on the Editor and Contributors	183
Bibliography	185

Introduction

by René Girard

Marcel Proust was born in 1871 of a Catholic father and a Jewish mother into a family of solid Parisian bourgeoisie. He was a gifted but sickly and neurotic child who, from an early age, displayed marked homosexual tendencies. After brilliant but desultory studies at a Paris lycée and at the university, the young man began to circulate in the intellectual and artistic upper class; he published a few minor essays, a thin volume of rather "decadent" prose, and some translations of John Ruskin. He also frequented assiduously certain salons of the old and aristocratic Faubourg Saint Germain. During that period, Proust doubtless felt and behaved like some of the bourgeois snobs he later created in *Remembrance of Things Past*. On the death of his mother in 1905, however, Proust literally renounced the world and dedicated the rest of his life to the creation of what is, perhaps, the masterpiece of French literature in the twentieth century. After more than a dozen years of continuous and often heroic labor pursued under the most deplorable conditions of health, Marcel Proust died at the task, leaving the last uncorrected volumes of his novel to be published posthumously, his literary fame already assured not only in France but in the entire world.

Like Montaigne, and more than Montaigne perhaps, Proust could have boasted that he, himself, was the substance of his book. This does not mean that Marcel Proust and Marcel, the hero and narrator of *Remembrance of Things Past*, are identical in the vulgar empirical sense, but that from a higher and more spiritual viewpoint, they are one. The book made the author no less than the author the book. The earlier works, however brilliant they may appear, are nothing but preparatory exercises and rejected first drafts of the great masterpiece. Any attempt to understand Marcel Proust, the man and his work, must therefore begin, as it must end, with *Remembrance of Things Past*.

In the beginning is Combray, a sleepy little provincial town of the Ile de France where Marcel (the narrator) spends the happiest moments of his childhood, at the home of his paternal grandparents. Combray is a world of tradition and ritual, rigidly caught in a complex middle class hierarchy, reminiscent of a latter-day feudal order. The village, still surrounded by the remnants of a perfectly circular medieval wall, lives apart from the rest of the world, not in time but in eternity, like a haven of poetry and joy which no evil can touch.

Combray is threatened, however, like every other paradise of childhood innocence. The dark forces of *snobisme* and erotic passion are seeking to destroy it. *Snobisme* makes its first appearance with Legrandin, a friend of Marcel's family who succumbs to a morbid fascination for the local gentry; sexual desire is introduced by Mlle Vinteuil, whose abnormal relationship with a woman friend turns the life of her father, the great musician Vinteuil, into a horrible martyrdom. From this point on, with the narrator himself or, exceptionally, with Swann, a wealthy bourgeois socialite, at the center of the stage, the great novel drifts further and further away from the blissful peace of the first Edenic descriptions. As we plunge deeper into the world of social ambition and sexual desire, a spirit of futility pervades. Marcel never begins the novel he plans to write. Eternity gives way to the hostile and corrosive time which Robert Champigny describes in his remarkable essay. The spirit of Combray seems utterly destroyed.

Throughout the novel, the desires—innocent as well as perverse—of Marcel and of the other characters are described in quasi-religious terms. Behind the coveted *something*, there is always a *someone* endowed with an almost supernatural prestige. Marcel yearns after a kind of mystical communion, with an individual, or with a group, dwelling, he believes, in a superior realm of existence and entirely separated from the vulgar herd. This *metaphysical* desire takes a different form in the various stages of the novel. Just as Combray huddles at the foot of its medieval church, so the first Marcel lives in the shadow of his parents, or of Swann, or of the great writer Bergotte, all of them towering figures whom the child imitates religiously in the hope of becoming one of them. Later on, through sexual desire and social ambition, Marcel again seeks *initiation* to a new and mysterious existence which he believes to be preferable to his own. Now, however, the benevolent gods of Combray have been replaced by malevolent ones—the smart hostesses who stubbornly refuse to send the passionately awaited invitation, the flighty boys and girls who inflict the torture of jealousy upon their admirers in inverse proportion to the pleasure they provide. Proust's metaphors, which he rightly saw were the most essential and original element of his art, reflect this change in the "religious" atmosphere of the novel. The images of Combray, usually borrowed from the Old Testament and medieval Christianity, express a vigorous but naïve faith. The world of *snobisme* and erotic passion, on the other hand, associates itself with black magic, with the bloody cults of fetishism, with such perversions of Christianity as witch-hunting and the Inquisition.

When the goal of initiation is reached, the awe-inspiring idol in-

Introduction

variably turns out to be as dull as anybody else and the divine flavor evaporates. We do not have to ask why possession kills such a desire, for the answer is obvious enough. Nothing human can satisfy it. The real question is harder to answer. Why is Proustian desire of this sort— why, that is, is it metaphysical? The answer lies in the psychology of man, as Proust understands it.

A child's veneration for his parents is intelligible enough. What surprises us is the adult's veneration for other adults, in which something infantile evidently remains. This is precisely what is suggested by an important scene at the very beginning of the novel. When Marcel goes to bed at Combray, he cannot go to sleep unless his mother comes up to his room and kisses him good night. The parents try not to accede to this demand because their child is nervous and sickly; he must build his "will power" or he will never become a "real" man.

One particular night, however, Marcel is so unhappy that he breaks the sacred family law and comes downstairs, begging for a last kiss. Instead of meting out the expected punishment, his father shrugs his shoulders and tells the mother to spend the whole night with her frightened little boy. Marcel is relieved, but he knows that something irreparable has happened. By transgressing the law they themselves have laid down, the parents have stooped to the level of the child and turned his weakness into their own. Marcel has lost faith in the gods of Combray. But this is no normal process of growing up, nor is it the end of the search for salvation through magical means. The child has to resort to other gods who will maintain, in their dealings with him, the unyielding domination which, up to that fateful night, was characteristic of his parents. Marcel's entire emotional life will become a *repetition* of the sleepless nights of Combray.

Included, of course, in this parental Götterdämmerung is the Law itself: bourgeois respectability, associated, in Marcel's eyes, with the world of the family. Once this has fallen, immorality and idleness must be worshipped in secret. The illusion of the *sacred* will be present whenever Marcel feels systematically excluded from pleasures which the family would consider forbidden. Here is a puritanism in reverse which is open, no doubt, to a psychoanalytical interpretation, but we must beware of considering Marcel a truly separate psychological entity. We have isolated him here from his fictional context in order to show that he systematically distorts reality. Let us now put him back into his context and it will become clear that reality, in the form of the snobs, contributes to provoke this distortion.

The snobs act as if the salon were not simply a place where people like to congregate for the purpose of gossiping and absorbing petits fours, but a sacred little world, entirely separated from the big one and infinitely more desirable. In this view, the salon is a temple of esoteric mysteries of which the snobs constitute the initiates, mysteries which would be diluted and lost if they were imparted to the unworthy. The rejected outsider is thus made to feel a victim of some earthly and mundane damnation. No wonder that these exclusive little cliques look to Marcel, prone as he is to metaphysical desire, like the *hortus conclusus*, the enclosed garden of mystical literature. He may himself be ill, but the snobs around him seem diabolically intent upon making his illness worse. Worse because social ascent in *Remembrance of Things Past* entails spiritual and physical degradation. Urged on by his desire and constantly turned toward a sterile future, the narrator is rendered incapable of real action or contemplation. Recollections from his happy childhood have become stilted and drily factual.

One day, however, the original Combray comes back through a curious phenomenon of *affective memory*. After a long and dreary day spent in seeking his so-called pleasures, the narrator comes home, and his mother serves him a cup of tea and one of those cakes which the French call *madeleine*. Marcel wearily dips the cake into the tea and, as the soaked crumbs touch his tongue, he feels miraculously delivered from his wretchedness. His bed-ridden aunt used to offer him tea and *madeleine* in the days of Combray. The renewed sensory impression provides a material bridge between the past and the present; the world of Combray springs back to life in all its original freshness.

The *madeleine* resurrects the serene and joyful Combray, huddled about its beautiful gothic church and protected from outer darkness by its perfectly circular wall. In retrospect, this Combray appears closer to the enchanted garden Marcel seeks than to all the experiences that follow. The salons are to Combray what a caricature is to the original. Combray, like the salons, is a world of ritual, but less self-consciously and less rigidly so; Combray is jealous of its identity but not to the point where outsiders become systematically excluded. Between Combray and the rest of the world, there may be perpetual misunderstanding but there is no open conflict as in the salons. Yet there is enough likeness between the two worlds to mislead an inexperienced observer like Marcel into thinking that the identity possessed by Combray must be possessed more abundantly by the salons. Their claim to being the "enchanted garden" appears a more substantial one.

This is a mistaken conclusion. Behind the tantalizing *noli me tangere* of the snobs, there is actually nothing but anxiety and restlessness. Mme Verdurin and her friends mimic a passionate attachment to their own "little clan" but, in reality, they are fascinated by the haughty Guermanteses, whom they profess to despise. All that unites the snobs of one salon is envy of another salon from which they feel excluded and which, in consequence, becomes the sole object of their desire. Far from being independent, the salons can be understood only in this "dialectical" relationship, whereas Combray is intelligible of and by itself. That is why there are many salons but only one Combray.

Introduction

Lured by the false promise of the salons, the narrator unknowingly turns his back on his true goal, the enchanted garden. A snob cannot find rest, even at the "top" of society, since there is always a place where he will feel unwanted and which he will therefore desire. The moment society crouches at his feet, the Proustian snob loses interest and turns elsewhere, even toward the underworld, like the baron de Charlus seeking his pleasure in the gutter. Consequently, whenever the snob moves forward, the enchanted garden recedes. In a world of insiders, everyone imagines himself an outsider. But since no one admits this truth, everyone becomes necessarily both deceiver and dupe, victim and torturer, excluding every other on the ground that he himself feels excluded. There is an element of imitative magic in this behavior and also a panic fear that one's own state of deprivation is going to be perceived, and the narrator undergoes it no less than the other characters in the novel: he learns to hide his true feelings; he learns to wear a mask of self-satisfaction and contempt.

Why should everyone feel individually guilty about a feeling of inadequacy which is, in reality, universal? To answer this question, we must go back to Combray. Marcel has rejected the bourgeois morality of his parents, except for one essential tenet which he is unable to question: he still believes that he must be a "real" man, self-reliant, independent, and strong. But what does it mean to be a "real" man in a positivistic world from which all things transcending the human have been banished? It means, in the last resort, that humanity must assume the attributes of divinity. This consequence of "God's death," seen clearly only by Nietzsche and Dostoevski before Proust's time is perhaps obscurely at work among those characters in the novel who are constantly seeking mystical union with a pseudo-divinity and must therefore be, at least subconsciously, committed to self divinization.

According to Nietzsche, God's death, by propelling human pride to new heights, will lead man to surpass himself and become a superman. Dostoevski is of a different mind. Man is not a god, Dostoevski asserts, and the individual man's inner voice will always tell him this truth. But this existentially irrefutable truth is powerless against the unanimous voice of a Promethean society, always urging its members to arrogate the functions of the divine. The result, for the individual, will be inescapable frustration. "Divinity" becomes what one knows one does not have, but what one must assume *les autres* do have. Each would-be superman will believe himself the only limited being in a society of demi-gods, and in his delusion will seek salvation from his divinized but envied fellowmen, with tragic and grotesque consequences for all concerned.

Proust is not prepared to take a direct part in this philosophical debate, possibly because, for him, God is simply too dead. But his snobs, like the Dostoevskian characters, would feel less inadequate if they were not so proud, if they did not expect the impossible from themselves. And the religious imagery of *Remembrance of Things Past* tells a story which is not fundamentally different from Dostoevski's own, tells it all the more objectively and strikingly because Proust does not perceive the metaphysical or even certain of the ethical implications of his vision, because he never abandons the level of "psychological" analysis. His shortcomings in the realm of existence, so shrewdly detected by Ramon Fernandez, here contribute to the value of his work.

For Proust as for Dostoevski, transcendence, which, in the past, separated the worshipper from the worshipped, now separates individuals from each other and forces them to live their relationships at the level of a corrupted religiosity. Everyone is led by amour-propre, Proust writes —by a self-centered love that leads *outward*, turning us into the slaves and imitators of others. Crushed under the weight of our Promethean pride, amour-propre has become like a centrifugal planisphere. As this centrifugal pride lures the narrator with the fallacious promises of *snobisme* and sexual passion, it takes him further and further away from Combray.

One may, of course, find moments of relief from this diabolical mechanism, ecstatic moments of peace provided by the contemplation of beautiful landscapes or by the great works of artists such as Bergotte the writer, Vinteuil the musician, Elstir the painter. But they cannot shut out actuality for long.

The grandmother, who has accompanied the narrator like a luminous angel of love and innocence during the years of his youth, falls ill and dies a horrible death. Then Bergotte dies. Then Albertine is killed in a riding accident after breaking away from the apartment where the morbidly jealous Marcel has held her a virtual prisoner. This last catastrophe marks the beginning of the worst period in the narrator's life. The sting of desire is gone, but instead of peace, apathy replaces it; the narrator resigns himself to a life of spiritual emptiness and ennui. Art itself has lost its power. Marcel gives up his long cherished plans to "reform his life" and become a great artist.

After a long period of illness, and for want of a better purpose, Marcel accepts an invitation from the Guermantesses. Upon his arrival, he again experiences a sudden and extraordinary blossoming of affective memory. The uneven cobblestones of the Guermanteses' courtyard take him back to a certain piazza in Venice; a little later, in an antechamber, the glossy surface of a starched napkin reminds him of his life in Balbec, a Channel resort where he had met Albertine; still later, he finds his whole childhood enclosed in the pages of a novel by Georges Sand, the same one which his grandmother had given him, many years before.

Once again, the present and the past are bridged; time is replaced by a sensation of eternal youthfulness, in violent contrast to the horrible spectacle of degeneration and decay offered by the guests of the Guermanteses, some of whom have aged so that Marcel hardly recognizes them. Marcel knows that his own body is going to die, but this does not trouble him, for his spirit has just been resurrected in memory. And this new resurrection, unlike the first one, is permanent and fruitful: it will be the foundation of the great work of art which Marcel had finally despaired of writing.

All directions are henceforward reversed in the existence of Marcel, all plans inverted: the quest for the "enchanted garden" has shifted from the outer to the inner world, from the future to the past, from dispersion to unity, from desire to detachment, from possession to contemplation, from disintegration to aesthetic creation. The outward and downward movement of pride is succeeded, as Richard Macksey points out, by an inward and upward movement leading back to Combray, back to the true center of the personality. Affective memory is only one aspect of a spiritual conversion which will not fail to provide the energy needed for the great work of art. The reader cannot doubt that the promise has been fulfilled this time, because the novel which is about to be written is also the one which is coming to a close.

II

Was *Remembrance of Things Past* born of a revelation, identical, or similar at least, to the one just described, which forms the subject of the last volume? Critics have traditionally said that it was, but this viewpoint has been weakened in recent years by the publication of unfinished manuscripts dating back to a period which, in the novel, is depicted as one of relative inactivity. Proust published very little between the dilettantish *Pleasures and Regrets* and *Remembrance of Things Past*, but we know, now, that these years were not spent in idleness. The three-volume *Jean Santeuil*—a somewhat heterogeneous collection of fictional texts in various stages of completion—has convinced several critics that *The Past Recaptured* owes little to the actual creative experience of Marcel Proust. On the other hand, although it is true that Marcel Proust had had some experience with the art of the novel when he finally plunged into *Remembrance of Things Past,* this fact does not prove that *The Past Recaptured* is pure invention. A comparison between the recently published manuscripts and the finished novel suggests that a real break did occur in the aesthetic life of Marcel Proust and that the event was, on the whole, faithfully recorded in *The Past Recaptured.*

In *Jean Santeuil,* we recognize the setting, as well as some of the characters of *Remembrance of Things Past,* but the style and spirit are different. Many brilliant pages of descriptive prose remind us of the good writers of the period, but the religious metaphors, so constant a feature in the later novel, are few. Love is present, but it is rosy and sentimental. As for *snobisme,* it is only an ugly fault that Jean Santeuil, the hero, condemns severely, even though he, a bourgeois, frequents the most aristocratic salons. Pursued by snobbish enemies, Jean Santeuil is always rescued at the last minute by protectors as well born as they are powerful; he therefore rises like a bright new star in the glittering firmament of society.

One need not be a great psychologist to suspect that the Cinderella outlook of certain of these chapters reflects the irrational hopes and fears of a *snobisme* of which Proust had not yet divested himself. The moral indignation of the Proustian hero is no proof to the contrary, for moral indignation may simply be one snob's way of expressing his resentment against other snobs who happen to stand in his way, rather than a true insight into the nature of *snobisme*. All the barriers of society come crashing down at the feet of Jean Santeuil, simply because he is a young man of remarkable talent and infinite charm, appreciated at his just value by almost equally talented and charming aristocrats. *Snobisme* thus plays a lesser role in *Jean Santeuil* than in *Remembrance of Things Past* and is more vigorously condemned. On this ground, some observers have concluded that it is a "healthier" novel, more "rational" in its outlook on people and society. They also note that its world is "closer to ours." This last remark may well be true—but Jean Santeuil's apparent health and rationality stem from Proust's failure to *perceive* the irrational and magical elements of his own approach to reality. *Snobisme* becomes universal in *Remembrance of Things Past* not because Proust is still obsessed with society but, on the contrary, because he has seen that it is a truly universal disease, and he can now assimilate, at least metaphorically, all its manifestations into the particular phase of it with which he is personally best acquainted.

Jean Santeuil is an ideal figure happily frolicking in the "enchanted garden" of Proustian metaphysical desire. This does not mean that Proust himself had reached his mystical goal at the time he wrote the novel, but only that he was still identifying it with the salons, to which Jean Santeuil has gained unobstructed access. Santeuil is therefore not so much a faithful image of what Proust really felt, as of what he hoped he would feel following frequentation of the salons and imitation of his current idols. The society Santeuil moves in—very different from that in *Remembrance of Things Past*—is divided in two halves: the first, which belongs to the hero and his aristocratic friends, is good, beautiful, and luminous; the second, which belongs to his enemies, is dark, ugly, sinister. This Manichean division means that introspection and observation are working separately, in the two separate halves of the world, at the expense of depth, color, and life. The hero's half is characterized by an empty and insipid perfection; the "enemy's" side by shadowy figures and grimacing caricatures.

How were the two halves of the Manichean world finally reconciled? This process can be followed rather closely thanks to some essays written

Introduction

by Proust just before *Remembrance of Things Past* and published in 1954 under the title *Contre Sainte-Beuve* (translated by Sylvia Townsend Warner under the title *On Art and Literature*, Meridian, 1958). In a chapter entitled "Conclusion," Proust expresses his conviction that he will never be a great writer. Then he notes that, at long intervals, he perceives certain new and mysterious bonds between people, things, or widely separated moments of his life, all of which previously had appeared unrelated. Perception of such synthesis is intensely pleasurable and is accompanied by a vivid impression of truth, but it shatters whatever confidence the writer had ever had in his literary talent.

In *Remembrance of Things Past* this same somber mood is attributed to Marcel during the period immediately preceding the aesthetic illumination. "Conclusion" must be read from the viewpoint of the yet to be written *Past Recaptured;* it is really a very early draft of this volume, although conceived at a much earlier stage of the experience, at a time when the Proustian "dark night of the soul" was still very dark indeed. But since it is more directly autobiographical, this "conclusion" reveals the purely literary aspects of the "dark night," which are omitted from *The Past Recaptured;* it shows us the two halves of *Jean Santeuil*'s Manichean world gradually coming together.

Professor Vigneron has shown that this literary drama is an echo of the real tragedy which Marcel Proust was living at that time. His mother was dead, and he thought that his conduct had been responsible for this tragic event. He felt an irrepressible urge to confess his guilt, in letters to his friends and even in the pages of *Figaro*. His despair was so intense that it frightened his friends. His already failing health being further impaired, Proust gave up his social life and retired to a cork-lined bedroom in his apartment on the Boulevard Haussmann, where much of *Remembrance of Things Past* was written. In *The Past Recaptured*, Proust insists that a great vision must be born in suffering. This and similar statements have been too much overlooked by those who feel that the effects of suffering on creative writing cannot be determined empirically. Guilt feelings, especially, do not enjoy a good reputation in our contemporary world. When they are not felt to be downright contemptible, they are viewed as symptoms of mental disturbance. But Proust felt differently; he was obsessed at the time with the structure of *Crime and Punishment,* which he recognized not only in all the novels of Dostoevski, and in those of Flaubert, but in *Don Quixote* as well. And Proust may well be right, in his own case as in that of these other novelists. If it is true that the aesthetically fatal division of the fictional world, as presented in *Jean Santeuil,* is a product of what we call metaphysical desire; and if it is true that metaphysical desire is a product of pride, we may have to conclude that whatever injures pride, whether it be guilt, suffering, or remorse, constitutes an important factor in the spiritual metamorphosis which turns a superficial writer into a great one. The two worlds of *Jean Santeuil* cannot come together unless Marcel Proust recognizes *himself* among the snobs. This is the price which must be paid for the alliance between introspection and observation. The experience is both a "sickness unto death" and a resurrection, for it is both the end of metaphysical questing and the end of metaphysical enslavement. The creator, at least temporarily free from an absorbing and sterile future, can turn back toward the past and breathe the flavor of the sacred in past desires, without the torture of actual yearning, and he can cast a lucid glance upon the errors and absurdities of this past. As Jacques Rivière perceived, the lyricism of the novel is inseparable from its psychological truth. *Jean Santeuil* and *Remembrance of Things Past* illustrate Simone Weil's distinction between those works of art which remain second rate, however brilliant they may be, because they do nothing but "enrich" their author's personality, and true masterpieces, which originate from an impoverishment, a mutilation of the unauthentic self.

The novelist's handwriting suggests that a sharp break occurred, in his life, just before *Remembrance of Things Past*. The change is so striking that even a casual glance can determine whether a page was written before or after the fateful period. All the available evidence confirms, therefore, the truthfulness of *The Past Recaptured*. The only departure from autobiographical truth is an apparent one—namely, the failure to mention previous contacts with the art of the novel. Proust modifies the letter of his experience in order to reveal the spirit. The metamorphosis of the writer had to be presented as a solemn entrance into literature, in order to acquire symbolic weight. It would be quite wrong to imagine a conflict between this aesthetic requirement and the autobiographical dimension of the novel. The novel uncovers a spiritual autobiography which is both more beautiful and more true than the literal one.

It is a fact that *The Past Recaptured* was entirely conceived, if not entirely written, before any other portion of the novel. This conclusion is, therefore, both an end and a beginning. If the novel is a "cathedral"—as Proust himself suggested—*The Past Recaptured* is the choir toward which all architectural lines converge and from which they all originate. Each event differs in meaning according to which "end" of the novel it is observed from. There are always two perspectives which must be brought together. Ideally, therefore, the novel should be read twice, with such a double reading as Charles S. Singleton has recommended for the *Divine Comedy*, which is also both the record and the fruit of a spiritual metamorphosis. In the first reading, we become acquainted with the progress of the hero; in the second, we fully appreciate for the first time, the viewpoint of the artist born from *The Past Recaptured*. But no novelist can expect so much attention from his readers. It is imperative, therefore, that the two perspectives be introduced and

Introduction

distinguished from the start. And yet it is impossible to reverse the chronological order. Proust solved the difficulty by extracting a small fragment of his conclusion and grafting it to the beginning of the novel; the scene of the *madeleine*. This scene, as we first meet it, seems to fall from heaven and to return to it, for it has no immediate consequences for the narrator's existence. It provides an image of a reality that is in the past from the viewpoint of the author, a promise of a reality that is yet to come from the viewpoint of the narrator. The *madeleine*, thus, is the *Annunciation* of *The Past Recaptured*. The novel has, indeed, the structure of a cathedral since, like a cathedral, it has the structure of a gospel.

The Proustian experience is often labeled Platonic because memory plays a great role in it and because the word *idea* is used repeatedly in *The Past Recaptured*. Platonism, however, evokes the notion of a serene and unbroken ascent toward the Ideal, bearing little resemblance to what happens in *Remembrance of Things Past*. Almost to the end, the dynamic element of the novel is amour-propre, which leads outward and downward from the relatively high starting point of Combray. This direction is reversed only in extremis, and the change cannot be logically explained. All we can say—and this remains an impression rather than a demonstrable fact—is that the downward movement had to be pursued in extremis before it could mysteriously reverse itself. Similarly, Dante went down to the bottom of his Inferno and, as he kept descending upon Satan's own body without ever turning around, suddenly found himself climbing toward Purgatory and Paradise.

The only possible analogy for the Proustian experience has been noted by Georges Poulet, and it is that of Christian grace. Critics like Georges Cattaui and Elliott Coleman have underlined the Christian aspects of *Remembrance of Things Past*. Others have protested, pointing out that Proust never made any effort to live according to Christian morality and probably did not even believe in God. This biographical fact does not, however, alter the aesthetic one, which is simply that, although Proust was an agnostic, his masterpiece espouses the Christian structure of redemption more perfectly than the carefully planned efforts of many conscientious Christian artists. Though the Christian significance of *Remembrance of Things Past* remained metaphorical for him, he viewed this metaphor as his supreme aesthetic achievement. After the naïve biblical symbolism of Combray, after the infernal imagery of *Cities of the Plain*, comes a third dominant religious symbolism in *The Past Recaptured*, the Johannic and Apocalyptic symbolism of spiritual metamorphosis. *The Past Recaptured* is a second birth and a last judgment.

None of this should scandalize a believer, or an unbeliever for that matter, especially in an age when the search for analogies between the creative experience and the most exotic mythologies has become an accepted topic of research. Even if Christianity were a myth it would still be less exotic than most, and we cannot reject out-of-hand, therefore, the possibility of its being relevant to certain forms of aesthetic experience. Mary Magdalen sitting by the empty tomb, the Emmaus pilgrims walking away from Jerusalem, are at first unable to recognize Christ who is speaking to them. This evangelical theme of a divine presence unidentified and yet effective—unidentified, perhaps, because it is particularly effective—is a familiar one to Proust. He makes use of it in his novel, in a non-religious context, but with the usual metaphysical overtones.

The Christian form seems to be present, in Western literature, whenever the hero-creator is saved from an idolatrous world by a spiritual metamorphosis which makes him able to describe his former condition. The work records its own genesis in the form of a fall and redemption. For Proust, as for Dostoevski and Dante, the fall and the redemption are opposed, yet dialectically joined. But the opposition is less radical for Dostoevski than for Dante, and still less radical for Proust. The metaphysical significance is lost first, then the ethical; to Proust, finally, the revelation is primarily aesthetic but it remains as irrational as ever. Or perhaps it should be called super-rational because, far from bringing irrationality in its wake, this illumination provides the rationality and order which a truly great art demands. Irrational subjective elements are finally distinguished from objective reality. Literature is raised to a level where most romantic and modern antinomies lose their relevance. *Remembrance of Things Past* is both poetic and didactic, lyrical and psychological, aesthetically autonomous as well as existentially truthful. A humanist like Albert Thibaudet feels no less at ease in the Proustian novel than a Christian like Charles du Bos. Henri Peyre finds romanticism in its pages and Jacques Rivière invokes the classical tradition. Georges Poulet is right to call *Remembrance of Things Past* a *Summa,* because all types of experience are explicitly or implicitly present in it. This universality is the fruit not of a weak eclecticism but of an authentic synthesis in which beauty and truth, so often enemies in art of the nineteenth and twentieth centuries, are reconciled. In some of his late theoretical pronouncements, Proust, who was not an abstract thinker, may still talk the language of the symbolist and the subjectivist; he may still oppose *his* truth to the truth of his readers; but this false prudence evaporates in the great moments of insight. As the novelist descends deeper into himself, he also descends into the hearts of all men. He cannot doubt, then, that truth itself is one.

Creative Agony

by Robert Vigneron

In 1905, at thirty-four, Marcel Proust, whom his friends affectionately or contemptuously call "Little Marcel," is a singular and unsavory character.

The flesh, in him, is weak and tormented. The product of the crossing of two races, the Beauceron strain and the Jewish strain intermingle in him without blending, and he is constantly torn between conflicting heredities. The prisoner of a masculine body, he has the nerves, the appetites, and the reflexes of a woman, and it is in vain that he tries to speak and to act like a man. As a child, he suffered from a recurrent hay-fever, which now presents the symptoms of nervous asthma. His condition forces him to lead a cloistered life, which in turn aggravates his condition. He no longer goes out, save for unexpected social resurrections and furtive escapades: he lives in reverse, deprived of normal sexual activity, sleeping by day, staying up or working by night, alternately overdosing himself with stimulants and sedatives. His originally nervous and melancholy temperament has now turned to neurasthenia and hypochondria; his humor is capricious and despotic.

He knows himself thoroughly; but in that unbalanced machinery mind has no control over matter. The son and brother of physicians, he is aware of his slightest symptoms, he diagnoses his pathological condition accurately, and he foresees its evolution and its consequences. Trained in self-examination and in psychological analysis, he has an equally clear insight into his character: he recognizes the innate and acquired tendencies of his humor, and he has observed all the moral habits that resulted from them. Sensitivity, delicacy, generosity; but also touchiness, distrust, egoism, deviousness; physical courage in the field, but also in-

"Marcel Proust: Creative Agony," *Chicago Review*, Spring 1958, pp. 33-51. Copyright 1958 by Robert Vigneron. This paper is based on the author's own chronological classification of the correspondence of Marcel Proust. A more detailed version in French, including the supporting evidence, was published in *Modern Philology*, November 1941, pp. 159-95, and March 1945, pp. 212-30. All rights reserved by Robert Vigneron. No part of this essay may be reproduced in any form without permission in writing from the author. Reprinted with the gracious permission of the author.

tellectual indolence and moral cowardice; deep filial love, but also abnormal tendencies and through them desecration of the image of a mother to whom he bears a striking resemblance: there is no quality, no flaw, no vice in him of which he is not fully conscious. But this lucidity is of no avail to him; out of those heterogeneous traits, he does not select, in order to subordinate the others to them, the ones that could constitute a definite, coherent, and stable character. For, when he was still very young, he realized that he lacked the quality without which there can be no order, no stability, no reform, no progress: willpower. And he abandons himself, according to circumstances, to the shifts of a sickly humor and to the whims of a wavering and untamed character.

To substitute for that inner framework, he unfortunately lacks the rigid armour of a profession or a vocation, which compels the most undisciplined humor and the most unpredictable character to conform to a certain pattern of behaviour and to present to society a consistent and responsible individual. He is a gentleman of leisure, without a role and without a mission in the world; he is a bourgeois, descended from two solidly established families; and he feels that the goods of this earth should be his naturally, as his birthright. He would like to be a writer, but he is only an amateur: for years he has been cluttering up his desk-drawers with abortive essays and sketches; with an inadequate knowledge of English, he has been working on a translation and exegesis of Ruskin, one volume of which has finally been published, without much success; and he occasionally writes for the *Figaro* quaint chronicles of an effeminate and obsolete elegance; but no one takes him seriously. He is half Catholic and half Jewish, and he feels equally out of place in the wealthy Jewish bourgeoisie to which he belongs through his mother, and in the old aristocracy into which he has gained admittance: no one is more keenly sensitive to the idiosyncrasies of the Jews, and yet no one more mercilessly derides the absurdities of the Faubourg Saint-Germain; he was one of the first to declare himself openly for Dreyfus, but, when contemptuously referred to as a young Jew, although a Catholic like his father, he did not dare deny it, for fear of hurting his mother. He is a deviate who, when attracted by a feminine face, pursues its resemblance in a masculine face, and slyly admits it in order to forestall condemnation by a society in which Athenian tastes are not openly admitted. For he is a *mondain* whose social position depends on opinion; and, as he cannot influence opinion either by the glamour of an illustrious name, or by the prestige of a great talent, or even by the zeal of an assiduous attendance, he has no other resource than flattery, intrigue, and falseness. He flatters passionately, frantically, with the blandishments of a harlot and the orgasms of a nymphomaniac. He lies with the cunning of a flunky and the finesse of a diplomat, to cover up the sins of negligence or the crimes of lèse-majesté into which he may be drawn by the shifts of his humor, the vicissitudes of his health, the tyranny of his concupiscence, or even sometimes the rebellion of his pride. For he may occasionally give vent to a long-contained rancour, or to his disgust with a worldly comedy whose futility, barrenness, and stupidity he fully realizes. But he promptly repents and humbles himself, and, in the sterility of a disoriented and vacillating existence, he resumes the inevitable cycle of apologies, flatteries, subterfuges, and lies.

The reason is that above all, in order to integrate and dominate all these heterogeneous elements, he lacks that which crowns an individual and constitutes a personality: the government of oneself. Not that he is completely devoid of a moral conscience; on the contrary, when still quite young, he passed judgment on himself, he perceived his absurdities and deplored his errors, he was haunted by sin and tormented by remorse. But, also when still quite young, he abdicated, by reconciling himself to that lack of will-power which distressed his parents and has now developed into a pathological abulia. He has not had the experience of passion, which perhaps would have saved him; nor, although he mourned for his father, has he had the experience of despair, which perhaps would have redeemed him. He is only the sport of humor, of caprice, and of snobbery.

Yes indeed, "Little Marcel." During the fifteen years between 1890 and 1905, the history of his life is apparently nothing but the history of his sycophancy; and his idol is Comte Robert de Montesquiou. It was during the summer of 1905 that he reached his highest point in Montesquiou's favor: the latter, brokenhearted by the death of Gabriel de Yturri, his most intimate secretary, and deeply touched by "Little Marcel's" sincere sympathy, imagined that he could find in him something like a reincarnation of his dead friend: so then, after many vicissitudes, Marcel found himself called to the right hand of the Master, to the place of the beloved disciple; Marcel, dear Marcel, little Marcel, whose destiny thus seemed to have reached its climax.

An irreparable loss, an excruciating despair, saved him from this indignity. For a long time he had realized that only a competent psychiatrist could cure him of his neurasthenia, his manias, and his vices. As early as the summer of 1904, he had thought of consulting a specialist; and, in the winter of 1905, he had about made up his mind to go to Switzerland and submit to a rigorous treatment at the hands of Dr. Dubois or Dr. Widmer; but, day after day, and week after week, he had always found new excuses to postpone his departure. By the middle of the summer, he had not yet managed to leave Paris; however, autumn was approaching, and he understood that he could not procrastinate any longer. But, in order to force him to act at last, apparently the intervention of his guardian angel, of his incomparable mother, was necessary; for it was she, it seems, who during the first days of September persuaded him to leave for Evian, from where he was to cross over into Switzerland to undergo his cure; and, with her habitual devotion, she accompanied him on his trip.

That was to be her last effort to save her son. For years, the physical infirmities and the moral failings of Marcel had been her obsession; and, since she had been compelled to abdicate before his unconquerable nervousness and give up all the plans for the future she had dreamed of for him, she had made herself his slave. She had encouraged his work in Ruskin; she had urged him to translate the *Bible of Amiens,* and, as he did not know much English, she had imposed upon herself the task of translating word for word the original text, filling with her fine handwriting several notebooks on which he then worked with Marie Nordlinger, Robert de Billy, and Robert d'Humières; and, after Dr. Proust's death, when Marcel had wanted to give up publishing this translation, she had urged him to go back to work on the proofs, insisting that it was what his father wanted and that he had been expecting this publication from day to day. She had favored his affair with Louisa de Mornand, the young actress from the Vaudeville, who sometimes came to see him late at night, after the theatre: when she knew in advance of such a visit, Mme. Proust obligingly retired early, in order to leave in complete freedom these two young people whom she could not help believing to be lovers. Perhaps she hoped that normal love affairs would succeed in curing Marcel of the sordid aberrations that she suspected; but, aside from a few spicy interludes, it seems that Marcel did not make of Louisa, who had a real protector anyway, anything more than a sort of *fausse maîtresse* designed to ward off any overt suspicion of his less orthodox amusements. In order to spare the invalid the slightest effort, there was no drudgery that Mme. Proust did not accept: he had her run his errands for him, sending her one day to Léon Daudet's to take him some package, another day to Neuilly to inquire about Gabriel de Yturri's health, giving her the task another time of escorting Marie Nordlinger back to Auteuil; and he depended on her to organize his dinner parties and invite his guests while he was sleeping. She watched over his rest and his work with untiring vigilance, maintaining the most profound silence in the apartment all day while he slept; but, if he stepped out of his bedroom, there was a floorboard in the hall that one could not walk on without its squeaking; and Mme. Proust, always on the watch, would hear it immediately and make the little sound with her lips that means: "Come kiss me." If after dinner, in the family dining-room where he sometimes worked in the evening, he received a visit from some young men, she would come in for a moment, with her usual discretion and tact, would say a few pleasant words to his friends, and before retiring would make some prudent recommendations: "Dear, if you go out tonight, wrap up well . . . it is very cold . . . take good care of him won't you, Mr. So-and-So?

he had a choking spell a little while ago." If he went out, his first words when he came back were: "Is Madame in?"; and, before anyone could answer him, there she was, waiting anxiously to see if he would come home without having too bad an attack, but not daring to speak to him for fear of making him talk if he felt short of breath.

It is certain that he loved jealously that too tender and too sublime mother, who put all her happiness and pride in making herself his servant; and, when he told her good-night, he kissed her with childish and passionate adoration. But this adoration was selfish and blind, as much as were unconsciously heartless and cruel the indolence with which he let himself be waited on and the weakness with which he surrendered to his vices. This ostensibly affectionate son did not notice that his mother was nearing complete exhaustion; and that, since the loss of her husband nearly two years before, it had been an effort every day more painful to survive him: an effort that she had attempted only for the sake of her children, and that she would soon no longer be able to carry on, so overwhelming was her weariness.

It was around the first days of September 1905 that Marcel, accompanied by his mother, left for Evian, feeling rather poorly, but nevertheless full of optimism, for he had just received a delightful letter from Mme. Straus, who had recommended him to Dr. Widmer. Two hours after their arrival, Mme. Proust had an attack of vomiting and dizziness that seemed to indicate some serious disorder. But that intrepid soul refused to be conquered. It was impossible to make her consent to see a physician or submit to any laboratory tests. In spite of those first symptoms, in spite of her recurrent dizzy spells, in spite of Marcel's supplications, she insisted for several days on walking down in the morning to the hotel lounge, even if she had to lean on two servants to keep from collapsing. As for Marcel, he was terribly worried about the condition and the obstinacy of his mother and he had fallen ill in turn. Finally, Dr. Robert Proust came for her and took her back to Paris; but she refused to let Marcel return with them. So he stayed several days longer at Evian, alone, with the agony of knowing that she was suffering far away from him, and the constant expectation of a telegram recalling him to Paris. "I hope that it will vanish like a bad dream," he wrote on the thirteenth of September to Marie Nordlinger, "but as long as it lasts I am very unhappy."

It was not a bad dream. The examinations and analyses made in Paris revealed that Mme. Proust was suffering from a severe attack of uremia, which had been aggravated by her railroad trip back to Paris. Marcel, no longer able to endure the torment of being away from her, or perhaps recalled by his brother, returned home. He found his mother in a state of extreme weakness, which still did not prevail over her indomitable will. She scarcely consented to see the doctor, she refused to take any medicine at all, for two weeks she had gone without any food; but she continued none the less having herself taken out of bed, bathed, and dressed every day. To animate further that faltering body, no doubt she still found some energy in her insatiable need, as blind and as irrepressible as an instinct, to continue watching over that son whom she still considered a little child: as the nun who was caring for her remarked, for his mother, Marcel was still only four years old. Many years later, to express his weariness when he felt that the strength of the writer in him was no longer equal to the demands of his work, the author of *Le Temps retrouvé* was to find an appalling comparison: "My work was for me like a son whose dying mother must still impose upon herself the weariness of worrying about him ceaselessly, between hypodermics and cuppings. She still loves him perhaps, but of this love she is no longer conscious except through the exhausting duty she has of taking care of him."

However, the patient showed a slight improvement, and the doctor assured that, if she managed to survive this attack, she would regain her former health. The improvement persisted; but recovery still seemed very far away: "Whatever hope the slight amelioration of these last few days gives us," Marcel wrote to Montesquiou, "the ascent will be so long from the abysses in which we were, that the progress of each day, if God wills that it continue, will be imperceptible." Marcel and Robert would have liked to tell and share that hope with their mother, but they were never able to: "Perhaps she wouldn't believe us. At any rate, her absolute calm prevents our knowing what she thinks and what she is suffering."

What she was suffering, if he did not know it, Marcel at least suspected, with horror. In a letter to Mme. Straus he had confessed his fears on that score: "She knows me so incapable of living without her, so completely defenseless before life, that if, as I fear and believe with anguish, she had the feeling that she was perhaps going to leave me forever, she must have known agonizing and atrocious moments, which it is the most atrocious torture for me to imagine." A torture of which, through an astonishing premonition, he had had a vicarious experience more than two months earlier, on the occasion of the death of the Duchesse de Gramont, the mother of Comtesse Hélie de Noailles, née Corisande de Gramont. The Duchesse de Gramont, née Rothschild, although converted to Catholicism, apparently had kept her Jewish faith and on dying had considered her separation from her daughter Corisande an eternal separation. It was around the first days of August that Marcel wrote to Comtesse Mathieu de Noailles about her sister-in-law, Comtesse Hélie de Noailles: "I remember her mother's devotion to her. The thought that her mother knew—or believed—that she was leaving her for eternity, that never again throughout the centuries would she see her, is a thought that drives me insane." And now the same tragedy was being reenacted in his own life; for Mme. Proust, who had remained openly faithful to the religion of her father and mother, also believed that she was going to leave for eternity that son who needed so desperately her incessant care and over whom she would have liked to be able to continue to watch from the world beyond.

The improvement did not last long. The imperturbable calm with which Mme. Proust had faced her own sufferings and the distress of her children, turned into a complete stupor from which it seemed that nothing could draw her again. Nothing except the maternal instinct, still on watch in that exhausted body which was slipping into nothingness, still able sometimes to galvanize for an instant the inert matter: "[My mother]," he related later, ostensibly referring to the grand-mother of his protagonist, "in the last days that preceded her death, when she had sunk into an immobility that nothing could disturb and that doctors called a coma, would begin to tremble for an instant like a leaf, they told me, whenever she heard the three rings of the bell with which I used to call Françoise, and which, even though I made them softer that week in order not to disturb the silence of the sick room, nobody, according to Françoise, could confuse with anyone else's ring, because of the manner I had and did not realize I had of pressing the button."

She finally died on Tuesday, September 26, 1905. Reynaldo Hahn, who had hurried to comfort his friend, was always to remember him, beside Mme. Proust's bed, weeping and smiling at the corpse through his tears. During the two days that he was permitted to keep her, he tore himself away from her only to write a few words to his friends. He wrote to Comtesse de Noailles on Wednesday, September 27, the day before the burial: "She died at fifty-six, looking thirty since her illness made her thinner and especially since death restored the youthfulness she had before her sorrows; she did not have a single white hair. She takes my life away with her, as Father took hers. She wanted to survive him for our sake and could not." And, counting the hours that remained until he would see her taken away, he added with heart-rending simplicity: "Today I still have her, dead but still receiving the marks of my love. And then I will never have her again."

The funeral took place on Thursday, the twenty-eighth, according to the Jewish ritual. The procession went directly from the apartment to the cemetery of Père-Lachaise; and then Marcel came back to the forever deserted apartment, alone with his grief. He had to take to his bed, and for days and weeks it was impossible for him to get up. To Louisa de Mornand, who had sent an enormous wreath, he found the strength to write his thanks; and it was to her also that he confided the first outburst of the despair and solitude of his soul: "You can guess in what distress I find myself, you who have seen me with my ears and my heart always alert to the sounds from Mother's room, to which I kept ceaselessly going back on any pretext to kiss her and where I now have seen her dead, still happy to have been able still to kiss her that way. And now the room is empty, and so are my heart and my life." Then he shut himself up alone with his memories. With all his heart, with all his strength, he tried to evoke the beloved shade; but it was in vain: "The very excess of my need of seeing her again," he confided early in November to Montesquiou, "prevents my seeing anything before my eyes when I think of her, except, for the last two days, two particularly painful visions of her illness." Those images, which haunted him when he was awake, became even more atrocious when he happened to doze off, because the censorship then ceased to operate: "I cannot sleep any more," he went on, "and if by chance I do fall asleep, sleep, less sparing of my pain than my wakeful intelligence, harasses me with atrocious thoughts which, when I am awake, my reason at least tries to mitigate and to obliterate when I can't stand them any longer." A few days later, it was to Mme. Straus that he explained this torture of memory: "When the anguish that accompanies it grows too sharp and makes me lose my mind, I try to divert it, to moderate it. But, these last few days, I have been able to sleep again a little. Then, in my sleep, my intelligence is no longer there to ward off for an instant a too painful memory, to mitigate the pain, to temper it with sweetness; then I am left without defense against the most atrocious impressions."

Sometimes, however, he achieved a moment of calm: it seemed to him that he was becoming accustomed to his grief, that he was going to take a new interest in life, and he reproached himself for it; but at the same time a new sorrow would burst on him, revealing to him thus the infinite variety of each of our affections, which at any instant innumerable associations of ideas may renew; for, as he explained to Mme. Straus, "one does not have one sorrow, regret takes at every instant another form; at every instant, suggested by a certain impression identical with a former impression, it becomes a new misfortune, an unknown pain, as atrocious as before." That multiplicity of sorrow, he experienced even more keenly when he could begin to get up and take a few steps out of his room: "I went into certain rooms of the apartment where I happened not to have gone back before," he wrote toward the end of November to Comtesse de Noailles, "and I explored unknown parts of my grief, that stretches out more and more infinitely the farther I go." But nothing perhaps made him experience more deeply the feeling of his irremediable loss than listening to the silence of the apartment, where the servants, trained by his mother, glided with noiseless steps like shadows: "My life has henceforth lost its only purpose, its only sweetness, its only love, its only consolation," he wrote early in November to Montesquiou; "I have lost her whose constant vigilance brought me in peace and in tenderness the only honey of life that I can still taste at times, with horror, in this silence which she knew how to maintain so completely all day around my sleep and which the habits of the servants trained by her still make survive, inertly, her now ended activity."

However pathetic they may be, these cries of grief are still the cries of a selfish grief, which, in the death of someone loved, deplores only its own loss and its own suffering. But in addition, as early as the first days of November, from that soul still so puerile and so cowardly there began to burst out also cries of shame and remorse, apparently so sincere that they perhaps foretold an imminent redemption. It was then, with an irresistible need of confiding and confessing his feelings, that he wrote almost simultaneously to Mme. Straus and to Montesquiou. To the former he recalled with what anxiety his mother, whenever he went out, waited for him so as to be sure that he came back home safely, and he confided the torture that those memories were for him now: "Alas, it is that worry, which increased her sorrow, that gnaws me now with remorse and keeps me from finding a moment's comfort in the memory of our hours of tenderness, a memory about which I can't even say that it is incessant, for it is in it that I breathe, in it that I think: it alone is all about me." To Robert de Montesquiou he confided, along with his own agony, the fear that he now felt of having been a constant cause of torment to his mother: "I have drained the cup of sorrow, I have lost her, I saw her suffer, I can be sure that she knew that she was leaving me and was not able to give me the advice that it was perhaps agonizing for her not to give, I feel that through my poor health I was the sorrow and the worry of her life." In his despair he even considered it a blessing to be the one to survive and suffer: "One thing alone has been spared me," he explained, "I have not had the torment of dying before she died and feeling the horror that that would have been for her"; but he wondered whether for his mother the agony of leaving him alone in the world was not even more frightful: "Leaving me for eternity, feeling me so little capable of struggling with life, must have been for her a very great torture also. She must have understood the wisdom of parents who, before dying, kill their little children."

This conciousness of having made his mother suffer so long from his egoism and his helplessness, finally gave him the courage to try to reform his life. He had no other ambition on this earth than to do what his mother would have liked him to do. He thought again therefore, toward the end of November, of his plan of undergoing a cure; and in the first days of December, after many tergiversations, he entered Dr. Sollier's sanatorium for nervous disorders, at Boulogne-sur-Seine. There he spent New Year's day of 1906; and, as he wrote a little later to Comtesse de Noailles, that day had on him a terrible power of evocation: "It brought back to me all at once recollections of Mother that I had lost, memories of her voice." A resurgence of memory which, by suddenly resurrecting that forgotten voice, made him feel again in all its bitterness the suffering of which he had had a foreboding many years before when hearing that same voice, then still alive, over the telephone: "Many times," he was to write later, "when listening to it thus, without seeing the one who was speaking to me from such a distance, I felt as though that voice was calling to me from the abysses from which there is no return, and I knew the agony which would grip me one day, when that voice would thus return, all by itself and detached from a body I would never see again, in order to whisper into my ear words that I would have liked to be able to kiss on lips forever turned to dust."

About the middle of January 1906, Marcel Proust left Dr. Sollier's clinic, still in a pitiful state. However, probably as an act of piety to the sacred memory of his mother, he took up again the Ruskinian studies that she had favored; and he put in final form for publication his translation of *Sesame and Lilies*, which appeared around June 1, preceded by the remarkable preface "On Reading" and enriched with copious footnotes. It was also through filial piety perhaps that he thought of going to spend the month of August on the coast of Normandy, where he had spent several vacations in the past with his mother, or that he considered a pilgrimage in September to the "calvary of Evian." But he finally went to Versailles, where he stopped at the Hôtel des Réservoirs; and he had hardly arrived when he fell sick, so that he had to stay shut in for almost five months. Moreover, the approach of autumn was to bring him new torments. As early as November 1905, he had realized that he would have to give up the family apartment on the Rue de Courcelles, which had become too large and too expensive for him alone. So in the early part of September 1906 he began to have his friends look for a smaller apartment to be available for occupancy on the October 15 moving day; and he finally fixed his choice on an apartment in the building on the Boulevard Haussmann which he owned jointly with his brother and his aunt: the same apartment in which his uncle Louis Weil had lived and died and which his mother had often visited. But, the apartment rented, the tribulations of the new tenant were far from being ended. He still had to move in; and he was unable to manage it before the last days of December. As he intended to move out again after a year, he did not take the trouble to get settled; and yet for more than twelve years he was to camp in that apartment on Boulevard Haussmann, in that bedroom whose shutters remained closed and whose walls were insulated with a thick layer of cork. There he was to conceive and work out *A la Recherche du Temps perdu;* but for the moment he was intellectually inert; of course he still read assiduously the *Figaro* and the *Débats*, but he had given up Ruskin, and he felt incapable of going back to the great work he had dreamed of some ten years before: "Are you working?"

he asked Marie Nordlinger; "I am not any more. I have ended forever the era of translations that Mother liked, and, as for translations of myself, I no longer have the courage for that."

But his lassitude, his worries, and his claustration were not an obstacle to his "philanthropy." Toward the end of November 1906 he had written to Robert de Billy that he wanted to find a position for "a young man of twenty-five, very distinguished and good-looking, with a good hand-writing, able enough at book-keeping, with very nice manners, very serious, but without any further education." Some weeks later, he was concerning himself with another protégé: he asked a certain Henri van Blarenberghe, whom he knew slightly and whose father during his lifetime was President of the Board of Directors of the *Compagnie des Chemins de Fer de l'Est,* for information about one of the employés of that company, in whom "one of [his] friends," it seems, "was interested." A vain attempt: on January 12, 1907, Henri van Blarenberghe answered in a somewhat puzzled tone: "I inquired about the possible presence of X . . . among the personnel of the Eastern Railway Company and about his probable address. I could not learn anything. If you are quite sure about the name, the person who bears it has disappeared from the Company without leaving any trace; he must have been employed there in a very temporary and accessory capacity."

It was on January 17 that Marcel received this disappointing answer which removed all hope of making a fuller acquaintance with the elusive employé of the Eastern Railway Company, in whom "one of [his] friends" was so keenly interested. Some days later, on Friday, January 25, he remembered on awakening that he should answer that letter from Henri van Blarenberghe; but he wanted first to glance at the *Figaro,* and he was beginning to read a news item which its title, "A Drama of Madness," seemed to make particularly enticing, when all at once he saw that the victim was Mme. van Blarenberghe, and that the murderer, who had then committed suicide, was her own son Henri, the same person whose letter Marcel was planning to answer. On Wednesday morning, January 30, he received a note from Gaston Calmette, director of the *Figaro,* asking him to write an article on that dramatic occurrence. He drafted it during the night from Wednesday to Thursday; he corrected the proofs and improvised the conclusion Thursday evening, and at midnight he dispatched the whole thing to the *Figaro,* with his permission to cut out all that they wished in the body of the article and the express request not to change a single word in the conclusion.

The article appeared the next morning, Friday, February 1, on the first page, with the title: "Filial sentiments of a parricide." Indeed, the beginning of the article is dull: the social relations of the Proust and Blarenberghe families leave the reader indifferent; the account of the inquiry about the employé of the Eastern Railway Company seems above all intended to reach through the *Figaro* a person singularly anxious of remaining unidentified; and the remarks on reading the morning paper betray a preciosity somewhat out of place under the circumstances. But, with the account of the drama itself, the tone changes suddenly, to assume a grave and tragic quality. The memories evoked are those of the fury of Ajax, the expiation of Oedipus, the despair of Lear. The reason is that, in this criminal who murdered his mother and then did justice to himself, Marcel wants to make us recognize a victim of ancient fatality: "I wanted to show," he explains, "in what a pure, religious atmosphere of moral beauty that outburst of madness and bloodshed took place, which bespatters it without succeeding in sullying it. I wanted to air the room of the crime with a breath from Heaven, to show that this was exactly one of the Greek dramas whose representation was almost a religious ceremony, and that the poor parricide was not a criminal beast, a monster beyond the pale of humanity, but, on the contrary a noble example of humanity, a man of fine intellect, a tender and devoted son, whom the most inescapable fatality—we will say a pathological fatality in order to talk like everybody else—forced, the most unfortunate of mortals, into a crime and an expiation worthy of remaining illustrious."

If he made such an eloquent plea to show us in that criminal who murdered his mother an innocent victim of tragic fatality, it was because Marcel recognized himself in him as in a mirror; it was because, in the bloody horror of that physical assassination, he found again, materialized, all the internal horror of the spiritual assassination that he had committed on his own mother. The remorse that, for more than a year, had not ceased tormenting him, he could no longer exorcise: once more, to escape for a moment from the harrowing consciousness of his guilt, "Little Marcel" had no other resource left than confession; and, irresistibly, in the last paragraph of the article, the dreadful confession gushed out:

"Henri, what have you done to me! what have you done to me!" Mme. van Blarenberghe had cried as she was dying of her wounds. "What have you done to me! What have you done to me!" Marcel repeated. "If we cared to think about it, there is perhaps not one truly loving mother who could not, on her last day, and often long before, address that same reproach to her son. Actually, we cause to grow old and we kill all those who love us, by the worries that we give them, even by the anxious tenderness that we inspire and to which we give incessant alarm. If we could see in a beloved body the slow work of destruction achieved by the heart-rending affection that animates it, if we could see the eyes grow dim, the hair, for a long time indomitably black, then conquered like the rest and turning gray, the arteries hardening, the kidneys obstructed, the heart overstrained, the courage to face life vanquished, the step becoming slow, and heavy the spirit that knows it has nothing more to hope for, when once it rebounded so untiringly with invincible hopes, the gaiety even, that innate and seemingly immortal gaiety which was such a pleasant companion for sadness, forever exhausted—perhaps the man who could see all that, in that belated moment of lucidity which the most chimerical lives can indeed have, since even Don Quixote's life had it, perhaps that man, like Henri van Blarenberghe after he had stabbed his mother to death, would recoil before the horror of his life, and would throw himself on a dagger or a gun, in order to kill himself immediately."

No confession could be more explicit, nor more public. It was to be the first step toward expiation and redemption of a soul once more convinced and desperately sick of its ignominy, but still floundering in its impotence and cowardice and destined to many failures and turpitudes before being at least temporarily touched by grace. At least this confession brought some immediate relief to a heart tortured by contrition. Two weeks later, to Georges de Lauris whose mother had just died, Marcel was able to promise that, after the first atrocious wrench, some serenity would be forthcoming: "When you had your mother," he wrote after the funeral, "you often thought of the days, which have now come, when you would have her no longer. Now you are thinking of the days, forever gone, when you had her. When you get used to the awful shock it is, to be forever thrown back into the past, then you will little by little feel her reviving, and coming back to resume her place, her whole place, by your side." This solace, he admitted, was not yet accessible to his friend; but in the meantime he advised him to remain passive, and to wait for the inconceivable force that had broken him, to help him a little. "I say a little," he explained, "because something will always remain broken in you. Understand this too, because it is a blessing to know that one shall never love less, that one shall never be comforted, that one shall always remember more and more." Five months after this effusion of a grief already less bitter and made more serene as it were by some secret absolution, Marcel resumed with even more confidence his consoler's role with another friend, Robert de Flers, who had just lost the admirable grandmother who had been a mother to him. When recalling the constant concern and the untiring devotion of Mme. de Rozière toward her grandson, when exclaiming that Death must be all powerful to have been able to part them, when refusing to consider this separation an eternal separation, he is thinking of his own mother as well as of his friend's grandmother: "What! two human beings in such complete communion that nothing existed in the one that did not have its justification, its object, its satisfaction, its explanation, its tender commentary in the other, two beings who seemed to be the translation of each other, although both were original creations, those two beings would have merely met for one instant in the infinity of time, in which they would be nothing to each other any longer, nothing more special than to billions of other beings? Is that really conceivable?" For his part, he writes, he will never be able to believe it altogether. He now confidently affirms that we never really say goodbye to those we have loved, because we never really leave them; and that nothing is everlasting, not even death. As he had done at the bedside of his dead mother, he now smiles through his tears: but at the immortal soul and not at the earthly remains, for he has now learned to believe in the mystic communion of the living and the dead: "Those we have loved most dearly, we never think of them, even when we are weeping most bitterly, without passionately smiling our tenderest smile at them. Is it in order to try to deceive them, to reassure them, to tell them that they should not worry, that we shall be brave, and to make them believe that we are not unhappy? Or is it not rather that that smile is the very expression of the endless kiss we are giving them in the Invisible?"

Less than two years later, Marcel was to experience his aesthetic illumination. In August 1892 he had written: "You are absorbed by success, you are enslaved by pleasure. But happiness can be achieved only in doing what one loves with the inmost longings of his soul." The perfect expression of the inmost longings of his sinful and tormented soul he had perhaps already found in *Middlemarch,* in the comforting words about the pursuit of "some object which would never justify weariness, which would reconcile self-despair with the rapturous consciousness of life beyond self." In December 1897, he had likened himself to Casaubon futilely compiling meaningless notes for a work he would never complete; and yet, for nearly twelve years, he had still kept on drafting apparently sterile episodes, sketches, and critical essays. In August 1907, he had discovered "Albertine," the person whom after his father and mother he loved most in this world, the one who was to reveal to him the anguish of passion and the torments of jealousy. Then, in May 1909, he finally attained the object of his quest: he conceived the main theme and outlined the general structure of his *magnum opus.* His remorse, his agony, his despair, his thirst for confession and atonement, were his inspiration and his driving force; the episodes, the sketches, the essays he had been accumulating for nearly fifteen years were the raw materials he undertook to integrate into a whole, by retrospectively giving them artistic unity in the light of his past memories and his present experiences. To be sure, his illumination was not a regeneration: he remained a frantic flatterer, an ingenious liar, and an incurable hypochondriac. But despair and remorse and passion had tempered him; and, failing the moral government he was never able to impose upon himself, at least the consciousness of his literary vocation subordinated in him some of the incoherent and contradictory elements, and made of him an artist, an artist according to Ruskin and Carlyle, an artist devoted above all to the work it was his mission to achieve. Thus, through the pangs of creative agony, did "Little Marcel" become Marcel Proust; and, when he wrote the first pages of *A la Recherche du Temps perdu,* it was a message of tender remembrance as well as an expiatory offering that, smiling through his tears, he was dedicating to his mother in the Invisible.

The Legacy of Proust

by Henri Peyre

English critics and admirers were, characteristically, the first to pay Proust a discerning and enthusiastic homage; a volume entitled *An English Tribute*, published as early as 1923, contains valuable contributions by Clive Bell, Joseph Conrad, Compton Mackenzie, Middleton Murry, Logan Pearsall Smith, Arthur Symons, Alec Waugh, and others. Several of the best recent appraisals of Proust have come from Great Britain and America. Between 1930 and the year 1941, when war-ridden England welcomed the two-volume new edition of *Remembrance of Things Past* (Random House, New York, 1941), ironical or severe attacks against the adulation of Proust poured in from English pens. A certain moral revulsion from the Proustian obsession with abnormal love was to be expected, even from post-Puritan England, and the lack in Proust of a social conscience or of any political enthusiasm for a better world was to be resented by the young Englishmen who 'thought continually of those who were truly great' and were inflamed by the Russian five-year plans and the Spanish republican cause. W. H. Auden and Louis MacNeice, venturing to appraise the literary stock market in their *Letters from Iceland*, prophesied—wrongly—'some further weakening in Proust.' Philip Guedalla had, much earlier, coined one of his bons mots in announcing that the vogue for Proust would hardly outlast a 'Marcel wave.' 'Water jelly,' exclaimed D. H. Lawrence to characterize that strange cold-blooded animal who scientifically and patiently dissociated ideas, emotions, and sensations. 'Ploughing a field with knitting needles' was George Moore's description of Proust. Aldous Huxley, one of the very few living writers who had the honor of a flattering mention in Proust's novel, placed some ungrateful lines in the mouth of one of his characters in *Eyeless in Gaza*.

> How I hate old Proust! . . . that asthmatic seeker of lost time squatting, horribly white and flabby, with breasts almost female but fledged with

"The Legacy of Proust." From *The Contemporary French Novel*, by Henri Peyre. Copyright 1955 by Oxford University Press, Inc. Reprinted by permission.

long black hairs, for ever squatting in the tepid bath of his remembered past . . . There he sat, a pale repellent invalid, taking up spongefuls of his own thick soup and squeezing it over his face . . .

The disappointment and the impatience that many expressed between 1930 and 1940, when the newness of Proust's psychology and poetry had worn off, can easily be explained by several converging causes. First came the mechanical working of one of the few effective laws of literature: the law of reaction of one generation against the previous one. Proust had appeared impossibly difficult in 1913—to the point where Gide himself had refused his manuscript for the Gallimard firm and where critic after critic confessed he could make neither head nor tail of *Du côté de chez Swann* (*Swann's Way*). But obscurity is short-lived in modern letters and was in this case. Ten years after Proust's death, most young readers declared Proust's writing occasionally involved and needlessly exacting, but hardly obscure—in fact, not enough so. Too many passages are too well written to suit the present fashion for bare simplicity, and for some the author falls too readily in line with the French tradition, which stems from Chateaubriand or even from Montaigne. Kafka and Joyce seem to many young readers to retain their 'virtue' of obscurity longer than Proust, now read as a classic the world over and revered as a model prose writer in many anthologies.

The personality of Proust as it came to be half revealed after his death (many letters probably still remain to be unearthed and many ugly secrets still to be brought to light) was a second source of disappointment for the early admirers of the novelist. It dawned on many that the author had lent much of himself not only to the narrator as a child crying for his mother's kiss and spoiled by his grandmother while vacationing in Balbec, but perhaps also to Mlle Vinteuil indulging in sadistic profanation of her father's image, to the morbid inquisitor into Albertine's past debauchery after the girl's death, and even to Morel, Jupien, and some of the most dubious or frankly discreditable characters in fiction. There were glaring contrasts in Proust's personality, polite to a fault and treating his friends to sumptuous aristocratic dinners, then repairing to some shady establishment where he would evince more concrete admiration for the handsome or vicious servants of the dukes and barons with whom he had associated. That ambivalence of the man in Proust obviously served the artist in him. He had good reason for forcing his own fictional characters into sudden contradictions or abrupt changes of personality that no gradual evolution could account for. Staid critics have been repelled or unconvinced by those dramatic metamorphoses that plunged Saint Loup or Gilberte into vice and exalted a former prostitute like Rachel to the pedestal of an actress loved and idealized by one of the most intelligent members of the aristocracy. In *La Prisonnière* (*The Captive*) Proust expressed his admiration for the buffoons and the women in Dostoevski, similar to people painted by Rembrandt, alternately exuberant in their humility and haughtily insolent, charitable to a point that hurts our Western idea of self-respect, then suddenly lecherous or drunken.[1] He compared Dostoevski's fantastic creatures to Rembrandt's 'Night Watch,' and implied, with his own characters in mind, that only the lighting and the costumes exalted to the status of visionary phantoms people who were perhaps average men and women.

Revelations, at first half-whispered and lately more frank, from friends and acquaintances of Proust threw some light on facets of Proust's personality that could not but disappoint the least squeamish among his readers. His high-flown compliments to women concealed a profound lack of interest in all but the superficial aspects of their nature. His interest in servants, chauffeurs, butlers, and elevator boys hardly sprang from social charity. Even his proverbially lavish tips were an unpleasant manifestation of his desire to be liked and to pay for his loves or for friendship. The publication of Proust's letters proved especially harmful to the cult that might have developed for the author of the most intimate novel of the century. He reserved his genius for his book, fearful as he was of dying before he would complete it, and veiled his life under a screen of flattering politeness that was little more than a defense reaction. There was a rare gift for mimicry in Proust's ability to observe and reproduce other people's idiosyncrasies, and not a little hypocrisy in the adolescent who had cultivated his disease in order to retain his mother's lenient love and who had to conceal from his beloved mother and from all those who were dear to him the less orthodox sides of his nature.

Other grievances harbored by many readers of Proust concerned his excessive preoccupation with sexual abnormality and his snobbery. Our moral notions are, it is well known, elastic, and the literature of the last two decades has accustomed many of us to a more than frank treatment of sodomy and Lesbianism. Jean Genet makes Marcel Proust appear rather tame. But even the broadest-minded among Proust's readers may protest, on aesthetic grounds, against a vision of the world that sets up abnormality as the norm. When practically every character in Proust turns homosexual in the latter part of the novel, we remain unconvinced and wonder how 'universal' such a vision can be. Proust, perhaps fascinated by Balzac, and in terms Flaubert or Zola might have used, defined himself in his last volume as an 'anatomist' and quietly wrote to one of his friends: 'I obey a general truth which prevents me from being concerned with friend and foe alike. The praise of sadists

---

[1] Claudel likewise acknowledged Dostoevski's enormous influence over him; he admired in him the rapid and sudden changes in the characters, through which they discover elements in themselves that simply were not there before—the way stressed by the biologist De Vries in which nature proceeds in its sudden mutations.

will distress the man in me when my book comes out. It cannot alter the conditions under which I experiment with truth and which I do not choose arbitrarily.'

Only naïve sociologists will demand from an artist that he depict the world as it is and be true to statistical proportions established by scientists. Obviously, the world of Balzac, that of Dostoevski, or that of Faulkner are no more normal, in other respects, than that of Proust. Even the France of Louis Philippe was less preoccupied with money than the characters in the *Comédie humaine* appear to be; and Temple Drake must have few prototypes among Southern American college girls. But Proust's saga-novel rests upon the assumption, occasionally made explicit by the author, that sexual anomaly and sadism are linked with moral goodness and superior intelligence. M. de Guermantes, unhappy enough to be afflicted with normal love habits, is a fool when compared with his extraordinary brother, M. de Charlus. Jupien, Proust assures us, was in truth highly gifted, whatever the average reader may think of the use to which he put his talents. The scene in *Swann* that shocked Edith Wharton and many French friends of Proust, where Mlle Vinteuil displays and spits upon her dead father's picture when indulging in Lesbian caresses, is strangely followed by an apology for sadism, in which Proust betrayed his hidden purpose. A sadist like her, he explains to his reader, is an artist in evil. She is a purely sentimental creature, naturally inclined to virtue, and, when yielding to evil momentarily, she merely 'escapes from her scrupulous and tender soul into the inhuman world of pleasure.' Elsewhere, in *A l'ombre des jeunes filles en fleurs* (*Within a Budding Grove*), he asserts that 'only in truly vicious lives can the moral problem be posed with its full anxious force.' There is much didacticism in Proust, and too much of it, less blatantly but more perfidiously than in Gide's *Corydon*, is devoted to proposing a justification of unorthodox sexual behavior and of effeminacy in some men, which remain exceptional in the eyes of many of us.

It seems hardly to be denied that Proust, in his youth at least, was a snob. He strove hard and long, he, a half-Jew, to be received into the most aristocratic Parisian circles. To this end he spared no effort of his naturally kind personality. He was almost obsequiously anxious to please; he was generous, but convinced that any affection is venal and could be purchased with enough presents and favors. But hundreds of writers in the past have been snobs and many are today, or inverted snobs in their brutality toward wealthy and well-mannered people and in their courting the popularity of the uncultured. Proust denied, in letters to Paul Souday and to his English friend Sidney Schiff (alias Stephen Hudson), that he was a snob. And he certainly outgrew most of his early admiration for the fashions, etiquette, and conventionality of the Faubourg Saint-Germain. He became ruthless in displaying their selfishness and their vanity. But he lost also 'whatever poetry there may be in snobbery,' as he had called it in writing to Lucien Daudet. In any case, snobbery exists; it is a powerful social force, occasionally a force for good. Proust deserves no blame for having turned his telescope, as he liked to call it, on that phenomenon.

He has, however, been severely taken to task for concentrating almost exclusively on the feudal nobility, the bourgeoisie, and the servant class. The charge is naïve and rests upon a misunderstanding. Neither Racine nor Kafka has depicted workmen on strike or humble housewives struggling with the Monday-morning laundry, and the depth and the truth of their work have not suffered thereby. Kitchenmaids and milliners have been known to admire such 'class products' as the Duchess of Guermantes and Gilberte; a New York commissioner of police, in 1950, was depicted by a weekly magazine as reading Proust at night in his kitchen while drinking (was it an antidote?) a glass of milk before retiring to bed. British prisoners of war, in 1940-44, displayed a passion for reading Proust, and it is reported that Proust had to be branded officially as dangerous to communism and as too subtly corrupt, even as an example of the decadent bourgeoisie, when his success in Russian translation frightened Moscow's cultural masters; proletarians had to be protected against his insidious poison.

Several brave critics, however, between 1930 and 1940, announced that Proust's fame was on the wane because he had sadly lacked a social conscience. Others ventured the thesis, in 1940, that he would remain as an illustration of French decadence and as providing the key to France's failure of nerves and to Vichy. Sociological maniacs, who flourish in some academic circles, maintained that Proust's survival would be attributable to his description of the ascending bourgeoisie absorbing the descending aristocracy. They overlooked similar assertions, which had characterized in closely parallel terms the memoirs of Saint-Simon, the satirical portraits of La Bruyère, Balzac's fiction, and many other famous works. In truth, the vision of the narrator, and of the author, having become gradually blurred by pessimism and by the stress on abnormality, is responsible for the changes in the characters and groups delineated by Proust. The fusion of the middle and upper classes had occurred a long time before Proust and would not have been a very original subject for a novelist. Just as convincing a case could be made for Proust as the champion of the servant class! He is tender to Jupien and Morel, lyrical in his irony over Françoise's culinary talents, and when a certain young man who had served him as a chauffeur died in 1914 in an airplane accident, Proust praised him in a letter to Gide as a 'young man with a delightful intelligence' who, with no culture and of a lowly estate, had written him 'letters which are those of a great writer.'

Proust's fame has survived these charges and others; it has emerged unscathed from World War II, from the new stress on *littérature en-*

gagée and on man's freedom in his denial of a God on whom to lean, and finally from the admiration for unanalytical American novels. If the convergent attention granted to a writer by scholars of all ages and by critics is a sign of his continued reputation, Proust has certainly received that tribute. At least twenty full books on him have been published in French and English since 1940. Proust's niece, by distilling very sparingly the notebooks left by Proust and hinting at further revelations,[2] has increased the curiosity of many for the details of Proust's life and the mysterious and critical years between twenty-five and forty when he elaborated his future work through fruitful waste of time. But the emphasis is no longer on the man, obsequious, tormented, hypocritical, self-centered, vicious as he may have been, and equally kindhearted, sensitive, secretly courageous, and extraordinarily intelligent. It stresses the long novel created by Proust, which proved to be greater than its creator.

An interesting French novel, in 1949, *Une Lecture* by Roland Cailleux, turned the Proustian novel itself into a fictional character. The protagonist of that book actually had his whole life changed by reading Proust. The author, Cailleux, and many who agreed with him, confessed that their own and many other lives had been determined at some critical moment by the intrusion of Proust's characters into their own careers. Only Balzacian creatures seem ever to have fascinated French readers to such a perilous extent. Contrary to what suspicious critics might expect, it is not the homosexual obsession suddenly irrupting into 'normal' lives that acted most potently upon devotees of Proust. For it soon dawns on the reader that, while Proust derives much that is universally valid and profound from his delineation of abnormal love, he has established those truths upon a fundamental lie; his most impressive scenes, such as those in which Albertine is kept prisoner, are too obviously incredible in their data. The hero of Cailleux's novel

[2] Other letters of moderate interest have come out in 1952-3. The most important posthumous work is *Jean Santeuil*, published in 1952, a long manuscript apparently composed between 1892 and 1903 or perhaps 1908 (and not just 1896-9 as claimed by the publisher). It was unfortunately badly edited, put together very arbitrarily and preceded, thus far, by a very inadequate introduction. It can be called a novel only in parts, for many of its chapters rather resemble portraits, sketches, comments on literature and politics. But several parts already give evidence of Proust's stylistic gifts and of his early awareness of some of the essential themes of his future work: the mother's kiss, the conventionality of the father, the son's revolt against his parents, the ambivalence between sadism and kindness in the imaginary novelist portrayed, the children's loves in the Champs Elysées, the death of love, jealousy. But neither Saint Loup, Charlus, Swann, nor Vinteuil is yet present. And Proust has not yet developed the type of fictional technique that felicitously blends the directness and intimacy of memoirs in the first person singular and the novelist's art through which he assigns full significance to the remembered past and recreates it imaginatively. *Jean Santeuil*, valuable as some of its chapters are, fails to come to life as a whole and to be lightened of the weight afflicting memoirs that adhere to reality too closely.

and many readers of Proust in actual life are much more struck by the critical about-face of the narrator in *A la recherche du temps perdu*. After many years seemingly wasted in social vanities and the melancholy conviction that he was unfit to devote himself to any serious achievement, the Proustian narrator suddenly shifted from the past to the future. He vanquished death, perceived the serpentine but sure direction of all his past life, and embarked upon artistic creation. Future Ph.D.'s will most certainly write theses on the beneficent moral influence of Proust's work.

The admirer of Proust need have little worry about the survival of Proust among the most eminent novelists. The difficulty lies rather in determining the most lasting reasons for that survival. We have enumerated the main grounds on which Proust could well antagonize or disgust the generations that followed him. Other flimsy assertions have been neglected, such as the prophecy, advanced by Léon Pierre-Quint in a disappointed or defeatist article in *Europe*, in 1935, that new generations being brought up in sports would find Proust distasteful. By the same reasoning, Joyce, Kafka, Eliot, and Sartre would hardly appeal to those who have practiced boxing, football, golf, and cricket! Proust has enjoyed an advantage that has not often been granted to great works and that the four authors just mentioned have been denied: he has had practically no imitators. Jean Stafford's *Boston Adventure* in America and Stephen Hudson's *A True Story* in England have been described as Proustian novels. In French, it would be hard to quote one book written unambiguously under Proust's influence. Proust has thus been spared the harmful tribute of disciples who caricature a great work and popularize it, a tribute from which Debussy, Cézanne, Matisse, and Gide have not been saved.

The legacy that Proust bequeathed French literature is as rich and diverse as the whole of his extant work and as the series of conflicting interpretations and misconstructions of which that work is susceptible. Among the manifold aspects from which one may look admiringly and with renewed wonder at Proust, a few, however, seem to us to deserve being singled out, thirty years after Proust's death. Others, which immediate successors of Proust had stressed, were soon dwindling into relative insignificance; or rather, they may well be the 'wrong reasons' that have always at first attracted the earliest admirers of great innovators to their least significant merits, as was the case, for instance, with Diderot, Baudelaire, Mallarmé, Henry James, and Yeats. Thus the so-called philosophy of Proust, which has been repeatedly referred to Plato, Schopenhauer, Schelling, and Bergson, seems to us today a secondary factor in Proust's originality. Hailing Proust as a 'forerunner' of Freud, whom chronologically he followed, or as a rediscoverer of Freudianism, of which he had probably never heard, is similarly irrelevant and injurious to Proust since Freudian psychoanalysis, epoch-

The Legacy of Proust

making as it is likely to remain, is being superseded by other doctrines and newer forms of soul therapeutics. It was equally naïve to multiply articles on the impeccable composition of Proust's novel, variously termed 'Wagnerian,' 'en rosace,' 'circular,' even a model of 'a perfect circle,' and 'Gothic,' like a cathedral of Ile de France. It is true that Proust stressed the ingeniousness of some of the props on which he was raising his structure, rich in gargoyles and buttresses and dark, suspicious aisles, and built many of his volumes with a view to the final aesthetic revelation of *Le Temps retrouvé*. But it is none the less true that few great novels, even Russian and American ones, are so liberally encumbered with digressions and extraneous accretions.

Whether organic structure, in spite of the immense prestige in which the word 'organic' seems to be held by many readers today, who approach literature with the minds of engineers, is an essential, or even an authentic, virtue in a novel seems to us a debatable point. Proust's tricks of *petites phrases* and leitmotivs and foreshadowings of the future evolution of his characters are in fact tricks and clumsy devices used by a writer who was far too mindful of the traditional French stress on composition and who could not help respecting Flaubert, Anatole France, and even Bourget (Bergotte has all the letters of Bourget's name but one) far too much. Lastly, to define Proust's position in literature as the crowning achievement of symbolism, as Edmund Wilson did, is to overemphasize one of the aspects of the early Proust and his theoretical aesthetics. Only rarely was Proustian symbolism artificial and intellectual, as the search for subtlety in correspondences had often proved to be with the minor symbolist poets. Proust himself liked to stress the naturalness and inevitability of metaphors not only in style but in our very perception and sensibility. 'Is it not logical,' he asks somewhere in his novel, 'through no device of symbolism but through a sincere return to the very root of the impression, to represent an object by another which, in the flash of an original illusion, we had mistaken for it.' But Proust, whatever he may have said in praise of dreams, of the imagination, of the magic lantern of his childhood reminiscences, of ethereal women's dresses, and of languid flowers, also stands the furthest removed from Henri de Régnier, Albert Samain, Maurice Maeterlinck, and other symbolists. A virile intellect, a relentless mental courage, comic realism, a grasp upon prosaic life, and the awareness that women are not blessed damozels nor marmoreal Herodiades, that men and even children are not angels of purity and innocent Pelleases—these were Proust's gifts also.

Proust possessed the primary privilege of the great novelist: he could, and did, create a variegated and haunting gallery of characters, the richest in French literature next to Balzac's. In spite of the philosophy that is generously lent to him, in spite of the psychological and moral didacticism, of which he was often guilty, and of the aesthetic theorizing in his last volume, Proust never created his characters in order to illustrate pre-existing views or as mouthpieces of his own ideas. Even Bergotte and Elstir are primarily real people. Elstir is the most complex and profound painter ever portrayed in fiction. Proustian characters are not all as convincing. The women who are loved (in what strange ways!) seem to have been endowed with the most elusive characterization. Odette and Albertine are almost negative in this respect. But Andrée, Oriane de Guermantes, Françoise (in spite of Proust's wearisome obsession with the language of his characters), the old aunts at Combray, Mme de Villeparisis, the narrator's grandmother—all are splendidly alive.

So are the 'flat' characters, as E. M. Forster calls them, of which any novel must count a good many, because they are actually flat in real life and are likely to become easily adopted as types. We dare laugh at them as we cannot do when we have discovered the true complexity of M. de Charlus or the tragedy of Swann frittering his life away not only, as he confesses somewhere, on a woman who was not worth it, but on empty social values from which he could not free himself. Proust is probably the greatest master of comedy since Dickens. M. de Norpois will for many decades remain the fatuous diplomat, Cottard the pompous doctor. Legrandin's nose, M. and Mme Verdurin's gestures, cruelty, and silliness are unforgettable. Proustian readers have actually been known to shed tears at St. Loup's disappointing evolution and death, and others to choke with sobs when reading the grave pages in *La Prisonnière* on Vinteuil's greatness or the Dantesque passage where Swann recognizes his own tearful eyes in a mirror while listening to the *petite phrase* and living over again his disappointed love for Odette in his torturing memory.

While Charlus is the incomparable hero of Proustian fiction, perhaps of twentieth-century fiction altogether, Swann, though less dominant in the saga, lays bare more clearly Proust's process of character presentation and delineation. Like all the others, he is a blend of several persons observed by the author in reality. He first appears to the narrator when the latter, a sensitive child, surrounds him with mystery and accumulates baffling contradictions on the wealthy neighbor of Combray. Proust depicts his physique in rapid touches, renders his language, gradually suggests him among his family, his sets of friends. Like most Proustian characters, Swann leads a double life and is himself ambivalent. He is one of the very few exceptions who, perhaps because he dies before the middle of the work, is never carried away in the infernal homosexual round. But he cherishes dolorous and languid women, Botticelli-like, in art, yet, in real life, concretely embraces Rubens-like cooks, servants, and unrefined country girls. He is addicted to dreaming and sharpens his acute nervous sensitiveness to the point of welcoming pain, but he is not capable of the effort needed to mature in solitude and

The Legacy of Proust

to create a work of art. He thus fills an essential function in the novel. He opens up the world of art to Marcel but fails to show him how to penetrate deeply into it, as Elstir will teach him. He points to the peril of living a purely mundane life and of being engulfed by it to the point of losing the ability to concentrate and to create. And he prefigures for Marcel all the tortures of sickly love, anguish, lack of will, and jealousy that will punctuate with their monotonous burden every subsequent passionate pilgrimage within the long novel. In the revelation of his characters, which is never continuously dramatic, Proust is gradual, second to no novelist, except perhaps Dostoevski. The character is imagined and magnified by the narrator long before he appears; then he reveals his several facets, always keeping some mysteries in reserve, and to the last he retains his capacity to astonish us and baffle us. Well may a discerning English critic, Raymond Mortimer, have declared:

> No novelist has made his characters more real to us than Proust, and we know much more about them than about any other figure in fiction. For this reason alone, I believe him to be incomparably the greatest writer who has flourished in my lifetime.

Much will doubtless continue to be written on Proust's psychological revelation and on his aesthetics, the two aspects of his work best calculated to tempt commentators. Both the psychology and the aesthetics of Proust contain much that is already being assimilated by other novelists and by a large portion of the public, even if that public has not actually read Proust. Our way of looking at nature and our manner of falling in and out of love and complacently undergoing the tortures of jealousy have today become definitely Proustian, so much so that the originality of the finest Proustian analyses are already blurred for the generations that have grown up in a Proustian climate. The secrets Marcel read in the sudden thrusts of involuntary memory have likewise lost some of their magic for us. Too many of us have thought ourselves favored with a Proustian revelation because dipping our cake into a cup of tea, smelling a woman's perfume, hearing the distant hum of a train in the night, or stumbling on a flagstone have, thanks to Proust, become meaningful events laden with what we seriously take to be half-mystical ecstasies. In truth, these multiplied episodes in which an involuntary reminiscence releases the Proustian narrator from his anguish and interrupts the otherwise inexorable flow of time do not constitute the most lasting part of Proust's revelation. They may indeed appear to some as a very frail and artificial foundation for the immense cathedral they have to support. Only the unusual depth of Proust's analysis and his poetical gift of transfiguration have saved such episodes, in the last volume, from appearing somewhat childish and arousing our disbelief.

Placed, however, in the course of the novel in general, these flashes of involuntary memory take on a different significance. The Dantesque voyage of the narrator through his childhood and his loves, through the turmoil and vanity of social life, even through the revelations of the spires of Martinville, of the hawthorn and of the medieval stones will end in futility. Society people are empty and cruel; the bevy of girls cycling about the beach is just as heartless; loved ones are mere pegs on which our illusions are hung for a brief respite; death is preying on us from all sides. But one involuntary memory suddenly reveals to the narrator the pattern for which his life had in vain striven. The past is recaptured, the essences shine from behind the painted veil of appearances, the hero's vocation is at last discovered. He composes his work and triumphs over death.

We have also disfigured Proust by our unjustified harping on the theme of his unconscious or latent Bergsonism. Since the task of men teaching young men is apparently to explain more than can be explained and to present annoyingly unpredictable masterpieces as linked to a society or to a philosophy, scholars and critics like to stress the unity of a culture or of an age. Their keenest joy is to discover a philosopher (Descartes, Hegel, Comte, Freud, or Dewey) who will be considered, preferably once he has been safely tucked in his grave, as having formulated the creed from which artistic creations of that age radiated. Bergson has been that scapegoat for the symbolist movement and for the aftermath of symbolism, with Claudel and Proust, even Valéry, presented as his astonished disciples. Proust's repeated denials availed but little, for a touchy author is always suspected of denying most vehemently what secretly pinches him most. The question of Proust's Bergsonism is highly complex and concerns us little here. Clearly, however, Proust does not stem from Bergson and cannot be explained by him. He differs from the philosopher of *Matière et mémoire* (*Matter and Memory*) radically in his conception of memory, in his neglect of the Bergsonian theses on freedom and on the heterogeneousness of cerebral and psychical elements in us, in his stress upon the past, and in his total disinterest in will power, in contrast with Bergson's orientation toward the future and toward action. Proustian aesthetics may remind us of the all-too-scarce passages in which Bergson (notably in *Le Rire* and in *La Pensée et le mouvant*, translated as *The Creative Mind*) had some lineaments of a Bergsonian aesthetics. But there again the parallel should not be strained.

Proust may more convincingly be presented as the Christ heralded by Bergson the Baptist. He was the novelist whom Bergson might have wished to appear and might have announced, even if the prophet did not hail the Messiah with enthusiasm when he finally arrived. For, however perfidiously Bergson may have been lauded by other philosophers for his literary style—a double or multiedged compliment on their

The Legacy of Proust

lips—he himself never confused the two separate provinces of philosophy and literature. In a passage of *La Pensée et le mouvant,* he declared: 'It is the province of literature to undertake . . . the study of the soul in the concrete, upon individual examples; the duty of philosophy, it seemed to me, was to lay down the general conditions of the direct, immediate observation of oneself by oneself.' In the same volume, in an essay on 'La Perception du changement,' Bergson had granted the artist a privileged function and added: 'What is the object of art if not to make us discover . . . outside and within ourselves, a vast number of things which did not clearly strike our senses?' And in his first work, *Les Données immédiates,* translated as *Time and Free Will,* he had praised the anonymous, bold novelist who might tear the deftly woven cloth of our conventional self and put us back in the presence of ourselves.

Proust's original vision may well remain priceless where it indeed rent the delusive veil that conceals true life from us. He escaped from the dull narcotic of habit, removed the superficial layers we have allowed to accumulate over our perception, espoused essences, and arrested time. He belonged, through some features of his genius, to the same family of minds that included Bergson, Rousseau, and Montaigne. He uttered diffident warnings against intelligence, also ingloriously treated by Bergson in *L'Evolution créatrice.* It is a saving grace for France, as Etienne Gilson has remarked, to count periodically some prophets who bid their countrymen to distrust the intellect and flout reason. But for them, it would be harder for Frenchmen to remain intelligent with the due corrective of humility.

More aptly than the much-abused adjective 'Bergsonian,' the broader word 'romantic' would designate the best in the Proustian vision. The romantics restored 'the pleasures of imagination' to the forefront. Romantic heroes, and, even more, romantic heroines, enjoyed the expectation of all joys, and particularly the sinful ones, far more than the fulfillment of such expectations; for reality regularly disappointed them. Like Emma Bovary after she had decided to seek the realization of her bookish dreams with pitifully selfish lovers, they confessed to 'experiencing nothing extraordinary' even in forbidden pleasures. But, and on another plane, imagination was the goddess worshipped by Coleridge, Poe, Baudelaire, and Proust. It alone constituted the whole of love according to Proust; it lay at its source in any case, and it provoked all other pleasures, transfiguring to secondary characters fleetingly colored by the narrator's magic lantern persons from M. de Charlus, Mme de Guermantes, la Berma, and Bergotte to Mlle de Stermaria or the dairy girl of whom he caught a glimpse from the train taking him to Balbec. Proust's claim to greatness lies in part in that irradiation of imagination, enriched by a retentive and transfiguring memory, which turns a weight of matter into gold, and transmutes vices, jealousies, and suspicions into beauty. The lyrical novel, in every language, has usually ended in failure. The Germans, the French (from Chateaubriand to Barrès), the English, including Walter Pater, George Moore, perhaps James Joyce himself, have regularly failed in their attempt to incorporate lyricism and a highly wrought prose into fiction. In his poetization of objects, persons, the cries of street vendors in Paris, and the butlers and lackeys standing in the antechamber of Mme de Saint-Euverte, Proust has succeeded in remaining a convincing and fascinating novelist and in filling the novel with all the poetry it can hold.

But Proust, like all writers who tower above mere talents and who retain their freshness through and despite generations of commentators, cannot be reduced to one formula. He unites in himself contradictory qualities. He 'pushed analysis to the point where it becomes creative,' said one of his earliest English admirers. On the one hand, he belongs with the romantics and the symbolists and goes beyond all of them in centering the whole of life and the whole of his long novel on art. The world, his own remorseful loss of past time, and his plunging into disease and vice receive their only possible justification in being suddenly raised, by the artist's magic wand, to the plane of an aesthetic phenomenon. On the other hand, Proust is a pitiless analyst of all that he uncovers in man, and of himself. He had been compared by the man who understood him most deeply among his contemporaries, Jacques Rivière, with Kepler, Galileo, or Newton. His sharp and cruel vision pierces through all our illusions. He dissociates, even more lucidly and relentlessly than the founders of psychoanalysis, the emotions of love, before which most philosophers, except perhaps Plato and Schopenhauer, had recoiled.

The miracle is that such analytical dissociation is not effected by separating the object from the subject but by a more intimate penetration into the object itself and a spiritualization of matter, which breaks up its material substance into atomic particles and infuses new life into them. The greatest virtue that Proust possesses can probably be best represented by one word—depth. Where others would have passed by, content with rendering the world of appearances, Proust dislocates, assimilates the shattered fragments, and reconstructs them. Like his hero Elstir, he spares no effort to 'dissolve that aggregate of reasonings that we call vision.' His own vision has the newness and the same quality of wonder as that of a child. But it is supplemented by memory, by knowledge of other artists who have already penetrated into the secrets of reality, by an intense concentration of the attention, and by knowledge. Proust probably appreciated the impressionists most among the painters of his age, but Cézanne, and before him Chardin, are those to whom he stands closest. His treatment of concrete objects (the brioches eaten at Combray after the Sunday Mass, the asparagus on Françoise's table, the telephone set at Doncières when he hears his grandmother's

The Legacy of Proust

voice transfigured by the instrument) has all the solidity and the multidimensional quality of a post-impressionist painting. And it retains motion or the potentiality of motion, grace, and elusiveness as well.

In a curious preface to *Tendres Stocks*, by Paul Morand, Proust wrote lines that may well apply to his own unique gift.

> In all the arts, it seems as if talent consisted in a greater closeness between the artist and the object to be expressed. As long as the closeness of the one to the other is not complete, the task is unfinished . . . In other centuries, we feel that there always had remained a certain remoteness dividing the object from the highest minds which hold discourse about it.

These words may well be the most fitting to designate the unique features of Proust's eminence as a novelist. He has most of the other qualities for which we praise the greatest of novelists.[3] In range, he cannot rank with Dickens, Balzac, and Dostoevski. In naturalness, Tolstoy outshines him. But his deep penetration both into reality and into man's emotions and thoughts is hardly equaled anywhere. As a foreign commentator, and one who is not partial to fiction or to French literature, the Spaniard José Ortega y Gasset declared:

> He [Proust] stands as the inventor of a new distance between things and ourselves . . . The whole of the novel that preceded him suddenly appears like a bird's eye literature, crudely panoramic, when compared to that delightfully near-sighted genius.

[3] In fact, a German critic, Ernst Robert Curtius, did not hesitate to write in the *Nouvelle Revue Française* issue devoted to Proust in 1924: 'He [Proust] excels Flaubert in intelligence, as he excels Balzac for his literary qualities and Stendhal for his understanding of life and beauty.'

Analytic Tradition

by Jacques Rivière

From Stendhal on, there occurred a continuous degeneration of our very ancient and deep-rooted faculty for understanding and translating feeling. Flaubert represents the point when this illness becomes noticeable and alarming. I do not mean that *Madame Bovary* and the *Education sentimentale* imply no knowledge of the human heart; but neither of the works gives us any new insight into the heart, or opens up before us any new aspects of it. In this author there is a certain intellectual heaviness in respect to sensibility, and he describes it poorly; he does not disentangle its threads; he no longer knows how to reach its caprices and nuances. For this reason, I think, we have the impression of standing still when we read these books, in spite of the fact that they "move ahead" so powerfully and that their style, as Marcel Proust so aptly remarked, reminds us of a conveyor belt.

A more advanced stage of the illness from which our sense of psychology suffered in the nineteenth century can be studied profitably in the early works of Barrès. They were the great undertaking of a writer who used himself as a subject: numerous, precise classifications of his emotions in order to proceed to as subtle and penetrating an investigation as possible. Strictly speaking, the result was of no value. In the three or four volumes of the *Culte du moi*, there is not the slightest embryo of any psychological discovery; from one end to the other, incense is burned before a truly "unknown God." In spite of his complete good will, in spite of the whole apparatus he sets up around himself, Barrès does not succeed in conquering the hermetic inner darkness that afflicts him.

Moreover, all around him at that period, the knowledge of self was diminishing. Never were people more eager to discuss intuition and less capable of using it, at least as far as inner material was concerned.

"Analytic Tradition" (Original title: "Proust and the Classical Tradition"). From *The Ideal Reader: Selected Essays by Jacques Rivière*, edited, translated, and introduced by Blanche A. Price. Copyright © 1960 by Meridian Books. Reprinted by permission of Meridian Books and The Harvill Press.

Analytic Tradition

Symbolism teaches poets, and novelists as well, a certain delightful manner of approaching the self only in a dream state. It is of very great importance to be blind. The effort to be made, if effort there is, is exactly the opposite to that of being clear-sighted. In order to make the reader vibrate more strongly, the emotions to be used for his delight will be touched only from the outside, with a sort of elated circumspection. They must be pressed, embraced, forced to yield all their sweet essence; but especially, they must not be penetrated, attacked, or dissolved. Whoever the writer may be, he exerts himself above all to be global; he is happy only when he succeeds in recovering, through suggestion and caresses, a moment of his soul in its entirety; he feels that he has accomplished his task only when he has succeeded in re-experiencing briefly that moment, just as it was, with no added understanding.

The psychological novel is permeated with lyricism; it is no longer a branch of the study of the passions; it is no longer used to portray character; with few exceptions it is now thought of as a mere volume of "impressions" of the soul, of "introspective landscapes."

At first glance, it may seem that Proust has done nothing but bring this genre to its perfection. What is his purpose if not to make his entire inner past come alive before the eyes of the reader? Is he not an amazing evocator of sensations and feelings?

Certainly; but there is the manner in which this is accomplished. To achieve his aim, he does not rely upon any magic wand. He will not "raise" his soul up before our eyes "from the depths of the waters" like a whole island completely outfitted. The title of his book, *A la recherche du temps perdu*, says everything; it implies a certain difficulty, an application, a method, an undertaking; it means that there is a certain distance between the author and his subject matter, a distance that he must traverse constantly by memory, reflection, and understanding; it implies a need of knowledge; it announces a discursive conquest of the reality pursued.

And in fact, from the very beginning, Proust abandons all those literary means that belong in any way to the world of enchantment. He is even somewhat severe in depriving himself of music; we see that he does not want to suggest, but to rediscover.

He grapples with feelings and characters through details; he does not abandon all intention of showing their contours and silhouettes, but he realizes that this must come, can come, only in the course of time. Nibble first. He is a rodent; he will make what seems to be a pile of debris until we can understand that it is, on the contrary, the material for a vast and magnificent construction.

I cannot sufficiently say how very moving I find his renunciation of every attempt to stir us, his patience, his diligence, his love of truth.

He picks up his pen by the proper end; first he sketches a small part, and little by little the rest comes of itself. He also makes me think of those machines that swallow very mathematically the piece of cloth or the sheet of paper of which they have been offered only the fringe.

He makes nothing appear unless he starts from within; he does not think of repeating the echo of lost Time; he tries only to give back to Time, little by little, its entire content. And he does the same individually for each emotion that he has experienced, for each character who reappears before his eyes. Immediately, he seeks their nuances, their intimate diversity; only by dint of discovering their differences does he hope to recall them to life.

Jacques Boulenger very subtly noted in *L'Opinion* that Proust portrayed others only "by retracing the reflection they had left in him," and thus went on to seek their image in the depths of some inner mirror, as it were. It is important to understand the implications of this process. However hard we may try, we can make no truly profound description of character unless it is based upon the narrow and solid understanding of ourselves. Before we can turn toward the outside with the hope of some chance of success, the analysis must have been etched strongly within. At least, this is the law among us French. What was lacking in Flaubert and in all the novelists of his school was the knowledge of how to seize themselves first. Because they wanted to be immediately and directly objective, they condemned themselves simply to placing objects in front of themselves, without animating them, diversifying them, lighting them up from within.

Proust sees all things, even those which are exterior, at the angle from which he sees himself. And as he has acquired the habit of refraction, his glance immediately decomposes, makes specific. He succeeds thus in never separating a human being from his detail, and in showing him to us always completely concrete, as rounded out inwardly as he is outwardly, astonishing but, at the same time, known.

The great classic tradition is what he thus renews. Does Racine not seek others in himself? Having once set his understanding upon the traces of his feelings, gradually, by their profitable interplay, he becomes a creator. And in this way only: nothing is raised up directly. By understanding, by analysis and knowledge, he gives birth little by little to different human beings. And before the eyes of the reader or of the spectator, these human beings, thanks to the progressive development of understanding within themselves, take form. In the very beginning, the poet turned his back upon their totality and refused to accept the appearance they might have assumed; he wanted only to absorb them better, to enter their souls as he had first entered his own, that is, completely armed with attention. From what other source do Hermione, Nero, and Phaedra slowly emerge before our eyes than from the depths

Analytic Tradition

of those feelings by which we see them being torn apart? Here there is no *creation* in the true sense of the word, but only invention, that is, something *found,* perceived, unraveled, a verification, so to speak, of the consciousness of another.

Proust goes back to this method, using a large canvas, working more slowly, more minutely, less dramatically. In everything, he once again finds the road inward. And he does so not by an effort of concentration and sleep, in imitation of the style of Bergson, but on the contrary, by the peaceful unfurling of lucidity and discernment. As naturally as a poet who, forgetful of himself, projects images before himself, so does Proust plunge into himself and ask questions, explore, guess, recognize, and gradually explain people and things to himself. His mind very gently eats away all that is obscure or opaque in his subjects, destroys all that refuses to be revealed, all that would tend to make just an impression. In this way he *invents* them merely by making an inventory, merely by the calm perpetuity of the attention he grants them. To produce his subjects, he demonstrates them. He tries to make them manifest on the page he is writing, and through ten thousand words, he goes in search of them. He does not acknowledge their shadows; these, too, must be filled with traits that can be and must be seized: for the lack of better, he will people them with his hypotheses.

His work moves in a direction contrary to that of romanticism, which unceasingly consisted in making people believe things without showing them. Through his intervention, we can expect an enormous deflation of our literature. In a little while it is going to become impossible to create any interest in the lump, to touch imagination directly. The writer will no longer be able to ask of the senses that faith upon which he was making increasingly tyrannical demands. He will have to explain himself, lay his cards on the table. And then it will be clearly seen that the great things are those in which there are the greatest possible number of little ones, that depth is in inverse ratio to size, and that genius is perhaps not so far removed from judgment and precision as we have come to think.

By relieving us of the lack of division in ideas and feelings, Proust delivers us from the enigmatic and the uncontrollable. He turns the stream back through the mill of our reason and once more puts in motion our faculty for reflection. Thanks to him, we escape from that sort of sensuous complicity or mystical conversation which was gradually becoming the only relationship we could engage in with a writer. Now we have reacquired a taste for understanding; once more our pleasure lies in learning something about ourselves, in feeling ourselves imbued with definition, in recognizing that we are more capable of being formulated than we had thought.

The great, modest journey through the human heart which the

classics had initiated begins again. "The study of feelings" once more makes progress. Our eyes open anew upon inner truth. Our literature, choked by the ineffable for a time, once more becomes openly what it has always been essentially: a "discourse on the passions."

Faces of Proust

by Albert Thibaudet

In literature as in history almost nothing happens as one had the right to expect; but when it does happen, one always finds good reasons for its happening in just that way: the kind of mind that imposes order triumphs where the prophetic mind had failed. During the war years everyone was waiting for the birth, almost any day, from the very travail of war, of a new literature. The result was very different.

Between pre-war literature and the literature of the generation brought up in war and by war, there seems to have been a peculiar oasis of disinterested literature, disinterested to the point of paradox: one of those spots of sunshine and blue water, with flowers and smiles, and white, ministering hands where, between descents into the battle, we spent our convalescence. Two names suddenly thrust themselves upon our attention, one, that of a poet, the other, that of a novelist: Paul Valéry and Marcel Proust. And if the coincidence of their fame is a work of chance, that chance, all will agree, worked in this instance like a great artist.

When the future Bishop Bossuet, then only twelve years old, preached at the Hôtel de Rambouillet at midnight, Voiture observed that he had never heard anybody preach either so early or so late. Valéry and Proust had made their first appearances very early, but their real *début* came now, very late. The young disciple of Mallarmé and the author of those *Plaisirs et Jours* presented to the public by Anatole France had entered into literature in the shadow of old masters more or less laden with literary fruit. And then, except for a few articles by one, a few translations from the English by the other, their voices had almost subsided. They had grown still in ways and for reasons that were also parallel. To "go into literature" means always, more or less, a descent into the world of practical techniques, of trade and exchange, a "come-down."

"Faces of Proust" (Original title: "Marcel Proust and the French Tradition"). Translated by Angelo P. Bertocci. From *From the NRF,* edited by Justin O'Brien. Copyright 1958 by Justin O'Brien. Reprinted by permission of Justin O'Brien and Meridian Books.

Now neither of the two had any intention of denying a realm of essences more precious than literature, the essences that were for one "pure poetry" and for the other "high society." Pure poetry and society they saw in detachment from everything else and especially from literature. That Valéry, a disciple of the high priest of the rue de Rome, was a mystic of pure poetry no one will deny. But the very idea of Marcel Proust as a mystic of "society" may raise a smile. And that marvelous character, Legrandin, of capital importance, may seem to give substance, in the work itself, to the derision in that smile. Yet it was a veritable transport of love, analogous to the mystic's transport, that made Proust yearn with his whole being, body and soul, toward the God of "society" life, the God desired in the ardor of youth, and finally embraced by passionate arms reaching out, one from Swann's way, the other from the Guermantes way.

We know now that that kind of thing can be encountered in real life. But how describe it so as to penetrate thick layers of obtuseness and irony? What dangers of radical misunderstanding! If they were to be incorporated in literature and reach a public sunk in habit and routine, with what kind of alloy must these imponderable essences be weighted? Valéry simply gave up on the whole idea. Satisfied with the test of his own gift, he left poetry to those capable of putting it to material use and stretching it out in discursive rhetoric. Marcel Proust might have done the same and plunged without a word into the unspeakable nature of "society," if a long illness had not kept him to himself, and if solitude, challenging him to come forth, had not torn away with imperious hand, in order to make them trophies in the museum of glory, the jewels bedecking the shoulders of life.

It is only then that, in his forties, he produced *Swann's Way,* which attracted little attention. It was talked of in some circles as an odd and original book, but no one guessed the astonishing renewal that was to spring from it. Without the war could this work have won a hearing, as it piled up its volumes and took on new depth, weight, levels of meaning, and meandered so deviously in its search for time past? Yes, almost certainly. But the war probably did not hurt it any. The resurgence of Valéry, who was of the same age as Proust, who had ceased to write almost at the same time, and who made his comeback at almost the same date, bears witness, as does Proust, of a certain dimly-felt need in the depths and the unconsciousness of our literary life. Nothing seemed more remote from public concerns and the clear light of consciousness than these two epitomes of a paradoxical leisure and detachment, these essences of pure poetic life and of pure "society" life. Precisely because they seemed infinitely remote, everybody saw them as stars shining through the storm. Art took on its old role as a means of escape. *A l'ombre des jeunes filles en fleurs* and *La Jeune Parque* went off together like parallel rockets, the poem's success in depth reflecting the novel's success in breadth of appeal. The analogy held between the two destinies, the dual resurgence at the same moment, the two essences.

But was it really a matter of escapism in this instance? The plastic arts and music were feeling at this same time a shock unparalleled in their history and were reacting in a violent movement against tradition. Do Proust and Valéry represent the same kind of break with French tradition? It hardly seems so. Part of the favor in which they were held is to be explained perhaps, in the public unconscious, by war-time psychology itself, by the intense desire to press to oneself whatever is most paradoxically pure, hidden, and mystical in the French treasure of tradition. I intend to speak only of Marcel Proust. He loved "society" as Mallarmé and Valéry loved poetry. He wrote a work which was to Romain Rolland's *La Foire sur la place* as Mallarmé's *Hérodiade* was to *La Grève des forgerons*. He participated in the defense of pure elegance just as did Valéry in the defense of pure beauty. And when I speak of elegance, when I take part for the whole, I expect my reader to add the necessary pinch of salt. Is there not, in the literature of each people, a place reserved and narrowly national, almost impossible of access for a foreigner? How are these secret gardens laid out and defended in literary and critical tradition? Are there not also, and at the opposite pole (I have just been speaking of *Jean-Christophe*) gardens that are public and almost international? However one may answer this question, whose terms need defining, Proust would seem to belong in gardens of a not very cosmopolitan sort. Some conscientious Englishmen have founded a Marcel Proust study club. That French "high society" should have inspired love and admiration in a Marcel Proust must be a source of no little astonishment to an English novelist. His wonder will grow less if he seeks the thread which binds Proust to an authentic tradition.

In the last six years it has become a custom in France to evoke the names of Saint-Simon and Montaigne in connection with Proust. Such an association does deserve to become a commonplace and a link in the chain of our literary history. We must think of Saint-Simon and of Montaigne in order to realize what depths of French experience underlie the work of Proust, and what a mass of time past is brought to mind by time recaptured.

Saint-Simon—this does not mean Saint-Simon alone. We know that his work, put together in such irregular fashion, includes three parts. The first does not belong to him. It is the diary of Dangeau, which is to the monument of literature as a whole what the little château of Louis XIII is to Versailles. Saint-Simon piled up over it first the *Additions au journal*, then he went over the whole thing and fused it together in his great search for things past, in the first part of the definitive *Mémoires*. The courtier's insipidity, the sanctimonious ecstasies of Dangeau in the royal presence move the Duke and Peer to a deep disgust and, not having the same reasons for prostrating himself, he shakes Dangeau down rather rudely, like a smug pear-tree. I should call Proust a Dangeau turned into a Saint-Simon. "Society" is for him, even to its very warts, what Louis XIV was, warts and all, for Dangeau (Any kind of worker is reduced by Proust to the rank of servant. He doesn't "belong"—I mean to "society." In the city Cottard has the rank of a celebrated professor, but in "society" what good is he except to make puns like all professors in the novels written in the XVIth Arrondissement?). This social world Proust sees with the many-faceted eye and renders with the style of Saint-Simon. The life of men and the life of style are in him the vibration of one and the same experience. This mode of picturing a world implies a world in the way the sentence is put together,—that synthesizing kind of sentence which seems indefinitely extensible and which holds in germ already, as in a homoeomery of Anaxagoras, all the complexity of the book, just as the book offers for our grasp all the complexity of life. A great writer does not think in terms of simplicity nor see in terms of simplicity, but he can be led to write in terms of simplicity, because style is free interpretation with a view to the effect to be produced and the result to be obtained, and because this effect, this result can consist in putting into the conclusion a simplicity missing in the premises. To write in terms of simplicity (I do not mean, to write simply) is to proceed with the aid of expressions that are discontinuous and whose connecting link is in the order and movement. Proust like Saint-Simon is one of those writers who, not seeing and not feeling in terms of simplicity, would shrink from writing in terms of simplicity as from an act of treason. Every sentence must preserve the complexity, the denseness, the emotional intensity or the descriptive joy which were in thought and image in the beginning. Having undertaken the task of bringing before the eyes and into the soul of the reader a tide of time and life in process, they would refuse to divide into drops this swelling tide as it advances bearing with it the creative urge that is one with its life and movement. In Saint-Simon the tide rolling in is a historical one, it is a crowd, the entire French court, and always, everywhere, it is the living soul of Saint-Simon in all its vehemence; with Proust, the tidal movement is in the individual psychology, a tide certainly of no lesser magnitude than in the first instance, but which needs, in order to make a total impact all along the way, no more than an individual soul, whether it be the author's or the unexhausted and inexhaustible soul of one of his characters. The rhythm of expression is in accord with the movement of this tide. A portrait by Saint-Simon, a portrait by Proust, even Swann's, extending over hundreds of pages, never leaves the impression, in all its wealth of substance and diversity, that is has exhausted the character's capacity to take an unexpected turn and spring a surprise. One must stop somewhere, and so they stopped, and not for want of a limitless vitality. Similarly, the sentence which carries their meaning stops only for negative reasons, because it too may not go on forever. Sentence structures give to an unlimited reality *de facto* limits which are not the *de jure* limits. The internal resistance that held off their completion as long as possible warns the reader against what is arbitrary in that completion, which must then be taken only as the best substitute available for a reality ever unfinished, on the march, ever advancing. The style lags behind the thought, its movement, multiplying distinctions, lagging behind the uniform, global, and indivisible movement of life in process. The very fact of such a lag illuminates strikingly what it lags behind. Style seems then a "second best," which functions as a perpetual reminder of the unattainable best.

Such a style is truly consubstantial to the thinking and living reality. Too consubstantial, one may object, to be clear and correct. It does indeed depend more on the writer's touch and organic sensibility than upon the easy flow of the pen-point. It was no chance that "style" got its name from the instrument utilized rather than from the moving hand that writes. But for a Saint-Simon or a Proust a style atomized and analytical is more like the labor of the scribe who expounds than of the man who lives. Saint-Simon in 1750 mentions a certain Arouet, "son of a notary of my father's, and who since then seems to have cut a figure in society." If he ever read that Arouet, his style must have seemed to him the style of a man who takes "note" of life, as a "notary" would, rather than the style of a man who lives it. And he would be more than a little wrong. As Voltaire used to like to say, in my Father's house there are many mansions.

At any rate, in the gallery of French styles since the *Provinciales*, a new category should be created for Saint-Simon and Proust—and it is hard to think of anybody else. This style, descending from that of the sixteenth century, probably did not follow the course to be traced by the genius of French prose. It remains unique. But the very fact of a Saint-Simon suffices to link Proust with some point of our rich literary diversity and to place him in a tradition. And Proust's style *à la* Saint-Simon is the product of a certain way of feeling life and evoking the past which also reminds us of Saint-Simon. The analogy is dual—in type of mind and in style. The common element underlying diversities of form in the author of the *Mémoires* and the searcher for time past was a style adapted to the nature of memory.

At first sight, the name of Montaigne seems less plausible in this connection than that of Saint-Simon. Proust's case, like Saint-Simon's, could almost be defined in terms of a breaking out of memory. Montaigne is careful to tell us that of all his faculties none was so lacking as memory. His *Essays* are ample confirmation. Montaigne cast the net of experience not over the world of men and the figures of his day but over himself and over that human predicament of which every man bears the effigy. In his book the only living portrait is himself. On the contrary, in the sections published so far of *A la recherche du temps perdu*, the author's own portrait is sketchy and dim, and not to be compared with Swann's or Charlus'.

Nevertheless, Proust the portrait-painter, author of memoirs, and novelist must not be allowed to overshadow the moralist. The day will come when his reflections on human psychology and morals will be brought together in a single book and we shall see clearly where he joins the great tradition of French moralists and students of human nature. This will be a discovery and embarrassment for certain intelligent critics who cannot bear to read him. From this point of view he can be considered the living representative of the family of subtle analysts which, since Montaigne, has so rarely been unemployed in France.

The sick-room has been for him what the tower was for Montaigne, and if the spirit of solitude has spoken to him and made him speak a different language, strange how that language will throw out images very evidently analogous to Montaigne's! Proust, like Montaigne, belongs to the family of image-creators, and his images, like Montaigne's, are generally images of movement. The plastic surface, the outer bark of things are for them only the external manifestations to be traversed in order to get at the inner movement which came to a stop or found expression in those things. The universe of Proust and of Montaigne is a projection of dynamic patterns with which the style, through the medium of images, aspires to coincide. Their style does not put movement into thought, according to the classical definition, but it puts thought into a movement which preexists, and which may inform, or be interrupted by, thought.

Criticism and Creation

by Walter A. Strauss

> Les beaux livres sont écrits dans une sorte de langue étrangère. Sous chaque mot chacun de nous met son sens ou du moins son image qui est souvent un contre-sens. Mais dans les beaux livres, tous les contre-sens qu'on fait sont beaux.
> Proust, *Contre Sainte-Beuve.*

Criticism for Proust was a means to an end. The germ and the fruit of this idea are contained in a quotation from *La Bible d'Amiens:*

> There is no better way of becoming conscious of what one feels oneself than to try to re-create in one's own mind the feelings of a master. For the deep-searching effort brings our thought, as well as his, into the light of day.

He found it to his advantage to use an author's text in the same way in which he intended his own novel to be read—as a sort of optical device whereby the reader can read himself. This process of making a text one's own necessarily implies an intermediate analytical and critical stage, in which the Proustian reader attempts to seize the essence behind an author's "vision." For the author's vision is not necessarily one which he can analyze consciously; the very texture of his writings is the result of a more or less mysterious process, in which the artist's inner organization imposes a secret and profound order upon his materials. In his critical studies Proust attempted to attune his ear to these secret rhythms. Writing to Gide about *Les Nourritures terrestres,* he observed:

> . . . Probably you will always be unaware of the most secret beauty of that book, for you know its content thoroughly, but you cannot hear its

---

"Criticism and Creation" (Original title: "Conclusion"). From *Proust and Literature* by Walter A. Strauss (Cambridge, Mass.: Harvard University Press, 1957). Copyright 1957 by the President and Fellows of Harvard College. Reprinted by permission.

rhythm. And the novelty of that book—a lasting quality, of course, since the new in art never lies in the realm of time—which takes hold of one even more effectively if one has put the work aside for a few years, this novelty is to be found above all in its rhythm.[1]

In order to capture this rhythm or accent Proust often casts his literary judgments in the form of analyses (discernments) rather than criticisms (judgments). Both are, for Proust, ways of discovering himself by means of discovering others.

In the above quotation, Proust uses the word "master" deliberately, rather than the more narrow "writer." All great artists have an aesthetic lesson to teach him. This statement requires no elucidation for the reader of Proust. *A la recherche* offers portraits of four representatives of the arts, Marcel's own patron saints: Bergotte, Berma, Elstir, and Vinteuil. Each one of these is studied in terms of his particular perfection, the theme of his art running as a leitmotiv throughout the novel, stimulating reflection and revealing some hitherto hidden aspect of the mystery of art. Speaking of Vinteuil and Elstir, Pierre-Quint observed that "existing on an almost divine plane, upon the heights where the Muses used to live, and resembling the Muses in having taken on human shape, they constitute the total image of artistic activity." [2] Bergotte's art serves at first as a literary ideal to the young Marcel preoccupied with literature; in Bergotte's works he discovers the first "key images" and the joy attending upon such revelations.[3] As Marcel matures he gradually leaves Bergotte behind, without losing his respect for the master, and gradually discovers his own literary vocation. The search for literary excellence finds successive incarnations in the Bergotte whom the reader meets in the first volumes, then the dying Bergotte, and finally the Marcel who discovers his own literary vocation and his aesthetics. Thus, in a broader sense, the early Bergotte parallels the refined but derivative Proust of *Les Plaisirs et les jours;* the dying Bergotte is what Proust would have been if he had not learned that style and vision are dual aspects of the same creative act. For, the dying Bergotte, grasping the secret of Vermeer's art, learns that the mystery of art may reside in a patch of yellow wall, just as it might be contained in the taste of a soaked *madeleine,* in a hedge of hawthorns, or in the shifting patterns of the Martinville steeples.

> . . . He fixed his eyes, like a child upon a yellow butterfly which it is trying to catch, upon the precious little patch of wall. "That is how I ought to have written," he said. "My last books are too dry, I ought to

[1] *Lettres à André Gide* (Paris: Ides et Calendes, 1949), pp. 60-61.
[2] Léon Pierre-Quint, *Marcel Proust* (Paris: Sagittaire, 1946), pp. 254-255.
[3] *Remembrance of Things Past,* I, 71-72.

Criticism and Creation

have gone over them with several coats of paint, made my language exquisite in itself, like this little patch of yellow wall." [4]

And the final incarnation of the writer is Marcel himself in *Le Temps retrouvé*, now to all intents and purposes identical with the Proust of *A la recherche*, grasping the significance of memory and art as ways of conquering Time, and converting this triumph into a vision of reality through the medium of artistic expression.

Elstir and Vinteuil, and to a lesser extent Berma, offer Marcel insights into the nature of art, which contribute to the clarification of his own aesthetics, for all the arts point to the same reality. As Curtius expresses it in his essay on Proust, ". . . The several arts are but different ways to the soul's kingdom, which is in a state of unchanging repose." [5] For Proust, they are the signposts along the path to eternity. And for this reason he constantly looked to the other arts for illumination along the way. Vermeer and Elstir taught him the secret of Space, Wagner and Vinteuil the secret of Time. Balzac showed him how the recurrence of characters can be used to tie a long novel together; Flaubert knew how to set Time to music, grammatically; Dostoevski knew how to split characters without disintegrating them. Tolstoi had the secret of being able to organize vast canvases by means of an intellectual pattern; George Eliot felt the poetry of humble existences; Ruskin taught him to beware of the idolatry of art; and Sainte-Beuve served as a warning against bondage to history and time and to the intellect. But even more important than the specific illuminations gained from all these masters is Proust's realization that all the creators of the world's literature are images of one and the same poet,

> that great poet who at bottom has been one single poet ever since the beginning of the world, whose intermittent life, which is as long as the life of mankind itself, had in this earthly life its tormented and cruel hours, which we call the life of Baudelaire; its hardworking and serene hours, which we call the life of Hugo; its vagabond and innocent hours which we call the life of Nerval and perhaps of Francis Jammes; its waywardness and debasement to ambitious purposes having nothing to do with truth, which we call the life of Chateaubriand and of Balzac; its waywardness and soaring above truth which we call the second half of Tolstoi's life, as well as Racine's, Pascal's, Ruskin's, and perhaps Maeterlinck's.[6]

The same thing could have been said of the painters and composers. The different arts, for Proust, are never categorized; he passes easily

---
[4] *Ibid*. II, 509.
[5] Curtius, Ernst-Robert, *Französischer Geist im neuen Europa* (Stuttgart: Deutsche Verlags-Anstalt, 1925), p. 66.
[6] *Contre Sainte-Beuve*, p. 193.

from literature to music to art, as happens when in his analysis of *Les Petites Vieilles* by Baudelaire he recalls the late works of Beethoven, and, significantly enough, in his explanation of the *phrases-types*, which are actually the outgrowth of Marcel's discovery of the "little phrase" in Vinteuil's music. The result is that Marcel's (and Proust's) method of scrutiny is essentially the same for all the arts; it always yields a glimpse of a more essential reality behind the actual language which the artist uses; and the result is always an enrichment of experience which stamps itself indelibly on Marcel's soul. It is this revelation of art that matters to the artist; as Proust observes in his essay on Baudelaire:

> ... the objective precision of a writer's judgments on an art other than his own are without importance. What matters, what sets him dreaming, is the fact of his admiration, even when it may be given to what is unworthy.[7]

As Marcel was to discover, the *phrases-types* of the various writers, painters, and composers always point toward the hawthorn blossoms, the steeples of Martinville, the *madeleine* and the other privileged moments in which a transcendent reality was revealed to him for a brief moment. Thus, when the artist begins to create, he draws on all his accumulated aesthetic experience, he sloughs off his temporal self and exchanges "his soul for the universal soul."[8] The contemplation of art leads Proust, inevitably, in the direction of mystical absorption.

The focusing of the artist's mind depends completely on the inner concerns of his psyche, even insofar as these concerns determine the form and style which can shape and express his inwardness. Proust, consequently, built his critical remarks about an author around certain facets of that writer that were of particular interest to him—the centrality of Gomorrha in Baudelaire, the sense of time in Flaubert, the recurrence of characters in Balzac, the idealization of the beloved in Hardy, the mystery of the women in Dostoevski, and so on. Each of these aspects of the various authors has its counterpart in *A la recherche du temps perdu*. Proust shows himself to be aware of the novelty of his critical method and its importance as a revaluation or in some cases even a resurrection of literary beauty: "I knew that it is not only over different works, in the long course of centuries, but over different parts of the same work that criticism plays, thrusting back into the shadow what for too long has been thought brilliant, and making emerge what has appeared to be doomed to permanent obscurity."[9]

To quote Professor Levin's words, Proust's "long apprenticeship in the arts had taught him that the greatest masters are hard to recognize,

[7] *Chroniques*, p. 218.
[8] *Contre Sainte-Beuve*, p. 352.
[9] *Remembrance of Things Past*, I, 1054.

that true originality must build up its own tradition." [10] This apprenticeship of necessity implies criticism, whether silent or expressed. Thus, criticism and analysis were a method of self-discovery for Proust. This explains why Proust practiced criticism from his youth up to the time when he began to write *A la recherche;* and it explains why one of the earlier conceptions of the work to be created took the form of a critical essay-*récit* about Sainte-Beuve. The later essays on Flaubert and Baudelaire, and the prefaces to *Propos de peintre* and *Tendres Stocks,* are replicas in one way or another of Proust's mature ideas on aesthetics, as set forth in *Le Temps retrouvé.* Indeed, it has been shown that Proust's own crisis occurred during the writing of the *Contre Sainte-Beuve.* "Sloth or doubt or impotence take refuge in an author's hesitation concerning the form his art is to take," he wrote in his notebook. "Is one to write a novel? a philosophical study? am I a novelist?" [11] Proust's artistic triumph lies in his having been able, by the end of the Sainte-Beuve experiment, to answer the last question in the affirmative. And thus the literary career of Proust after *Jean Santeuil* can be described as an enormous cycle that begins with the posing of a number of aesthetic problems, which only criticism could begin to solve; Ruskin and Sainte-Beuve are the catalysts here. Then follows Proust's definitive discovery of his artistic vocation and its fulfillment in *A la recherche.* And this work closes on a note of artistic certitude, which comprises the solution to the problem as originally posed.

To be sure, as we look back to *Jean Santeuil,* we can see that the germ of Proust's idealistic aesthetics was already there. In that novel Jean Santeuil muses at length about the relation of art to life, and about the nature of artistic creation. Proust's most cherished ideas are already sketched out there. The value of literature does not lie in a (naturalistic) use of materials but in the way in which the writer "operates" on his materials. The ironic relationship of life to art is compared—with Platonic overtones—to the difference between shadow and prey; and those who seek reality by embracing life and leaving behind the realm of art are substituting the illusion of material possession for the reality of spiritual possession, "les choses n'étant possédables que par l'esprit." [12] The artist's rendering of the reality as he perceives it takes the form of impressions, and the way in which these impressions are organized in the artist's consciousness remains mysterious to him, so that he can never explain to others how the amalgamation took place.[13] Proust's great achievement as a literary critic lies in the fact that he attempted to elucidate the mystery, without dispelling it—because for him art,

[10] Harry Levin, Introduction to *Letters of Marcel Proust* (New York: Random House, 1949), p. xvi.
[11] Quoted by M. de Fallois in his preface to *Contre Sainte-Beuve,* p. 35.
[12] *Jean Santeuil* (New York: Simon and Schuster, Inc., 1956), p. 253. Cf. also p. 426.
[13] *Jean Santeuil,* pp. 204 and 239.

like religion, needs its mysteries. And the contact established with this mysterious essence—the spiritual "homeland"—of another writer, and leading to self-discovery, is an experience of great joy, a kind of ecstasy comparable to the elation accompanying the *unio mystica*. The artist who has just discovered himself, notes Proust,

> dies instantaneously in the particular and begins immediately to float and to live in the general. He lives only by means of the general: it animates and nurtures him . . . But so long as he is alive, his life is one long ecstasy and happiness.[14]

We understand now Proust's repeated emphasis on the mystery of things and of art, even though at times the word appeared unnecessary and perhaps obscure. For him the whole web of human experience is suffused with this essence, which only memory and art can liberate. The process of this liberation is the highest metaphysical and aesthetic achievement of which the human soul is capable. The conquest of this reality is the highest ethical aspiration of the artist and brings with it the promise of an absolute felicity.

But the final distillation of Proust's aesthetic creed comes at the end of *A la recherche*. The principal points of the essay-within-the-novel center around the writer's, particularly the novelist's, art, the relationship of art to reality, and the problem of style. In Proust's scheme of things these three aspects are closely interlinked, culminating in a triumphant and apocalyptic vision of art: "art is the most real of all things, the sternest school in life and truly the Last Judgment."[15] It is as if art had become a mode of salvation for him, demanding its own *askesis*, whereby the artist might successfully purify himself of what was material and temporal in him. It is strange—and in no way accidental—how often Proust uses the vocabulary of theology to parallel his own aesthetic journey. This characteristic is by no means the same as the "religion of art" of the fin de siècle, though that was perhaps Proust's point of origin. The religion of art is transcended and becomes, instead, a religion *through* art, an *itinerarium mentis in Artem*.

Because the involuntary memory and the contemplation of "things" had afforded Marcel an insight into the "hidden essence" of things, across the vastness of Time, Proust felt convinced that the writer's sole raison d'être was to penetrate more deeply into this reality. The quest, he knew, was difficult:

> To read the subjective book of these strange signs . . . no one could help me with any rule, for the reading of that book is a creative act in

[14] *Contre Sainte-Beuve*, p. 303.
[15] *Remembrance of Things Past*, II, 1001.

Criticism and Creation 59

which no one can stand in our stead, or even collaborate with us. And therefore how many there are who shrink from writing it; how many tasks are undertaken in order to avoid that one! Each happening, the Dreyfus case, the war, supplied fresh excuses to the writers for not deciphering that book—they wished to assure the triumph of right, rebuild the moral unity of the nation, and they had no time to think of literature.[16]

This truancy from literature for which Proust is here reproaching many of his contemporaries, notably Barrès, is further aggravated by their espousal of a realism without depth, a kind of journalism, against which Proust's own great work is so eloquent an argument. Reality is to be measured by the degree of penetration attained by the writer, not by the objects selected.

The literature that is satisfied merely to "describe things," to furnish a miserable listing of their lines and surfaces, is, notwithstanding its pretensions to realism, the farthest removed from reality, the one that most impoverishes and saddens us, even though it speak of nought but glory and greatness, for it sharply cuts off all communication of our present self with the past, the essence of which the objects preserve, and with the future, in which they stimulate us to enjoy the past again.[17]

Realism, he concludes, is not a matter of reproducing observed things photographically and cinematographically, nor need the writer fill up notebooks with facts and with sketches: the synthesis of his accumulated observation is made subconsciously, not by a calculated arrangement of notes. ". . . The writer finds that he, too, has been making a sketchbook without knowing it . . . it is the feeling for the general which in the future writer automatically selects what is general and can therefore enter into a work of art." [18]

It would be wrong to regard these ideas merely as a reaction to naturalism and the "literature of notation" and to assign Proust the critic a place beside antinaturalists like Bourget and de Vogüé; Proust is rather expressing a conviction intended to be applicable to all great artists of all time. It is for this reason that he considers all great art classical—a statement which does away with the textbook classifications into movements and schools. Whether he is justified in overthrowing these cherished academic distinctions is somewhat beside the point here; the important thing is that for him all true art is, by definition, classical, and that true art is constantly being renewed, with the result that the history of all art is a succession of classical artists and works. Since this notion equates the terms "classical" and "timeless," the concept of literary movements is merely useful to designate the timely (historical)

[16] *Ibid.* [17] *Ibid.*, II, 1005. [18] *Ibid.*, II, 1016.

side of literary creation. Thus, the term "school" has only a relative significance, as Proust explained in a letter to Rosny:

> "Schools" . . . are only a material symbol of the time it takes for a great artist to be understood and placed among his peers, for the repudiated *Olympia* to hang next to Ingres; for Baudelaire, the judgment against him reversed, to fraternize with Racine . . .
> As soon as the innovator is understood, the school for which there is no longer any need is disbanded. Besides, no matter how long the school lasts, the innovator's taste is always much broader. Hugo vaunted Romanticism as his school, but appreciated perfectly Boileau and Regnard. Wagner never regarded Italian music with the severity of the Wagnerians.[19]

A literary school might thus be defined as a propaganda organization designed to make its new ideas acceptable to the public. The proper place for such ideas is to be found within the framework of intellectual history. Proust assumes all along something that literary history has amply borne out, something of which he himself was only too aware: that new writers, by virtue of their novelty, find acceptance difficult. Since every classicism is a renewal not only of vision but also of the way in which this vision finds expression—"the continuity of styles is not compromised but guaranteed by a perpetual renewal of style" [20]—he observes that every renewal of this sort requires a new effort. In his Preface to Jacques-Emile Blanche's *Propos de peintre* he spoke of those new artists who prove themselves worthy successors of the past "because they begin their lives by being situated in the future," producing works "at which one must try to look down the perspective of the years that they anticipate, bringing that modification of the sensibilities for the development of which it is time, precisely, that is needed." [21] A statement summarizing Proust's attitude is found at the conclusion of the Preface to *Tendres Stocks*, this conclusion being intended as a final answer to Anatole France's complaint that good writers had disappeared since the end of the eighteenth century.

> The truth . . . is that from time to time a new and original writer appears . . . The new writer is, as a rule, rather exhausting to read and difficult to understand, because he is forever finding new relationships between things. One follows him half-way through a sentence, but then one's endurance gives out. One feels the reason to be merely this, that the new writer has a more agile mind than one's own. It is with original

[19] *Letters of Marcel Proust*, pp. 382-383.
[20] In "Sommes-nous en présence d'un renouvellement du style? . . . ," *La Renaissance politique, littéraire, artistique* 9:6 (July 22, 1922).
[21] *Marcel Proust: A Selection from his Miscellaneous Writings* (London: Allan Wingate, 1948), p. 242.

Criticism and Creation

writers as it is with original painters. When Renoir began to paint, no one recognized the objects which he set himself to represent. It is easy, today, to speak of him as having an eighteenth-century spirit. But, in saying that, people omit the time factor, and forget that, even in the middle of the nineteenth century, it took a long time for Renoir to be accepted as a great painter. If they are to succeed, they have—the original painter and the original writer—to proceed much in the manner of oculists. The treatment administered through their paintings or their literature is not always pleasant. When it is finished, they say to us: "*Now look!*" and suddenly the world, which, far from having been created once and for all, is created afresh each time that a new artist comes on the scene, is shown to us in perfect clarity—but looking very different from the one we knew before.[22]

Since Proust's belief is that the vitality of literature depends on a continuous renewal of style, his idea of style is necessarily broad. This is one of the great virtues of his criticism: his sense of style seems almost infallible, as his pastiches and his numerous stylistic analyses have adequately shown. Rejecting all that is artificial, rhetorical, and decorative, Proust exalts the style in which the authentic impression, the natural progress of the mind are reflected:

> As to style, I have endeavored to reject everything dictated by pure intellect, everything that is rhetoric, embellishment and, more or less, any deliberate or mannered figures of speech . . . to express my deep and authentic impressions and to respect the natural progress of my thought.[23]

Thus he explains in his Preface to *Tendres Stocks* that it is better to use no images at all if the "inevitable" image fails to suggest itself to the writer:

> . . . An image that is merely approximate is a failure. Water (in given conditions) boils at a temperature of 100 degrees. At 98 or 99 the phenomenon does not occur. In such cases it is better to do without any images at all. Set somebody in front of a piano for six months on end, someone who knows nothing of Wagner or of Beethoven; let him try every possible chance combination of notes on the keyboard; this fumbling will never produce the Spring theme from *Die Walküre* or the pre-Mendelssohnian (or, rather, infinitely super-Mendelssohnian) phase from the 15th Quartet.[24]

A writer's conscious effort to be original belongs in the same category and, in Proust's eyes, is equally reprehensible. Writing for the sym-

[22] *Ibid.*, pp. 221-22.
[23] *Letters of Marcel Proust*, pp. 405-406.
[24] *M. P.: A Selection*, pp. 222-223.

posium on style in the *Renaissance politique, littéraire, artistique* on July 22, 1922, he remarks:

> I in no way "give my support" (to use the very phrasing of your inquiry) to writers "preoccupied with originality of form." A writer should be exclusively preoccupied with his impressions, or with ideas to be translated into words.[25]

On the other hand, he welcomes a writer's originality in using the French language. As the style is renewed, the language too undergoes a renewal; for Proust, what is finest in the French language is due to the efforts of its great writers:

> This idea that there is a French language that exists outside of the writers who use it and that must be protected is fantastic. Each writer is bound to create his own language as each violinist must create his own "tone." . . . I prefer—and it is, perhaps, a weakness—those who write well. But they start to write well only on condition that they are original, that they themselves create their own language. Correctness, perfection of style do exist, but not this side of originality, but through and beyond it . . . The only way to defend the language is to attack it! Because its unity is created only by the neutralizing of opposites, by an apparent immobility which hides perpetual, vertiginous activity. For one "holds one's own" and cuts a fine figure in comparison with writers of the past only inasmuch as one has tried to write quite differently. And when one wants to defend the French language, one actually writes quite the opposite of classical French. For example: the revolutionaries Rousseau, Hugo, Flaubert, Maeterlinck "hold their own" beside Bossuet.[26]

This preoccupation with language in all its aspects—the written language of his predecessors which he made his own in the pastiches with such astonishing virtuosity, as well as the spoken language of others which he imitated in the drawing rooms and later in *A la recherche*—can be noted as early as *Jean Santeuil*. There Proust offers his readers an object lesson on style by having Professor Beulier criticize Jean Santeuil's dissertation; the pasage reads like an extension of "Contre l'obscurité" into fiction:

> ". . . No doubt you, like everybody else, have experienced the noble pleasure which certain scents can produce. It would be very much more interesting if you tried to indicate what the smells were. See how flabby and vague your phrases are. You say—*there one could breathe in heady odours from lilac and from heliotrope, rich with a wealth of obscure suggestions.* In the first place, leave *suggestions* alone, if all you can tell

[25] "Sommes-nous en présence d'un renouvellement du style?", p. 6.
[26] *Letters of Marcel Proust*, pp. 180-181.

Criticism and Creation 63

us about them is that they are *obscure*. If you can't throw any light upon them, you'd better say nothing at all. And don't mix up the scent of the lilac with the scent of the heliotrope. You must know that one catches the fresh smell of the lilac only after rain, whereas the heliotrope does not give the fullness of its scent—which is very subtle—except when the sun is on it . . . ." [27]

It is unfortunate that Proust did not decide to retain this passage in *A la recherche*, because it would have fitted so well into the pattern of Marcel's "invisible vocation." It also illustrates how Proust began with Symbolism and left it behind in order to achieve a new kind of "classical" precision.

But the beauty of the great authors does not depend alone on their ability to renew the language. Language and style depend on something more comprehensive—on what Proust calls "vision." As early as 1904, at the beginning of his liberation from Ruskin, he had defined the absolute beauty of certain things as "a kind of blending, a kind of transparent unity." [28] This passage already contains the nucleus of Proust's mature formulation of literary style, more fully outlined in an interview with E.-J. Bois of the *Temps*, on the eve of the publication of *Du côté de chez Swann*:

> Style is in no way an embellishment, as certain persons seem to think; it is not even a matter of technique; it is—analogous to the way painters use color—a quality of vision, the revelation of a special universe which each one of us sees, which the others do not see. The pleasure which an artist offers us is to acquaint us with one more universe.[29]

In his last period Proust saw the writer's problem as one of overcoming the contingencies of objects by establishing the necessary relationships between them. In *Le Temps retrouvé* the idea is elaborated as follows:

> An hour is not merely an hour. It is a vase filled with perfumes, sounds, plans and climates. What we call reality is a certain relationship between these sensations and the memories which surround us at the same time (a relationship that is destroyed by a bare cinematographic presentation, which gets further away from the truth the more closely it claims to adhere to it) the only true relationship, which the writer must recapture so that he may forever link together in his phrase its two distinct elements. One may list in an interminable description the objects that figured in the place described, but truth will begin only when the writer takes two different objects, establishes their relationship—analogous in the world of art to the sole relationship in the world of science, the law of cause and

---

[27] *Jean Santeuil*, p. 163.
[28] *Correspondance générale* (Paris: Plon, 1930-36), II, 86-87.
[29] Quoted in Robert Dreyfus, *Souvenirs sur Marcel Proust* (Paris: Grasset, 1926), p. 292.

effect—and encloses them in the necessary rings of a beautiful style, or even when, like life itself, comparing similar qualities in two sensations, he makes their essential nature stand out clearly by joining them in a metaphor, in order to remove them from the contingencies of time.[30]

The whole language of these pronouncements on the secret beauty of literary style is conceived in terms of the art of the genre painter: the emphasis on objects, their relationships, the importance of light, the over-all harmony. One thinks of Chardin, of Vermeer, of Rembrandt here, and of Proust's recurrent allusions to their art; and, following Proust's analyses, we recognize the *phrases-types* as symbols of the "unité transparente" and their applicability in painting as well as in music and literature. The metaphor is the device which gives permanence to objects and frees them from the temporal and spatial contingency. When Proust defines style in the essay contained in *Le Temps retrouvé*, he once more speaks of the painter's art and the writer's art simultaneously:

> . . . For style is for the writer, as for the painter, a question, not of technique but of vision. It is the revelation—impossible by direct and conscious means—of the qualitative differences in the way the world appears to us, differences which, but for art, would remain the eternal secret of each of us. Only by art can we get outside ourselves, know what another sees of his universe, which is not the same as ours and the different views of which would otherwise have remained as unknown to us as those there may be on the moon. Thanks to art, instead of seeing only one world, our own, we see it under multiple forms, and as many as there are original artists, just so many worlds have we at our disposal, differing more widely from one another than those that roll through infinite space, and years after the glowing center from which they emanated has been extinguished, be it called Rembrandt or Vermeer, they continue to send us their own rays of light.[31]

"We have as many worlds at our disposal as there are original artists." The artist is a world-builder: like Elstir, he refashions the Creation by giving its components new names—that is to say, metaphors[32]—and the reader's purpose is to discern the qualitative differences among these worlds; the critic's function is to help him achieve this purpose. The critic's first task is to see—"to see distinctly where other people see only indistinctly." [33] This recalls the definition of the critic's primary function given in the preface to *La Bible d'Amiens*—to aid the reader in discerning the artist's unique characteristics. But, it will be remembered,

[30] *Remembrance of Things Past*, II, 1008-1009.
[31] *Ibid.*, II, 1013.   [32] *Ibid.*, I, 628.
[33] "Un Professeur de Beauté," *Les Arts de la vie* 4:67-69 (July-December, 1905), p. 74.

Proust felt that the critic could go beyond this simple function of guide and become a sharer, so to speak, of the artist's vision, "to reconstruct the peculiar life of the spirit which belongs to every writer who is obsessed by his own special view of reality." [34] All Proust's mature ideas on art, as summarized in *Le Temps retrouvé*, are already implied there: literature growing out of a writer's contact with reality; the writer as a visionary; and the necessity which forces the writer to create (". . . we are not at all free in the presence of the work of art to be created" [35]).

To what extent did Proust himself fulfill this twofold function of the critic? In many cases, he contents himself with merely acting as a guide. This is especially true of the pastiches, in which his primary purpose was to fix the *traits singuliers* of certain literary styles. And yet even here Proust often probes more deeply; when he makes Renan use a word which, to his knowledge, does *not* appear in Renan's writings but which seems to him "extrêmement Renan," is he not probing into Renan's inner nature, into the "special view of reality" which, according to Proust's analysis, obsessed Renan? In a similar manner, the Flaubert pastiche attempts to recapture Flaubert's particular intelligence, not only his style; and the Saint-Simon pastiche recreates not only the Duke's excited violence but also his "Dostoevskian" aspect. In other words, Proust tends to move closer and closer to the second, the higher, function of the critic; his sensibility is not satisfied with a description of the characteristics of a writer, but strives to penetrate into the writer's inner organization.

The critic's function of guide to a certain author is analogous to the writer's apprenticeship to that author. The critic explains the author's style, whereas the writer adopts it, draws from it what he can assimilate, then purges himself of the style. Like Stevenson, Proust delighted in playing the sedulous ape to authors of the past:

> . . . the best advice I can give to my fellow-writers is that they would be well-advised to indulge in the cleansing, exorcising, pastime of parody, when we come to the end of a book, we find that not only do we want to go on living with its characters, with Madame de Beauséant, with Frédéric Moreau, etc., but that our inner voice, which has grown accustomed, through the long hours of perusal, to follow the Balzacian or Flaubertian rhythm, insists on talking just like those authors. The one means of escape from the toils lies in letting the influence have its way for a while, in keeping one's foot on the pedal and permitting the resonance to continue: in other words, in embarking upon a deliberate act of parody, with the object, once we have got the stuff out of our system, of becoming ourselves again, instead of spending the rest of our working lives producing *unconscious* parodies. But deliberate parody must be spontaneous. When I

[34] *M. P.: A Selection*, pp. 24 n.-25 n.; *Pastiches et mélanges*, pp. 108 n.-109 n.
[35] *Remembrance of Things Past*, II, 1002.

set about producing my own, rather detestable, parody of Flaubert, I did not stop to ask myself whether the "tune" ringing in my ears owed its peculiar quality to a recurrent series of imperfects or of present participles. If I had bothered about that, I should never have got the thing on paper at all.[36]

This observation has a curious similarity to Malraux' analysis of the importance of the pastiche in his *Psychologie de l'art*. For Malraux, "every artist's career begins with the pastiche"; it is the artist's first attempt at a participation in the world of art. ". . . The pastiche is a gesture of fraternity."[37] Proust, to be sure, emphasizes the cleansing effect of the pastiche, which permits him to get the persistent throb of an author's rhythm out of his system; but in a certain sense, the pastiche, for Proust too, is a kind of initiation rite which must be accomplished before artistic maturity and mastery are possible.

From the pastiche to the analysis there is only a small step; what the pastiche writer often does unconsciously he may also do consciously afterwards in the form of a critical essay, at which point he approaches the critic *voyant*.

> The human mind can never be satisfied unless it can manage to achieve a clear analysis of what, at the moment of composition, it produced unconsciously, or can re-create in vital terms what, till then, it has been merely analyzing.[38]

In the writer—that is to say, in Proust himself—reading leads to analysis, which in turn leads to re-creation. The critic, as has been observed, acts as the artist's lesser double. His scope of effectiveness lies rather in the realm of the intelligence, whereas Proust relied by preference on intuition and sensibility. Nevertheless, the image of the highest type of critic which he offers us is also attuned to the intuitive basis of artistic creation.

Proust is most interesting and most successful as a literary critic when he goes beyond the basic function of the critic. As has been shown, he is never altogether content to be a mere guide. In the preface to *La Bible d'Amiens* he begins by saying that he is trying only to satisfy this basic function of the critic. Nevertheless, toward the end of the essay on Ruskin, he begins to ask himself how the insincerity in Ruskin's writings can be accounted for; this question gives rise to the "Post-Scriptum," in which he tries to penetrate into the problem of "reconstituting Ruskin's spiritual life." Proust knew—and this perception is

---

[36] *M. P.: A Selection*, pp. 233-234.
[37] André Malraux, *The Psychology of Art*, II, *The Creative Act*, tr. Stuart Gilbert (New York: Pantheon Books, Inc., 1949), p. 145.
[38] *M. P.: A Selection*, p. 234.

also his answer to Sainte-Beuve—that through the work of art he could glimpse the inner structure of the artist:

> ... In fact, is not a work of art something like a sphygmogram, which records our pulse automatically, of our soul's inner rhythm, and all the more vital for the fact that we do not perceive it ourselves? [39]

This very conviction enables Proust to venture on dangerous territory— as the critic whom Proust has in mind always must—to show us the particular vision which a great artist offers the reader. The procedure is used with remarkable skill in the Flaubert and Baudelaire essays and in "Sainte-Beuve et Balzac"; it is essentially the same as the *phrases-types* analysis of Barbey d'Aurevilly, Stendhal, Hardy, and Dostoevski; in other words, it is Proust's method par excellence for arriving at the essence of an artist's contact with reality and the metaphors which his vision dictates to him. If Proust seems sometimes too daring or too sweeping with his *phrases-types,* it should be kept in mind that his critical method is always inextricably bound up with his artistic intuition. In this respect, too, his literary criticism moves along the same path as his literary art. Fallois is entirely correct in saying of Proust's method of criticism that it "destroys the customary boundary lines between art and criticism." [40]

Proust had a way of "using" literary criticism to deepen a character. Here literary criticism plays a role subordinate to character portrayal —Proust knew that the intellectual side of an individual revealed many traits not directly revealed in his actions. Thus, when Block's or Charlus' or Madame de Villeparisis' literary opinions are presented in some detail, Proust is not criticizing the writer in question but revealing the personality of the critic. To be sure, such opinions may on occasion coincide with Marcel's (and Proust's) own, but the emphasis is always on the character in the novel. Marcel himself occupies a somewhat complex position in the novel; as an intermediary between Proust and his material, he represents Proust the child infatuated with Georges Sand as well as the early, groping Proust, then the maturing critic, then the writer of an article for *Le Figaro,* then the matured literary critic, and finally the artist who is going to write the novel that Proust has just finished. Thus, Marcel represents the transitory as well as the permanent literary opinions of Proust; only in the latter portions of *A la recherche* does the dividing line between Marcel's and Proust's literary opinions become tenuous. The area in which it occurs may be said to be the revelation of the Vinteuil Septet and the *phrases-types* passage, both in *La Prisonnière.* And in the

---
[39] *Sésame et les lys* (Paris: Mercure de France, n. d.), p. 93 n.
[40] *Contre Sainte-Beuve,* p. 50.

opening pages of volume II of *Le Temps retrouvé* the congruence is all but complete.

The importance of Proust's personal interests in his choice of topics for critical commentary has already been pointed out. Similarly, the somewhat disorderly arrangement of the critical essays can be accounted for by the corollary that Proust let his memory, his associations, and his interests guide him in the arrangement of his material. The subjective, Proustian element of these essays is forever betraying itself; and the essays themselves often read like Proustian sentences, magnified several times, with their interlocking and parenthetical components. For behind Proust the critic stands, like a guardian angel, Proust the artist, dictating to the critic what is important, what is interesting, and what is relevant to the artist. Or, to put it somewhat differently, Proust is both pilgrim and guide in the ascent of his own mountain of Purgatory; and after the arduous discipline, the guide can finally abdicate his office, leaving the pilgrim purified, self-reliant, and able to work out his own salvation. The salvation, to be sure, was a literary one. Yet there are few writers in the world's history to whom literature has meant so much and whose devotion to art has been so religious. Few books have been so uniquely impregnated with literature, so dependent on the literary consciousness for their inner rhythm. And so it is right, after all, to call *A la recherche du temps perdu* a cathedral: not only because of its structure and its impressiveness but also because its very center is occupied by a most splendid altar dedicated to the glorification of literature.

The Inhuman World of Pleasure

by Germaine Brée

Geographically close to Combray, Tansonville and Guermantes are equally prominent on the narrator's map of his own "enchanted realms." Linking him to these two worlds are the people who live there, and whom he actually sees: Swann, Gilberte, and the Duchesse de Guermantes. They are for him at once real and imaginary. As an adolescent and a young man, they seem to him like magicians whose favor would assure his entry into the domain of his dreams. Anyone who belongs to these worlds becomes the object of his passionate curiosity, not because of themselves, as he would have it, but because they seem to him guardians of the keys of paradise. In this way the narrator takes his place in the social scheme, and gravitates toward these two different spheres, of which both, according to the social values of Combray, are outside his orbit; the "solid bourgeoisie" does not mix with the aristocracy to which the Guermantes belong; Swann has hopelessly lost caste in their eyes by his marriage. The narrator categorically reverses this unwritten social law; the people who are rejected by Combray have for him an irresistible attraction: they are inaccessible. In addition, they have a glamorous aura which seems to the adolescent the very essence of social superiority: wealth and elegance in the case of Swann, ancient lineage in the case of the Guermantes.

In spite of the convictions of his immediate milieu, and even in opposition to them, the narrator feels himself compelled toward a "worldly" life. In order to make his way into the society of the Swanns and the Guermantes, he breaks down the gentle, unspoken resistance of his mother and grandmother by using the emotional blackmail which he had discovered to be so effective one evening in Combray. And so he follows the path of flight from Combray, and embarks upon a course which impels him to sacrifice everything to the fulfillment of his

"The Inhuman World of Pleasure." From *Marcel Proust and Deliverance from Time* by Germaine Brée (New Brunswick, N. J.: Rutgers University Press, 1955). Copyright 1955 by The Trustees of Rutgers College in New Jersey. Reprinted by permission of Rutgers University Press and Chatto & Windus Ltd.

phantasies and his desires. He is led to violate the social boundaries which the "virtues" of Combray have defined for him, and to lead a life which is in direct opposition to them. As he moves further and further away from Combray, the stable core of his life recedes. He leaves his home territory by degrees, venturing first into Swann's milieu. "Our Combray society couldn't have been less worldly. Association with Swann was a step in the direction of sophistication." [1] Taking advantage of the "social looseness" of life at a seaside resort where various social groups "mix," [2] he also begins to make his way, through Mme de Villeparisis, St. Loup and Charlus, whom he meets in Balbec, toward the world of the Guermantes. He comes into contact with various other groups of all types which are represented among the motley inhabitants of the Grand Hotel, such as the young bourgeoises of the "little set" or the Jewish colony to which the Blochs belong. He discovers an infinitely enlarged and quite new social universe which he explores with burning interest.

This social barrier breached, he penetrates, thanks to the Guermantes, into the heart of the Faubourg St. Germain. Then, during his second stay at Balbec, he runs into fantastic and innumerable imbroglios, myriad threads of which cross and re-cross from one social milieu to another in a veritable comedy of errors and fortuitous events, until the day when, as in a vaudeville show, a flurry of marriages sanctifies the real but disguised unity of Proust's social world. This only takes place after Proust has dragged all these worldly people who were excluded from the bourgeois society of Combray into a dizzying downfall. Like the narrator, we shall then have seen, in mirrors or through the half-open doors of houses of questionable repute like Jupien's, a dark region where on a strange footing of equality, princes, businessmen, and valets meet, avoid each other, or spy upon one another. The "virtues" of Combray have taken their revenge.

From its beginning in Combray, the narrator's world is limited to his own field of vision, that of the well-to-do middle classes and of the aristocracy with their respective satellites, their servants on the one hand, artists and intellectuals on the other. If through Françoise and her daughter, Jupien, or Morel, we catch a glimpse of other classes, it is only in passing. Proust concentrates his attention upon the "upper classes" of society and their social life. Except in its social aspects, he almost entirely ignores their professional life. In the Proustian world an individual can be both a Guermantes and a senator, a military officer or even an ambassador, just as he can be a bourgeois and a doctor, engineer, professor, civil servant, writer, or artist. The Proustian characters are not as idle as they are often said to be, but they interest Proust only

[1] *A la recherche du temps perdu*, I, 398.
[2] *Ibid.*, pp. 468, 517.

The Inhuman World of Pleasure

in their social relationships because in the world of wealth and leisure "social relationships attain their purest form." [3]

As a whole, Proustian society is classified according to certain general principles which remain fixed. The peasant Françoise easily distinguishes between the social levels of the laboring class, the middle class, and the aristocracy, to each of which appertain certain privileges and obligations. Inside her own class she establishes an inflexible hierarchy and a well-defined code of manners which are the expression of certain definite values. The other two classes live according to rules which she does not understand very well, but about which she has certain simple and inflexible notions: the middle class "owes it to itself" to be rich, and to look it; the aristocracy to be royalist, and toward them Françoise owes it to herself to show her independence. She looks at them from a distance with a curiosity tinged with dislike, but without the slightest desire or the slightest aspiration to belong to their class. This attitude is roughly that of the great-aunt, of Tante Léonie, or of the Prince de Guermantes, each in his own sphere. For the narrator's great-aunt only one social milieu is worthy of consideration: that of the solid middle class which is characterized by the almost hereditary exercise of certain honorable, well-remunerated professions, administrative or intellectual, and by respect for solid values, both material and moral. The gradations of superiority within the middle class are a matter of occupation and fortune. To be, like Swann, the possessor of a substantial upper-middle-class fortune, and to spend a lifetime collecting bibelots and paintings and hobnobbing with the aristocracy is a disgrace. To be a worthy member of his class, Swann should have undertaken the respectable occupation of stockbroker. The narrator's great-aunt surveys the social scene with complacency: she receives from the inhabitants of Combray the respect due her, and regards the aristocracy with a rather vague irony, and with a certain scorn as well, because she confuses it with the demimonde which is frivolous, spendthrift, and immoral. For the Prince de Guermantes and his class, aristocracy is a matter of name. The name is the mark of the family's past, of its lineage and its rank in the feudal and monarchic order. People so "named" thus belong, each in his place, to high society. A hierarchy is established. At the top are individuals bearing the most illustrious heraldic name, such as Guermantes and families related to them, and the name itself confers an absolute superiority. In the eyes of the prince, all individuals who are not "named" are equal from the aristocratic point of view—they do not belong to "society."

Belief in a hierarchy creates within each group a veritable miniature Versailles. The shadow of Louis XIV and of the world of Saint-Simon is thrown across each echelon: Charlus, heaped with honors, receiving the

[3] III, p. 670.

eager homage of the Faubourg St. Germain; Tante Léonie, flanked by Eulalie and Françoise; Françoise lording it over the butler and the valet, or the manager of the Grand Hotel framed by the respectful crowd of bellboys, waiters and valets. The individuals at the top of their hierarchy enjoy a prestige which they do not question, and exercise over those inferior to them a certain capricious tyranny which confirms their rights: Françoise's tyranny over the scullery maid, Tante Léonie's over Françoise, Charlus' over the Faubourg St. Germain. Around these centers veritable court plots are hatched, intrigues of precedence and self-interest comprehensible only to those who know the tacit code which governs the group. However, like Françoise in relation to the two classes above her, like the great-aunt and the prince, the bourgeoisie and the aristocracy have certain vague conceptions and elementary impressions about one another which are prompted by total ignorance or outright hostility. Secure in their well-defined conception of their own rights and prerogatives, the individuals of one class look askance at those belonging to another. They fail to make any distinction between "degrees" and regard them with the sly, ironic complacency of the narrator's great-aunt, or with the vague kindliness of the Princesse de Luxembourg when Mme de Villeparisis introduces the narrator and his grandmother to her:

> The Princesse de Luxembourg had given us her hand, and from time to time, as she conversed with the Marquise, she would bestow a kindly look upon my grandmother and myself, a look that contained that embryonic kiss which is put into a smile reserved for babies out for an airing with their nurse-maids. Indeed, in her anxiety not to appear to belong to a sphere higher than ours she seemed to have miscalculated the distance between us and by an error in adjustment, her eyes beamed with such benevolence that I could see the moment approach when she would stroke us with her hand as she would have stroked a couple of friendly animals which had stuck their heads between the bars of their cages at the zoo . . . But she said good-bye to Mme de Villeparisis and put out her hand to us with the intention of treating us in the same way she treated her friends, as intimates, and to put herself on our level. But this time she had doubtless promoted us in the hierarchy of creation, for her equality with us was indicated by the Princesse to my grandmother by that tender, maternal smile one gives a little boy when saying good-bye to him as to a grown-up. By a miraculous stride in evolution, my grandmother was no longer a duck or an antelope but what Mme Swann, a passionate anglophile, would have called a "baby." [4]

From its own sphere, each group views the others through a strangely distorted lens which gives rise to a body of errors: the middle-class group, for instance, thinks that the Marquise de Villeparisis and the

[4] I, 484, 485.

Princesse de Luxembourg are "two hussies of the kind that it is difficult to avoid in spas." The principles according to which the people within each group classify themselves do not carry over from one group to another, nor does the knowledge of how these distinctions are made. Their mutual relations are a veritable "comedy of errors," full of the blunders, mistaken identities, and muddles of all kinds, from which Proust draws the material for his social comedy. So it is that when the flower of the aristocracy of the Faubourg St. Germain are invited by the Baron de Charlus to Mme Verdurin's, they behave with the most blatant crudeness—even though theoretically their social relationships are built upon a strict code of politeness:

> Having come there partly out of friendship for M. de Charlus and partly out of curiosity to see a place of this kind, each duchess went straight to the baron, as though he were the host, and said within earshot of the Verdurins, who naturally missed nothing: "Where is the old girl? Must I really be introduced to her? I do hope that at least she won't have my name put in the papers tomorrow; my family would never speak to me again. What! It's that white-haired woman? Why, she looks quite presentable . . ." and each having found a number of friends, they gathered in little groups that watched with ironic curiosity the arrival of the "faithful," finding nothing to criticize but an occasional odd hairdo . . . and, in short, regretting that this salon was not very different from those they knew and feeling the disappointment of society people who, having gone to a dive to see Bruant in the hopes of being rudely greeted by the entertainer, find themselves welcomed by a courteous bow instead of the expected chorus: "Look at her! Look at her puss! My gawd, what a mug she has!" [5]

Social distances are thus based upon the premise that the people whom we do not know are different from us. This belief dehumanizes social reactions, creates a viewpoint which is distorted, sometimes to a preposterous degree, and introduces into society the comedy of incongruity in attitudes, opinions, and gossip. Charlus, for instance, whose easy insolence is nourished by his unquestioned belief in the superiority bestowed upon him by his noble birth, seems to the uninformed narrator a shady and somewhat alarming character; the Marquise de Villeparisis looks to Odette like a little old woman who might easily be a concierge, and Mme Verdurin states positively that the Duc and Duchesse de la Trémoille eat with their fingers.

Nothing is further removed from these rather spiteful deformations than the distortion, similar in origin but of a very different kind, manifest in the narrator's view of society during the period when a "social springtime" enraptures him. This vernal glamour of society is due to

[5] III, 167.

his "curiosity about all ways of life hitherto unknown," [6] a curiosity which is particularly piqued by anything related to the two sumptuous "realms" near Combray. The appearance of Gilberte Swann in the Champs-Elysées marks the narrator's point of departure toward that "society" which still seems mysterious to him. Irresistibly drawn by the prestige that glorifies the name of Swann in his eyes, it is toward the Swanns that he directs his avid curiosity. Everything that seems to him to have the slightest contact with them, to belong in their lives, be it merely by a simple proximity, or an association of ideas, becomes, like Mme Blatin, a focus of attention and attraction, a center around which gravitate all the various feelings which agitate him. "Plunged in a restless sleep," he says, "my adolescence enveloped in one long phantasy the whole section of the city where it first contained my dreams," [7] the section where the Swanns live. This vague restlessness becomes focused on Gilberte, and he names it love. The obsession which springs from this love is not enough to assure the narrator's entry into the Swann salon; that entry is brought about by chance, but it is because of his love that his introduction to the Swanns becomes a real social "migration." His love for Gilberte is the magic carpet by means of which he crosses the gap which he had mentally established between himself and the Swanns. But he does not lose his place in the Swann's milieu when his love for Gilberte dies; he remains in their world.

If originally he frequents the Swanns so that he can see Gilberte, that which keeps him there after he no longer wants to see her is a purely social element, the attraction of elegance, of social prestige, which, although he is unconscious of it, also plays a large part in his love. This attraction had already oriented his childish dreams toward a certain way of life, the opulence of which seems to him to reveal an inner wealth, an exquisite treasure reserved for an élite, inaccessible to ordinary mortals. It is through its atmosphere—that of a chatoyant, animated tapestry— that social life first exerts its charms upon the adolescent narrator. These charms are epitomized in the voluptuous and brilliant scene that unfolds "between quarter past twelve and one o'clock in the month of May" [8] in the Allées des Acacias in the Bois de Boulogne. There is the pure show of social life, an urbane, luxurious spectacle which is an end in itself and has no other spectators than the actors who take part in it. It is a gratuitous display of opulence, but of an opulence which utilizes life and the means gained by wealth for the sole purpose of extracting from them an ephemeral and perfect creation; woman is its focus and elegance its criterion. Elegance in itself creates momentarily an autonomous assembly of people set apart from the toil of everyday life, as well as from its cares, its suffering and solitude. The ritual develops merely to perpetuate its own existence. At least so it appears to

[6] I, 470.   [7] *Ibid.*, p. 342.   [8] *Ibid.*, p. 445.

the dazzled eyes of the narrator when he comes first to see and later to participate in that perfect flowering of affluence, Odette Swann's morning walk in the paths of the Bois de Boulogne. The Bois is the classless realm which belongs to a special social ilk: the women on the fringe of high society, or the demimondaines, both cultivated in the hothouses of Parisian elegance in "the era of the horse and carriage."

"But most often . . . as I had learned that Mme Swann took a walk almost daily in the Allée des Acacias, around the Grand Lac, and in the Allée de la Reine Marguerite, I guided Françoise toward the Bois de Boulogne." It is there that the pageant of worldly elegance unfolds, there that all social Paris meets, forming a retinue for the beauties then in vogue:

> I thought that the beautiful—in the hierarchy of feminine elegance— was determined by occult practices into which they [the women] had been initiated, and that they had the power to create it; and I accepted beforehand, as a revelation, the aspect of their attire, their carriages, the thousand and one details which to me were like the agents of an inner force that gave the cohesion of a masterpiece to this ephemeral and moving pageant.[9]

It is, however, upon Mme Swann that the adolescent boy's "troubled" and "reverent" gaze rests:

> Suddenly, on the gravelled path, late, unhurried, and luxuriant as the most beautiful flower that blooms only at midday, Mme Swann appeared, radiant in a costume always a bit different, but as I recall, usually mauve; then at the moment of her brightest radiance she raised and unfurled at the end of its long stem the silken banner of a large parasol that matched the shimmering petals of her gown. A retinue surrounded her: Swann, four or five clubmen who had come to call on her in the morning or whom she had met on the way; their dark mass attentive, performing the almost mechanical movements of a squad immobilized in a setting around Odette . . . made her stand out, frail, fearless . . . like the apparition of a creature of a different species, of an unknown race with an almost martial strength that made her seem a match for her multiple escort.[10]

So "Mme Swann, majestic, smiling, amiable, advancing down the avenue in the Bois," passed by in a veritable apotheosis, hailed universally. Each salutation "released . . . like clockwork the gesticulations of minor characters who were none other than Odette's entourage, with Swann the first to lift his topper lined with green leather, with the smiling graciousness he had learned in the Faubourg St. Germain." [11]

The world of elegance here, as in all its ceremonies, is focused to such an extent upon the woman that the men of her entourage, al-

[9] *Ibid.*, p. 294. [10] *Ibid.*, p. 442. [11] *Ibid.*

though distinguished, are reduced to little more than automatons. The extravagant ritual which takes place before the eyes of the narrator in the Allée des Acacias in May is peculiar to elegance. The ceremonial life of society in all its forms exerts upon him the same fascination: that of large hotels and restaurants, of salons, of dinners, of afternoon and evening receptions, as well as the ceremonial of the kitchen. These rituals seem to the adolescent the very essence of social life; they are apparent in fashions or liveries, in fixed and almost mechanical ceremonies such as Odette's outing, in the behavior of waiters at a fashionable restaurant. Each change of scene brings the young man into contact with a form of life which at first appears to him stylized, and in which people behave with the ordered and beguiling grace of dancers in a ballet.

These ceremonies, which he observes from the outside, appear to define a way of life in which everything is choice; they are, he thinks, signs of a mysterious life oriented toward some precious goal unknown to him. The social concept of his parents, content to belong to the solid middle class, gives way to an entirely different attitude which is essentially adolescent. Everything that belongs to his world is depreciated, everything that differs from it acquires value. He is ashamed of Françoise when he compares her with Gilberte's English governess, and his grandmother's familiar habits cover him with confusion before the personnel at the Grand Hotel in Balbec. He feels himself compelled to appropriate the new ceremonies, and participate in them, whether by using Odette's anglicisms, eating chocolate cakes which make him sick, or playing hunt-the-slipper with Albertine and her friends.

The social universe is split into two, the ordinary world, his own, and the extraordinary world, which alone interests him. Any group which behaves self-confidently, and from which he is excluded, is society as far as he is concerned. The individuality of anyone belonging to any of these groups is enhanced for him because of the marvelous atmosphere which radiates from the coterie itself, and which transforms any member of it into a creature of a special species. Thus, "surrounded by monsters and gods," [12] the narrator observes the evolutions of these groups with wonder, timidity, and longing. In "the delightful anxiety of partaking in an unknown way of life," [13] he unconsciously experiences the feelings which initiate and maintain all social ceremony. He scorns his own social group, and creates fictitious social values based solely on his ignorance and on the attraction that emanates from an apparently self-contained and closed coterie. These feelings all amass around the worldly passion par excellence, complex and protean—snobbery. They also determine the continual gravitation of one group toward another, and of individuals toward the groups. Each time that a social gap is crossed, the group previously mysterious when viewed

[12] I, 505.   [13] *Ibid.*, p. 470.

from afar falls into the depreciated domain of the known, and another group acquires prestige.

For the narrator a whole world of emotion revolves around these encounters. When young St. Loup, heralded by Mme de Villeparisis and already a legend of worldly success, appears in Balbec, the passionate curiosity with which the adolescent narrator observes him transforms him at first into a young sun god:

> One afternoon of scorching heat I was in the hotel dining room which had been left in semi-darkness to keep out the sun, . . . when . . . I saw a young man with piercing eyes, tall and slender, his head held high on his long neck, his skin and hair so golden that they seemed to have absorbed all the sun's rays. Clothed in a plain white suit of a thin material that suggested, no less than the darkened dining room, the heat and glorious weather outside, he walked quickly by. His eyes, from one of which a monocle kept falling, were the color of the sea. Everyone looked at him with curiosity, for the young Marquis de St. Loup-en-Bray was noted for his elegance.[14]

The young sun-god, who is to become an intimate and devoted friend, is rapidly transformed into a monster of "innate hardness" and "insolence" when he passes the narrator without greeting him, "his slender body just as inflexibly straight" as when seen before, "his head just as high, his glance indifferent." [15] The "monster" St. Loup is simply the form taken by the narrator's frustration because he is not at once able to make the acquaintance of the young Marquis. Precisely at that moment, the adolescent experiences the power of that unique motivation which activates the whole social movement from the top to the bottom: to "become acquainted" with a person or group, or to refuse to "become acquainted." Everyone in the social game is looked upon as a connection desirable or undesirable, established or virtual, past, present or future.

The members of the middle class who engage in this game are close enough to the aristocracy to be aware that it exists; they recognize an aristocrat because he bears a name preceded by the nobiliary particle "de." It is essential for a socially ambitious member of the middle class to close the gap which separates his name from the "noble" name, and to make the acquaintance of someone who has the coveted "de." The Faubourg St. Germain as a whole seems to the bourgeoisie a citadel which is defended by the aristocracy and can only be taken by assault. In *A la recherche du temps perdu*, a sub-rosa social "war" is carried on which Proust presents at length, and most humourously. The Verdurin clique is a war machine, scientifically armed; within it all the ruses and strategies of assault are developed. In the center of the Faubourg St.

[14] *Ibid.*, p. 504.   [15] *Ibid.*, p. 505.

Germain, grouped around the Duchesse, the aristocracy defends its positions. Its defenses, however, are weakened from the inside by psychological tendencies which are common to all human beings: curiosity, the fear of boredom, the need for diversion, and self-interest. The Verdurin phalange assures its rise up the social ladder by cleverly playing upon these weaknesses.

Extremely rich, the Verdurins give sumptuous receptions. They counterattack worldly snobbery with an artistic or political snobbery which gradually attracts attention; they combat aristocratic exclusiveness with intellectual exclusiveness. The clique makes its appearance in the social world as a unit strongly organized around its "chief" and his lady, with an acknowledged code tyrannically enforced. People who are not in the group are "bores." Its sole avowed aim is the creation of an agreeable and stimulating life for the "faithful." But its implacable progression in time reveals its true goal. As a social organism, it proceeds by successive assimilations and automatic expulsions. The appearance of a new element within it and the identical quality which marks each successive acquisition clearly show where the group is headed: Swann, Forcheville (whose "de" delights Dr. Cottard), Charlus, then, little by little, the whole Faubourg are absorbed until Mme Verdurin after her husband's death finally reaches the heart of the aristocratic citadel and marries the Prince de Guermantes. Everything is used in this assault: Swann's love for Odette, Charlus' passion for Morel, Elstir's genius, Vinteuil's sonata, the Dreyfus affair, the war, Morel's talent. As soon as they deviate from the invisible route that "Ma" Verdurin is following, Swann, Charlus and Elstir are coldly eliminated. The little clique is not concerned with human beings as much as with the rôle they play in the coterie's social strategy, a rôle to which they must entirely submit themselves; the Verdurins are never concerned with the real value of an individual.

For the Duchesse de Guermantes social art consists not only in forming a salon closed to all but the most exclusive aristocracy, but in arranging to bring into it, to a cleverly calculated degree, people of a different kind, like Swann. She gives the aristocracy the impression that what counts in Oriane's salon are spiritual values, and that her salon is not like the others. She enhances this impression by making herself inaccessible. To make Oriane's acquaintance, or to have her as a guest at a soirée, becomes an event in the Faubourg St. Germain. In Oriane's salon certain signs also appear which indicate where it is going. The need for novelty and diversion push the Duchesse further and further afield, away from the Faubourg until at the end of the novel, she has wandered far outside her own class. She now sees only artists and actresses on the fringes of society and only hesitates still a little between Balthy and Mistinguett through fear of the Duc. In both cases the social battle is waged around a group, a coterie which, because it has the

The Inhuman World of Pleasure

reputation of being exclusive, creates around itself a zone of attraction and that climate of prestige in which snobbery flourishes.

Proust shows that the laws of society are always the same as he describes all the phases of worldly ascent and descent through countless salons. Behind the ritual of salon life, the game of human relationships —complicated and sharpened by the game of social relationships—continues to be played from individual to individual and from group to group. The narrator discovers it slowly, and he himself is subject to its laws: attractions and repulsions, invitations and refusals, intertwine in all directions, determining meetings, factions, friendships, evolutions and revolutions of individuals in relation to one another. Society forms a sort of biological culture in which individuals can try out all the means by which they can make contact with one another, a medium in which emotions are experimented with freely; it is essentially the sphere of relativity. Love is born there, friendship is cultivated, as well as the whole gamut of sentiments, running from generosity to cruelty, which accompany the desire to please and to dominate. But, more than anything else, what flourishes in all its forms is the need for "diversion" in the Pascalian sense of the word.

"Diversion" for society people is the art of using others for the sole purpose of satisfying one's needs and disguising one's boredom. Where affections are concerned, this exploitation can be admitted neither to oneself nor to others. That is why Proust's characters hide, dissemble, and betray one another. They lie to themselves and to each other under various pretexts, hiding their real motivations, which may vary from the needs created by a habit which has become automatic to the exacting demands of homosexuality. In the Proustian world the constant reshuffling of social sets becomes apparent when Proust juxtaposes characters whose presence side by side is in itself the sign of a social mutation: Swann seated next to Odette in the Verdurins' salon; Bloch at the Marquise de Villeparisis' tea; Charlus travelling with the "faithful" in the little Balbec train; the narrator chatting with Mme Swann under her parasol as "under the reflection of a wisteria arbor," or dining at the Duchesse de Guermantes'.

It is also conveyed by the variations, which can be infinitely sudden and numerous, that one person undergoes in his apparently stable relations with another person: Swann's relations with Odette, the narrator's with Albertine. Instead of being organized around a social hierarchy, society in this sense seems to the narrator a vast jungle where everyone ferociously pursues his own gratification. In so far as this is concerned, there is no distinction between the Verdurins and the Guermantes. Their social universe is the same, regulated by a strong generic need to be amused, to organize their lives with a view to immediate pleasures. This exigency is the Trojan horse by means of which all social citadels are taken and all class conventions foiled. The narrator, once he has entered the Swanns' milieu, remains there; in the same way, once someone has been introduced into society to satisfy its demand for amusement, he remains there despite displacements and disfavors, as do Bloch and Morel, participating only in the general gyrations of the social kaleidoscope.

Possessing both money and leisure, left entirely to its own devices, the social set has only one deep-rooted desire: to be protected from the emptiness of existence and to draw from the sterile and disquieting substance of life a mask which is reassuring and flattering to itself. Carried along in the toils of pleasures, all of them worldly, the members of society experience a violent aversion when confronted by the slightest unpleasantness. It is infinitely more important to avoid unpleasantness than to respect the values of a social, moral, or intellectual code, or to grapple with spiritual problems. It is for this reason that, even while these people make a point of cultivating the emotions, they cannot tolerate the blossoming of any deep feeling, any more than that of a real talent or a vigorous intellect. They want neither to understand nor to know, only to be adorned and amused. In society Brichot's knowledge becomes pedantry, Cottard's curiosity expresses itself in lumbering absurdities, and Swann turns into an amiable dilettante; no solid values are tolerated. Proust emphasizes this characteristic of society in his portrayal of the unconscious behavior of his characters, pointing out the disparity between their words and their acts, or the disparity between the truth and their distortion of it.

Among the numerous dinners, teas, and soirées described in the novel, there is one soirée that is particularly important both because of its position in the very center of the book and because of the space allotted to it. It is the ball at the Princesse de Guermantes' which consumes about two hundred pages between the moment when the narrator reads the invitation: "The Princesse de Guermantes, née Duchesse de Bavière, will be at home on . . . ."[16] to the moment when he leaves the Duc and Duchesse at the end of the ball to find Albertine.

Closely connected with the account of the ball is an episode which runs through an almost equal number of pages, and which concerns the Duc and Duchesse de Guermantes only:

> The day on which the Princesse de Guermantes was to give her party I heard that the Duc and Duchesse had returned to Paris the day before. It was not the Princesse's ball that brought them back; one of their cousins was seriously ill and, besides, the Duc was most anxious to attend a fancy-dress ball that was to be held that same evening at which he was to appear as Louis XI and his wife as Isabeau of Bavaria.[17]

[16] II, 387. [17] *Ibid.*, p. 390.

The Inhuman World of Pleasure

A ball, a fancy-dress party: these are social obligations, imperative pleasures—secondary, however, when compared with the important social obligations entailed by the death of a relative. The two obligations coincide, and a single act, the return to Paris, fulfills both. But it is not long before they are in direct conflict. As the Duc and Duchesse, after returning from the ball, prepare to dress for the fancy-dress party, M. de Guermantes is confronted by two cousins who are faithfully keeping guard on the stairs in front of his door:

> "Basin, we felt we must warn you that you must not be seen at the ball: poor Amanian died just an hour ago." The duke felt a momentary alarm. He could see the delights of the ball snatched away from him . . . now that he had been told of the death of M. d'Osmond. But he quickly recovered and flung at his two cousins a retort in which he declared, along with his determination not to forego his pleasure, his inability to assimilate the niceties of the French language: "He is dead! Surely not, it's an exaggeration, an exaggeration!" [18]

And the fancy-dress party is not sacrificed.

This episode, from its introduction to its conclusion, is an intrinsic part of the account of the Princesse's soirée and its theme reappears intermittently. As the time of the fancy-dress party draws nearer, Osmond's death becomes more imminent and the attitude of the Duc harassed by two opposing obligations, becomes more transparent. It becomes progressively clear, from the discreet beginning of the tale to its end, that in the Duc's mind a common standard prevails with respect to the two opposing events, and that as far as he is concerned pleasure definitely takes precedence over mourning. All the Duc's worldly acumen is brought into play so that the ill-timed death will not interfere with his own pleasure.

During the afternoon that precedes the ball, the Princesse de Silistrie comes to see the Guermantes, who are back in Paris chiefly, they claim, because of their cousin's illness:

> She spoke sadly to the Duc of a cousin of his . . . whose health had been very bad for some time and who was suddenly much worse. But it was evident that the Duc, though full of pity for his cousin's lot, and who kept repeating "Poor Mama! He's such a nice boy," but it was clear he was still hopeful.[19]

A little later, the two cousins, Mme de Plassac and Mme de Tresme, "came to call upon Basin and declared Cousin Mama's state left no more hope." [20] The problem is posed:

[18] *Ibid.*, p. 493.   [19] *Ibid.*, p. 393.   [20] *Ibid.*, p. 393.

The Duc called back the footman to ask whether the servant he had sent to enquire at his cousin d'Osmond's had returned. His plan was simple: as he had reason to believe that his cousin was dying, he was anxious to have news of him before his death, that is to say, before he was obliged to go into the customary mourning. Once protected by the formal assurance that Amanian was still alive, he would high-tail it to his dinner, to the party at the prince's, to the ball where he would appear as Louis XI and where he had a most promising and exciting rendezvous with a new mistress. And he would not send again to enquire about his cousin's health until the next day when all the fun would be over. Then, if the cousin had died during the night, he would go into mourning.[21]

In order to ensure the complete success of this little strategy of etiquette and propriety, M. de Guermantes orders his valet to disappear: "Go out, go wherever you want, paint the town red, sleep out, but I don't want to see you until tomorrow morning." If d'Osmond's death cannot be prevented, its announcement will at least be delayed; and the Guermantes make a brilliant entrance at the ball. "Some well-intentioned people threw themselves upon the Duc to prevent his entering: 'But don't you know that poor Mama is at death's door? He has just been given extreme unction.' 'I know it,' answered M. de Guermantes, pushing aside the importunate person in order to enter. 'The last sacrament produced the best effect.' "[22]

The final "You're exaggerating" of M. de Guermantes is thus only a stronger declaration of his persistence in preventing the social conventions which surround death from interfering with his pleasure. Proust dwells at some length upon this incident, and emphasizes it; he does not hesitate to exaggerate to the point of absurdity the Duc's reactions and retorts, and his complete complacency. The importance of the episode seems markedly greater when we note that the story reappears, in a more or less modified form, three times in the course of the novel.

On the evening of the famous fancy-dress ball, the Duchesse Oriane, as she is about to enter her carriage, learns from Swann that he has only a short time to live. " 'What are you saying,' said the Duchesse, stopping for a second on her way to the carriage and raising her beautiful blue eyes, which were grieved but full of doubt."[23] Startled by Swann's words, she hesitates, but is hustled along by the Duc. "Mme de Guermantes continued determinedly toward the carriage and repeated her previous farewell to Swann. 'We'll have to speak about that again, you know. I don't believe a word of what you're telling me, but we shall have to talk about it. You have been frightened by some silly fool.' [24] and the Duc, as he was leaving, bellowed from the door to Swann who was already in the courtyard: 'And don't let yourself be taken in by those idiot doctors. What the devil! They're nothing but

[21] *Ibid.*, p. 394.   [22] *Ibid.*, p. 450.   [23] *Ibid.*, p. 406.   [24] *Ibid.*, p. 407.

The Inhuman World of Pleasure 83

silly asses. You're as healthy as the Pont-Neuf. You'll bury us all.' "[25] Although the same word is not repeated the conclusion is the same: Swann and the doctors are exaggerating. But when the Duc suddenly catches sight of Oriane's shoes his hurry to be off disappears; and Swann, the Duchesse's favorite friend, who is now close to death, sees, more clearly than the Guermantes' dying relative, that going to a ball in slippers of the right color is more important to them than a word of sympathy to a doomed friend.

These two episodes, so close to one another, are juxtaposed for a definite purpose. The second raises the question of the claims of friendship in the face of death, and reflects on the attitude of the Duchesse as well as that of the Duc. Somewhat less automatic and brutal than the Duc's, Oriane's attitude and her words are, nevertheless, so exact a repetition that one is tempted to see in them an expression of that philosophy which characterizes the "Guermantes species" and to which they all conform, each in his individual manner. Yet the trait does not belong solely to the Guermantes'; their reaction in the face of death reappears in an entirely different milieu, that of the Verdurins.

The habitués of La Raspelière are arriving for the usual Wednesday dinner: "But à propos of the young violinist," continues Brichot, "I was forgetting, Cottard, to tell you the big news. Did you know that our poor friend Dechambre, who used to be Mme Verdurin's favorite pianist, has just died? Isn't it awful?"[26] The "faithful" exchange a few words on the subject and then resume their own topics of conversation until their arrival at La Raspelière, where the question of mourning comes up. What will Mme Verdurin's reaction be? Will the dinner be put off? M. Verdurin decrees that it be ignored. " 'What, you're still talking about Dechambre?' said M. Verdurin, who had preceded us and who, seeing that we were not following him, had come back. 'Look here,' he said to Brichot, 'there must be no exaggeration in anything.' "[27] Dechambre's death, the reaction of the Verdurins and their coterie to that death are described in ten pages of the novel and culminate with the word already used by the Guermantes. After this the evening flows on quite peacefully.

And finally there is the soirée given by Mme Verdurin in honor of Morel for the aristocratic guests of the Baron de Charlus, the soirée which occurs just after the death of the Princesse Sherbatoff, an inseparable friend of the Verdurins. "Just as we were going to ring the doorbell we were overtaken by Saniette, who told us that the Princesse Sherbatoff had died at six o'clock." The guests enter, remove their overcoats and are welcomed by M. Verdurin. "M. Verdurin, with whom we condoled on the subject of the Princesse Sherbatoff, said to us, 'Yes, I know that she is very ill.' 'But she died at six o'clock,' exclaimed

[25] *Ibid.*, p. 408.   [26] *Ibid.*, p. 606.   [27] *Ibid.*, p. 611.

Saniette. 'You always exaggerate,' Saniette was told curtly by M. Verdurin who, since he had not called off the reception, preferred the hypothesis of illness." [28]

Obviously Proust is repeating the same anecdote deliberately. In each of the four cases he juxtaposes a social event and a death. In each he depicts a contradictory situation in which social convention demands that the conventional sentiments of either family or friendship be respected; and finally we have a barefaced evasion of convention, denoted by the same word "exaggeration," applied to the state least susceptible to that description, death. Could this repetition have been unconscious, merely vague reminiscence? Proust makes use of his anecdote in different ways, but perfectly symmetrically: twice with the Guermantes, twice with the Verdurins. This symmetrical repetition seems to indicate that Proust has some purpose in mind, and is not writing haphazardly. The repetition of the episode has a value in itself for because of it the anecdote acquires a meaning it would not possess had it appeared only once.

By repeating his anecdote, Proust relates the Verdurin group to the Guermantes group, and shows that their reactions are identical. It is a concrete yet subtle demonstration. Two different groups in identical circumstances might react once in the same way by mere chance; but when the reaction is repeated not only within the framework of each group but from group to group, it can scarcely be a chance reaction. Proust sets up this evidence to make us realize that despite all their individual differences, the Guermantes and the Verdurins are alike. The behavior described in the four successive and distinct incidents becomes progressively impersonal and automatic. The gestures seem to be isolated from the individuals, and to belong properly neither to the Duc nor to M. Verdurin; the words are not spoken reflectively, but mechanically. We come to think of these reactions as particular not to any individual but to a "group," a "species," of which the Duc and Duchesse are one specimen and the Verdurins another.

This species flourishes in society and unites Odette with Albertine, with the Duchesse, with the Verdurins, and with all the Guermantes. It is ferociously egotistical, anarchical even, and this explains the unproductivity of society, and its "prodigious aptitude for the disruption of class distinctions." The men accepted by the world of the Guermantes "had usually been brilliant men; but though gifted for a career in the arts, diplomacy, parliament or the army, they had preferred the life of the coterie." [29] Such a life does not tolerate a genuine talent which is not instantly employed to give pleasure. It is really the individual quest for pleasure which determines the apparently chaotic changes in the social kaleidoscope of Proust's world.

[28] III, 154-55.   [29] II, 412.

The Inhuman World of Pleasure

One pleasure is supreme above all others in this world. Before the narrator goes to the reception of the Prince and Princesse de Guermantes, he sees a meeting between Jupien and Charlus, and a whole aspect of Charlus' personality and relationships becomes clear to him. We are introduced first to the world of Sodom, and subsequently to the world in which Sodom and Gomorrha merge. The essential unifying factor of the Proustian social world is now revealed: the covert game of sex, especially in its forbidden form, homosexuality. In this respect Proust, possibly unconsciously, proves the force of his own aesthetic theory; his own particular "inner" world tyrannically imposes its values upon his work. The narrator's view of life is now not unlike the one he entertained as an adolescent when he lived "completely surrounded by monsters and gods." For underneath the trappings and rites of society, underneath the worldly game which it pretends to play so solemnly, Proust gradually delineates another reality. Essentially neither bourgeois nor aristocrats, the inhabitants of the Proustian world are equivocal beings, man-like women and women-like men, androgynous, hermaphroditic. They bridge all social gaps in order to meet each other in the hazardous game which they are always playing among themselves. They flout the laws and conventions of society, laying themselves open to insult and misunderstanding. They live in a picaresque world; events are unforeseen, and everyone moves through a maze of disguise, improvisation, and mistaken identity.

Instead of leading him to a knowledge of the "occult laws" of his "enchanted realms," the narrator's exploration of society ultimately leads him to discover the cities of Sodom and Gomorrha, reborn and surreptitiously allied. The inhabitants of these cities, dogged by the need for secrecy and subterfuge, obsessed by their desire, cannot achieve any enduring happiness. More than all the other Proustian figures, they live in the "inhuman world" of an ever more demanding sensuality which can only be satisfied by others as fugitive as themselves. Vulnerable from every point of view, they flourish in an atmosphere of blackmail and dissimulation which leaves its mark upon them. And they in turn mark the society which surrounds them: St. Loup marries Gilberte because he needs money to keep Morel, whom his uncle has already pushed into society. Jupien's niece, having become Mlle d'Oléron and a noblewoman, marries the young Marquis de Cambremer, thus sanctioning Charlus' affair with Jupien. Albertine through her "affairs" establishes a vast network of "contacts" in which Morel and his friend the chauffeur are involved in a rather shady way. And it is the Prince de Guermantes whom Charlus, spying upon Morel's movements, could have discovered as a rival. The virtuoso Morel, son of the narrator's uncle's valet, loved by the Verdurins, adored by Charlus, associated in Albertine's pleasures, is the character around whom the whole ambiguous network of homosexuality develops.

The narrator's imagination had endowed the inhabitants of the social world with a special aura; they were unknown, mysterious. When he becomes intimate with these people and thinks he knows them, he gets used to them and they lose their aura. Homosexuality then gives them a disturbing, deeper dimension, and a new and mysterious complexity, but this time it is the complexity of reality, less harmonious than that of imagination and infinitely more unruly.

The Princesse de Guermantes' soirée is the climax of the narrator's social ascension. It is also there that Swann makes his last appearance in society, and that the narrator first understands Charlus' personality. Swann disappears and Charlus embarks upon a Balzacian career which is more and more marked by his homosexuality. As a child peering through the gates of Swann's grounds in Tansonville, the narrator had seen Charlus at Odette's side. Odette, framed by Charlus and Swann, is already a sort of symbol of the society he will come to know. Swann, sensitive, cultured, talented, devotes his life first to social dilettantism, then to a love which combines the spice of artistic dilettantism with that of sensual dilettantism. Charlus is drawn outside his native milieu by homosexuality, which slowly usurps his personality and finally absorbs him completely. Always accompanied by his mother and by Françoise, the narrator crosses the territory of the Swanns and the Guermantes without permitting himself to be absorbed by them. Behind these two prodigious creatures, Swann and Charlus, emerges Proust's own countenance, surprisingly illuminated by this juxtaposition. Swann and Charlus, Charlus who develops when Swann disappears, could not these be the two great temptations that society offered to Proust, the two principal beings within himself to whom it appealed: the "little Proust" of the salons and the alarming Proust who for so long kept young men like Agostinelli, "imprisoned" in his apartment? Could not Swann and Charlus be personifications of the two forces which for a long time deflected Proust from his path, triumphing in him successively; Swann during the period of his "social spring," Charlus in the shadows at first but more and more triumphant? And could not the narrator's mother, pale reflection of the dead grandmother, and Françoise, constitute the symbols of those "virtues" of Combray, the concern for real values, the dogged industry, by which the "virtues" of Combray and the "vices" of society are finally synthesized in the work of art? Swann and Charlus are characters far more powerful in stature than the narrator. Their social career reflects a bitter experience; its tragic overtones are plain.

As he tells the story of the illusions and dreams of his narrator, Proust reconstructs the characteristic aspects of a whole era. Because of his love of imagery, reinforced by his theory of the image, he delights in describing lavishly the passing forms of fashions, of customs, of manners which are all part of the ceremony of social intercourse; his detailed evocations firmly locate his world in historical time. Precisely because it is not concerned with real values, the society which he depicts—fleeting mirror of images and opinions—lives for the moment. Consequently, it reflects the outer aspects of an era, transitory, quickly lost, yet aspects which were then more "present" than any other. It restores those elements of the tangible world which defy definition because they are constantly changing. Mme Swann's costumes are no more superfluous ornaments than the "joyful sensations" described at such length. Worldly ritual imposes its fragile mask upon the Proustian characters, placing them in their own time. Though they are not concerned with it, it nevertheless endows them, already so remote from us, with a compelling charm. This charm does not, however, prevent Proust from emphasizing the cruelty of the social comedy. He derives from it an austere moral code the meaning of which is made clear by the twin failures of Charles Swann and the Baron de Charlus.

Images as Instruments

by Georges Cattaui

It is, I believe, no accident that Proust evokes "Celtic beliefs," Medieval legends of Geneviève de Brabant, and chivalrous traditions when writing of love. Platonizer that he was, Proust, anticipating the studies of Denis de Rougemont, had felt the need to probe the occidental concept of a courtly love haunted by the absolute and forever unsatisfied. To claim that Marcel, like Tristan, does not really love Albertine or that Swann does not love Odette would not be overbold. Both Marcel and Albertine desire to feel themselves loved and are content to live their ardent dream. They do not require each other in order to nourish their passion. It is not the lover's presence that is needed, but rather (shades of Mallarmé and *Majnoun Leila!*) his absence. Separation becomes the very consequence of passion. Thus transpires the mysterious indifference of Marcel and Albertine, who remain conspirators isolated in the depths of the same dream. Their adoration of love itself conceals a still more terrifying passion. For this strange couple unknowingly aspire to nothing less than death. The source of their suffering and martyrdom is neither the "other" person nor the love of that person. It is rather the enamoured "ego," held a contemplative prisoner of itself while struggling vainly to close the divine cycle.

This spiritual "narcissism" and solipsism are as evident in Proust as in Valéry. Albertine is loved like a mistress, a sister, a daughter, a mother, and a *double*—just as his own shadow or reflection is coveted by Narcissus. It is above all during her pure, childlike "sleep" that Marcel ultimately finds in Albertine the secret intimacy, delight, and appeasement for which he has yearned. She does not only live *with* Marcel, but *in* him. She is perpetually woven into his dreams and coalesces with the unbroken recitative of half-liturgical, almost Gregorian street cries which combine to form for us the leitmotiv and incarnation

"Images as Instruments" (Original title: "Proust et le Temps"). Translated by Russell Pfohl. From *Marcel Proust* by Georges Cattaui. Copyright 1952 by René Julliard, Editeur. Reprinted by permission.

of her presence. Possession, withering all things encompassed by its embrace, is aware of its own futility and changes to disinterested lucidity. The drama of desire and imagination becomes a faintly melancholy, subjective mysticism wherein it would be possible to discern traces of Albigensian and Catharian illuminism. I am even tempted to detect in Proust's attitude a certain echo of oriental mysticism. (Whether a Buddhist or Sufistic mysticism, I cannot say.) Proust tries less to satisfy desire than to efface and deaden it. And the time he recovers is above all a time he annihilates. He does not wish to attain things themselves, but their essence; or rather, like the Arabian poet, he seeks their absence. Imprisoned and consoled within his daydream, Proust savours the tears and pleasures belonging to the childhood solitude which he has recaptured.

What reader does not see that the Proustian quest in many ways evokes the aspirations of Gnosticism and Orphism? In the absence of forgotten rites handed down to us by Neo-Pythagoreans and Cabalists, we rediscover in Proust, as in most Romantic poets, the nostalgic longing for primitive unity and for this Dionysian passion which symbolizes, through successive and individual deaths, the resurrection of universal life. "The rather bewitching and very imprecise idea of Orphism" fascinated Proust as much as Goethe, Nerval, or Rilke. "The magical notion that some hidden vital principle and tendency toward a higher life may be attributed to each living and inanimate thing; that an intelligence seethes within every element of reality and that it is not impossible to act with the mind upon all things and beings in so far as they too possess an intelligence: such a notion belongs to those ideas which simultaneously evince a kind of primitive reasoning and an instinct essentially creative in realms of poetry and personification." This definition by Valéry might well have been Proust's own. And his entire work, like that of Ovid, could have borne the title *Metamorphoses*. What does this vast cycle of the novel reveal to us if not avatars, transfigurations, and magic charms reminiscent of spells cast by sorcerers and wicked fairies? Metamorphoses of social sets and coteries (the Guermantes, the Blochs, the Verdurins) agitated by continual movement; metamorphoses visible in changing criteria and hierarchies, the force of ascending and descending currents, the phenomena of osmosis, the fusion of social classes, and the corrosive action of Time; metamorphoses of objects effected by the consciousness and realized in turn by art, "Elstir, who was unable to contemplate a flower unless he had first transplanted it in this interior garden where we are forced to remain forever"; finally, metamorphoses of people who are transformed hour by hour before our eyes because the author, unlike most earlier novelists, has taken care "to protect his personages against a simplification of the drama." The vulgar "M. Biche" suddenly turns into Elstir, the painter; Miss Sacripant, "the lady in pink," is by turns

Odette de Crécy, Madame Swann, Madame de Forcheville, the mother of the Marquise de Saint-Loup-en-Bray, and ultimately the socially formidable mistress of the aged duc de Guermantes; the once arrogant Palamède de Charlus is now only a broken old man who glances timidly about while muttering in the street. . . . One sees so many reversals and vicissitudes! Madame Verdurin and Morel humiliate Charlus but are in turn humiliated by the Queen of Naples; Odette de Crécy, formerly snubbed by Oriane, has come to be the latter's implacable and triumphant rival. We are reminded of the *Chad Gadya! Chad Gadya!* in the Jewish *Haggada*, where the water puts out the fire-that-burnt-the-stick-that-beat-the-goat-that-ate-the-cabbage. . . . Such is the perpetual cycle of oriental cosmogonies, the vacillating world of bad dreams which revolve in circles. And such indeed is the infernal hallucination that we witness at the Guermantes' reception, where an entire symbolism of dreams is rediscovered.

Before Sartre, Proust, in his own evocation of the absurd, depicted man as "alienated before all things but especially before himself, unable to repossess himself or to give up the attempt; too wretched ontologically to do without his mask, powerless to discover one that he can endure, and too weak to remove his disguise so as to play his role unhindered." But who then, besides Pascal, will cause "the All of God" to blaze forth against man's nothingness? When shall we see arduous self-examination succeeded by an epoch of contemplation? As one contemplative has shown, the power of analysis, in itself liberating, often merely leads to a mediocre struggle toward autonomy among contemporary thinkers, descendants of Kierkegaard and Nietzsche. Here, as in other areas, "modern man possesses extremely developed means that remain entirely unrelated to the authentic virtue of the mind employing them." Is this not precisely one of the artist's tragedies? Hegel, Hopkins, and Proust thought so. It is not, Proust notes, the most gifted or learned man who is the greatest creator, but "he who is able to become a mirror and thus reflect his life, however ignoble." This observation, born of deep humility, sets Proust apart from the Romantics who wanted their poets to serve as lawgivers for Mankind. The narrator of *Remembrance of Things Past* appears to us in all his weakness. But this is what constitutes his strength and brings him nearer to Christianity than many professed members of that faith. Jacques Madaule has asked whether Proust may not possibly be included among the members of this invisible Church "whose walls are manifested only in living stones." Certainly one of the characteristics of Proust's work is the absence of God. However, it is perhaps out of respect, loyalty, and modesty that Proust declines to mention God. Simone Weil would say that, for want of a personal knowledge of divine life, such reticence is perhaps best. . . . Still, Proust has explored a spiritually authentic universe. And doubtless we have no right to claim that the sacrifice of his life to his work

Images as Instruments

was performed in vain. Has the Creator not willed such lucidity and keenness of vision? Let us heed the writer's own exhortation and recognize therein nameless echoes emanating from the highest of Christian aspirations:

> Happiness is beneficial for the body but it is grief that develops the powers of the mind. Moreover, even if it did not each time disclose to us a law, it would nevertheless be indispensable for bringing us back to the truth, forcing us to take things in serious vein, by uprooting each time the tangled growth of habits, skepticism, flippancy, indifference. It is true that grief, which is not compatible with happiness or health, is sometimes prejudicial also to life. In the end, sorrow kills. At each fresh, overpowering shock we feel another vein stand out and develop its deadly swellings along our temples, beneath our eyes. Thus were produced little by little those terrible, grief-ravaged faces of the aged Rembrandt and the aged Beethoven, whom everyone used to scoff at. And the pouches under the eyes and wrinkles on the brow would be nothing if there were not also the suffering in the heart. But since forces can change their nature and sustained heat become light and the electricity of lightning record a photograph, since the dull ache at our heart can raise, as it were, a banner for each fresh sorrow, the permanent symbol of an inner image, let us accept the physical injury it inflicts because of the spiritual wisdom that it brings; let us allow our body to disintegrate, since each fresh particle that breaks off, now luminous and decipherable, comes and adds itself to our work to complete it at the cost of suffering superfluous to others more gifted and to make it more and more substantial as emotions gradually chip away our life. Ideas take the place of sorrows; when the latter are transformed into ideas, they at once lose part of their noxious effect on the heart and from the very first moment the transformation itself radiates joy.[1]

[1] *Remembrance of Things Past*, II, 1020-1021.

Religious Imagery

by Elliott Coleman

The early part of *A la recherche du temps perdu*, and the early life of the narrator, are suffused by the light of a liturgy. It seems always to be Holy Week, or the Month of Mary, with the walks to and from Mass or special devotions in the church of Saint-Hilaire at Combray, in which he first recognized a fourth dimension: that of time; with those walks into the country on Sunday afternoons, Swann's way, and the Guermantes' way.

"During May," recounts the narrator, "we used to go out on Saturday evenings after dinner to the 'Month of Mary' devotions. . . . It was in these . . . services that I can remember having first fallen in love with hawthorn-blossoms." He continues:

> The hawthorn was not merely in the church, for there, holy ground as it was, we had all of us a right of entry; but, arranged upon the altar itself, inseparable from the mysteries in whose celebration it was playing a part, it thrust in among the tapers and the sacred vessels its rows of branches, tied to one another horizontally in a stiff, festal scheme of decoration.

When the boy turns to the woods and walks out toward the estate of Gilberte's father, the whole path "throbbing with the fragrance of hawthorn blossoms," he finds that the hedges of hawthorn trees resemble a series of chapels, "whose walls were no longer visible under the mountains of flowers that were heaped upon their altars." The scent that reached him was as rich and as circumscribed in range as that which had swept round him before the Lady-altar. He shaped his fingers into a frame so that he could see nothing but hawthorns. The vague sentiment they aroused this time struggled to free itself, to "float across and become one with the flowers, and I could not call upon any other flowers

"Religious Imagery." From *The Golden Angel* by Elliott Coleman. Copyright 1954 by Elliott Coleman. Reprinted by permission of Academy Guild Press, Fresno, California.

Religious Imagery

to satisfy this mysterious longing." Just at this moment Marcel's grandfather calls him to look at a hedge of pink hawthorn.

And it was indeed a hawthorn, but one whose flowers were pink, and lovelier even than the white. It, too, was in holiday attire, for one of those days which are the only true holidays, the holidays of religion, because they are not appointed by any capricious accident, as secular holidays are appointed . . . which have nothing about them which is essentially festal. . . . High up on the branches, like so many of those tiny rose-trees, their pots concealed in jackets of paper lace, whose slender stems rise in a forest from the altar on the greater festivals, a thousand buds were swelling and opening, paler in color, but each disclosing as it burst, as at the bottom of a cup of pink marble, its blood-red stain, and suggesting even more strongly than the full blown flowers, the special irresistible quality of the hawthorn tree, which, wherever it budded, wherever it was about to blossom, could bud and blossom in pink flowers alone. Taking its place in the hedge but as different from the rest as a young girl in holiday attire among a crowd of dowdy women in everyday clothes, who are staying at home, equipped and ready for the 'Month of Mary,' of which it seemed already to form a part, it shone and smiled in its clear, rosy garments, a Catholic bush indeed, and altogether delightful.[1]

The little *madeleine* itself, which, dipped in a cup of hot lime-flower tea, provides a taste and an aroma that set in motion all the "vast structure of recollection" is finally remembered to have been tasted first in the serenity of those Sunday mornings at Combray when the little boy used to visit the room of his aunt Léonie before going to Mass. This delicate, scented wafer is described by the narrator as having a "religious" look about it; and it will always come to mind on those continual occasions of the author's use of the wafer of the Holy Sacrament as a symbol or comparison—as even when he is describing the kiss of Albertine.

Trees and Spires: Trinities of Images

One Sunday afternoon . . . Marcel sits up on the coachman's box [in the carriage of the Combray physician] and in the windy sunset at a bend in the road he catches sight of the twin steeples of Martinville. Of course they are church steeples; nothing else on that landscape would have been so plainly visible. But something new and strange happens. As the carriage progresses and the angles of perspective change, a third steeple, that of the church at Vieuxvicq, a village separated from Martinville by a hill and a valley, comes into view with the other two spires

[1] *Remembrance of Things Past*, I, 107.

and stands up beside them to form a triad. As the narrator gazed at these "three flowers painted upon the sky," he suddenly experienced "that special pleasure, which bore no resemblance to any other." The carriage jolts along and now, in noting their changes of aspect and their sunny surfaces, Marcel feels that he is not penetrating to the full depth of his impression, "that something more lay behind that mobility, that luminosity, something which they seemed at once to contain and to conceal. . . ."

What is happening here is a religious experience which the narrator cannot consciously or intellectually realize but which becomes real in his art. The number three is necessary for him, whether it be for a Calvary or for a Holy Trinity. The need is there for a third spire to move like a bright ghost into place; otherwise the conditions of ecstasy would not have been conferred. And of singular importance is the twilight vision of the three spires as one. Perhaps we should pause to read renunciation and death in the comparisons to birds and maidens, but the theme that triumphs is life and joy. The spires spring to the sky in nobility, and the boy begins to sing at the top of his voice. . . .

Of desperate importance are the Three Trees of Hudimesnil. It was a Sunday in early summer on the Channel coast. . . . "Suddenly," says the narrator, "I was overwhelmed with that profound happiness which I had not often felt since Combray; happiness analogous to that which had been given me by—among other things—the steeples of Martinville. But this time it remained incomplete. I had just seen, standing a little way back from the steep ridge over which we were passing, three trees, probably marking the entrance to a shady avenue, which made a pattern at which I was looking now for the first time. . . ."

It must be pointed out that the immediate conditions under which he saw the Three Trees were practically identical with those under which he had seen the Three Spires. In both instances he was in a carriage moving along a country road, and his own motion gave the objects of his vision motion. It was the trees that came toward Marcel but he could not stop to meet them. It was as if they turned with earth and the nature of things, whereas his conscious direction was the opposite from theirs. As they came close to him, the wind blowing through them, "in their simple passionate gesticulation I could discern the *helpless anguish of a beloved person who had lost the power of speech.*" (Italics mine.) This is different, once more, from the live voices of dead spirits calling from trees, as in the Celtic legend he once related. Again the Three Trees were like one person who "feels that he will never be able to say to us what he wishes to say and we can never guess. . . ." The carriage "was bearing me away from what alone I believed to be true, what would have made me truly happy; it was like my life."

The Three Trees, waving despairing arms, were at least this articulate: "What you fail to learn from us today you will never know . . . a whole part of yourself which we were bringing to you will fall forever into the abyss." That was what Marcel thought they said. He was to find out much more, though never to know all of it. It is to be remembered, if we are to feel the impact of his final sentence, that the narrator had already lost any conscious religious faith: ". . . I was as wretched as though I had just lost a friend, had broken faith with the dead, or had denied my God."

Orchestration of the Images: The Golden Angel

The source of the Visions of Three, including Bergotte's books arranged angelically three by three in the lighted windows at his death, is finally confirmed in music by an equation: the seven-fold widening of the Little Phrase of Vinteuil's Sonata into the orchestration of the Septuor —"the boldest approximation of the bliss of the world beyond"—which affirms the existence and persistence of the soul.

On the pinnacle of the towering Campanile of San Marco stands the figure of a golden angel, once fallen, to be sure, but restored in the first decade of this century. The narrator of these novels records his vision of it on a visit made to Venice before he had accepted his Vocation. He had arrived in the night and had gone to his hotel.

> When at ten o'clock in the morning my shutters were thrown open, I saw ablaze in the sunlight, instead of the black marble into which the slates of Saint-Hilaire used to turn, the Golden Angel on the Campanile of San Marco. . . . I could see nothing but itself, so long as I remained in bed, but as the whole world is merely a vast sun-dial, a single lighted segment of which enables us to tell what o'clock it is, on the very first morning I was reminded of the shops in the Place de l'Eglise at Combray, which, on Sunday mornings, were always on the point of shutting when I arrived for mass, while the straw in the market place smelt strongly in the already hot sunlight.[2]

Because it had a natural air and also an air of distinction, because it was notable for an absence of vulgarity, pretension, and meanness, the gray stone steeple of Saint-Hilaire in Combray had "shaped and crowned and consecrated every occupation, every hour of the day, every point of view in the town . . . like the Finger of God Whose Body might have been concealed below among the crowd of human bodies, without fear of my confounding It, for that reason, with them." The church itself, the "dear, familiar friend," whose influence pervades all the life of the early chapters, renews its own identity in that of its glittering counterpart above the Adriatic Sea, where memory is entrusted to porphyry and

[2] *Remembrance of Things Past*, II, 821.

jasper: just as the curé who was amateur philologist and would have his joke merges into the aged figure of the archbishop of the last sentence of the book, and just as the Calvary that was long ago reflected in the moonlight of a country pond is finally mirrored from that only solid part of him, his metal cross.

. . . The golden angel of Saint Mark's, floating between earth and heaven, so bright that it was almost impossible to fix it in space . . . sums up what is for me a discovery; something I did not recognize on first reading *A la recherche du temps perdu*; something I did not know existed in that world until I was urged to travel there again. The Golden Angel, symbol of religion and of art, of aesthetics and morality is, like so many unconscious gifts of Marcel Proust, clear and incomparable.

The central imagery, the vital metaphors, the abiding symbols of this work, both conscious and unconscious, are one continuing story. Without them the art of Proust would have been an art without a central reference; at the best the seal of timelessness would then indeed have become the seal of time. The little *madeleine* and the cup of hot lime-flower tea of Sunday mornings, the red and white blossoms of hawthorn in the month of May, the gardens of flowering pear, the Three Spires of Martinville, the Three Trees near Balbec, the paradisal Phrase that half-explained them all, the uneven stones in a courtyard that summoned them all back, these and a circle of angels are the recreation of a religious impulse. They are the form of *A la recherche du temps perdu*.

Only a poet-linguist of his language could estimate the immense action of the author's conscious struggle; only a pastoral psychologist the vaster struggle of the soul; but when we read the symbols the artist arrived at and find they represent a liturgy of hope, we understand better how one great work of the imagination was made possible. And whether or not we share its impulse, we have learned something of relationships in art. Among guardian angels, there is something to be said for those of gold.

Intuition and Philology

by Leo Spitzer

We recall the marvelous "Overture for a Public Holiday" of that chapter in which Proust frames the morning awakening of Marcel and Albertine with the street cries of Paris, celebrating the awakening of the metropolis (*La Prisonnière*, Pléiade, III, 116 ff.; Scott-Moncrieff, II, 459 ff.). The alternate feelings of attraction and repulsion experienced by his hero, confronted with the devious and mendacious character of Albertine, the author succeeds in orchestrating not only by the skillful variations (modulation from major to minor) imposed by these psychological fluctuations and lapses, but also by the introduction of the voices of the City, weaving a symbolic counterpoint. Marcel hears in them now an invitation to the joys of external life (pleasures of the palate, of the ear, etc.) which he savors by the side of his beloved, now the call addressed by the yawning, dark gulf of vicious, sensual life to this woman who is ever on the verge of succumbing to it. In the condensed descriptions of these traditional cries which the novelist gives us, one idea stands out with an insistence no doubt intentional: the identification of the musical cries with the chants of the Catholic Church, a conceit expressed not only for its own sake by an acute observer, but one which here corresponds to the preoccupations of his hero. Into these cries, suggestive of quite "terrestrial" fruits, there creeps a sort of religious *basso continuo,* emphasizing the supraterrestrial rights in the name of which Marcel would hold Albertine back from the edge of the abyss. Certain abrupt, staccato breaks evoke most particularly for Proust's "historic ear" the mixture of declamation and of song which is peculiar to the music of old churches:

. . . the old-clothes man . . . intoned: *"Habits, marchand d'habits, ha . . . bits"* with the same pause between the final syllables as if he had been

"Intuition and Philology" (Original title: "L'Etymoligie d'un, 'Cri de Paris'"). Translated by Catherine and Richard Macksey. From *The Romanic Review* XXV. Copyright 1944 by Columbia University Press. Reprinted by the gracious permission of the editor and publisher.

intoning in plain chant: *"Per omnia saecula saeculo . . . rum"* or *"resquiescat in pa . . . ce"*. . . . And similarly, . . . a vegetable woman, pushing her little hand-cart, was using for her litany the Gregorian division:

> *A la tendresse, à le verduresse*
> *Artichauts tendres et beaux*
> *Arti—chauts.*

I should like to treat here briefly the origins of this last "cry," adding to the "historical description" of the novelist the philologist's etymology. Perhaps the former will be confirmed and a bit broadened by the considerations to be presented here: beginning with the modern form I shall attempt to trace it as far as possible into the past.

We know that Proust's verbal orchestration of the *Cris de Paris* was preceded by the musical orchestration of the same cries in Charpentier's opera *Louise* (performed in 1900). At the end of the second act, the cries of open-air vendors—motifs intermingling in an impressionist manner and symbolizing the City which serves as background for the action—join the duo of the lovers. The cry of the old-clothes man is there, along with that of the artichoke woman, which takes the form:

> *Artichauts, des gros artichauts,*
> *à la tendress', la verduress',*
> *et à un sou,*
> *Vert et tendre, et à un sou,*

in which Proust's assonance is replaced by the (imperfect) assonance *artichauts-sou*, but in which we find the same rhyme *tendress'—verduress'*. Charpentier even allows the act to close on this verse evocative of cool verdure and of springtime love (*à la tendress', à la verduress'*), but, less concerned than the novelist with the history of the cries and with their ultimate meaning, the composer transcribes here (as, too, for the old-clothes man) only the vocal elements of the cry without recording its prosody, that "ritual suspension" which for Proust links these accents of modern Paris with the Catholic past of old France.

It is evident that the two versions of the cry, heard by Proust and by Charpentier, are but the surviving fragments, varied in the manner of the common people who love to *zersingen* as the German Volkslied scholars say, of songs which formerly had a more perfect or more complete form. By a stroke of fortune the *Petit Dictionnaire du Peuple* of J. C. L. P. Desgranges (1821), published exactly a century before Proust, gives us a more satisfactory form: *La tendresse, la verduresse, trois liards la pièce,* comprising a perfect rhyme. Here is the entry of the dictionary, which was studied by M. Gougenheim in his complementary thesis *La Langue populaire dans le premier quart du XIXe siècle:*

La Verduresse. Voilà du français de marchands d'artichauts qui crient dans Paris: *La tendresse, la verduresse, à trois liards la pièce.* Tout cela est charmant quant à la rime; mais pour s'exprimer exactement, il faudrait qu'ils disent: *La tendreté, la verdeur.* [This is the French of artichoke vendors who cry in Paris: *La tendresse, la verduresse, à trois liards la pièce.* All very charming as for the rhyme, but to express themselves accurately they would have to say: *La tendreté, la verdeur.*]¹

With all due respect to the orthopedists of the language, not only the rhyme but precisely the formations in *-esse* have an archaic flavor which we must be careful *not* to regularize. Obviously this cry must be fairly ancient since it alludes to the *liard,* a coin of the old Monarchy which has not been minted since the Revolution (1792) and which was withdrawn from circulation in 1856 (*Larousse du XXe siècle*). But we can go back even further, precisely because of the formation of *tendresse,* which, today used only in the figurative sense, in Old French could mean "tenderness," "the fact of being tender (in the physical sense)"; Godefroy gives an example from *Le Roi Modus.*

A further consideration, this time of a literary order, takes us back again to the Old French period. G. Thurau, in *Der Refrain in der französischen Chanson* (1901), page 485, mentions our 19th-century cry (in the altered form *Un sou la pièce—La tendresse—La verdurette,—* which we can obviously correct to: *verduresse*) as one among the variant refrains of the *re(n)verdies,* that lyric genre of spring *romance* or *ballade* (dancing song), presenting in a setting of verdure and of flowers either the nightingale, symbol of Love, or Love himself. We remember that it was Gaston Paris who baptized the genre *re(n)verdie,* because this word "expresses admirably both its setting and its theme" (*Mélanges littéraires,* page 556). Furthermore, according to Paris, since joy at the return of spring was the central theme of Old French lyricism, this genre must have been one of its oldest manifestations, linking it with the Pagan May festivals. Unhappily these songs "sung by girls and young women, dancing at the calends of May," with their "gay, springtime" spirit, cele-

¹ It is the two suffixes *-té* and *-eur* which even today would come to mind if a Frenchman were in search of neologisms: cf. the two substantives derived from *sombre* which Pichon (*Le Français mod.* VI, 301) cites as examples of spontaneous derivations heard in 1932-1933: *sombreté, sombreur,* the first more abstract (in the sentence: . . . *ici ce n'est rien comme sombreté,* 'the point being the fact of darkness'), the second indicating rather a certain intensity (in the sentence: *Etait-il* [the place] *d'une telle sombreur?*) The suffix *-euse,* on the other hand, is absolutely unproductive of new formations today, except in the figurative sense (cf. *rudesse, délicatesse*): Meyer-Lübke, *Hist. fr. Gr.,* II, 72, observes that a word like *robustesse,* coined by Th. Gautier, is not a sign of life in the suffix, but rather a symptom of the poet's wanting to enrich the language by means of archaic formations. It is the very 'gratuitousness' of *verduresse* which gives it charm: the flowering of the suffix *-esse* restores to the prosaic *verdure* a living grace, but one which carries the nostalgia of yesteryear.

brating "simply the month of May, the rebirth of nature, verdure, flowers, the song of birds"—these songs have not survived; but we find their echo in Latin or German lyrics of the *Carmina burana* or in refrains. Many of these refrains, which are the "stock formulae" of the genre (just as the word *alba* is indispensable to the lyric so named), have been catalogued, after G. Paris, by Thurau. Among them appears the root *vert*, or one of its derivatives:

> Se part de froidure
> Que cist bois sont boutonné
> Et plain de verdure
> La bonne amor m'asseure . . . ;—
> Quand repaire la verdor et la prime florette;—
> A la renverdie, au bois!
> A la renverdie;—
> Verdure le boys, verdure

Often the scene of the dancing, greensward or meadow, is evoked in popular songs by the phrase *sus la verdure* (or *sous le bois, la feuille; sur le gazon*); and often the word itself is provided with fanciful refrain-suffixes through which the lyrical gaiety seeks expression: *Verdurette, oh! verduron!; La verduron don don, A la verduron, durette.* Those dancing gaily on the green must have been tempted to include in their song the gathering of certain spring herbs, and thus Thurau cites, after E. Rolland:

> Oh! verdin, verdillette,
> Pour cueillir cresson
> Verdillette, Oh! verdillon,
> Oh verdin, verdin, verdillette.

We can now safely conclude that the cry of the artichoke vendors was originally a *renverdie* of the kind just cited, but adapted to their commercial requirements. In the dancing song they found the idea of returning spring, with its invitation to love and to dancing on the green (*A la tendresse—verduresse*), and the idea of the gathering of plants (*Pour cueillir cresson > artichauts*); by adding a price (*à trois liards [à un sou] la pièce*) they produced a nice rhyme. The word *tendresse*, originally linked both with love and with nature-reborn, must also have been understood, probably as far back as the Old French period, as describing the tender young plants. The traditional elements of the strophe thus acquired a new value. Curiously enough it was not the word *pièce* which suggested the rhymes *tendresse—verduresse;* rather *verduresse* (associated with *tendresse*) was the older element, and it was the spring song

Intuition and Philology 101

which made it possible for the vegetable vendors to proffer their wares in a poetic guise. Thus poetry cleared the path for tradesmen. The outdoor vendors were able to capture in their cry all of the matutinal poetry of the old May songs; even appropriated to a very practical end this poetry did not lose its bloom. And it is a very French trait to let the gratuitousness of poetry coexist with avowedly practical interests—the latter being thus transposed into poetry. And perhaps poetry, which in the old songs celebrated greenness as the reveling place of young and tender love, perhaps this poetry survives in the form of *tendresse pour la jeune verdure*—the vendor looks with tenderness on his merchandise (*artichauts tendres et beaux!*), which he appreciates as a poet—a popular poet, of course, for whom the aesthetic and the lucrative aspects of nature's fruits are not dissociated. I shall always remember, with an amazement which does not fade with the years, that insistent and moving cry of the open-air Parisian florists with the roguish eye, who speculate on . . . —no, that isn't the word!—who incorporate into the business of earning a few sous the age-old French need for beauty:[2] *Achetez de la violette, de la violette jolie et pas chère!* Calculation—poetry? No, there is no conflict: the poet, too, calculates his effects, and the man-in-the-street is a poet even as he calculates. And this poet of the common people is a traditionalist: he adapts, he varies the given recipe—so that an intellectual poet, in this case Proust the novelist-poet, can still relish and thereby make us relish the original savor. Ah! if Proust had known the "etymology"[3] of this cry, how happy he would have been to hear echoes of twelfth-century France in the modern streets of the noble quartier Saint-Germain, in which his hero, loftily intellectual, dwells with the earthier Albertine—how happy to reflect with disenchanted bitterness

[2] The preposition *à* in *À la verduresse, à la tendresse* is obviously the same as the one which invites *au bois, à la renverdie*. Thence the *à* of other cries: *À la barque, les huîtres, à la barque,/À la romaine, à la romaine,/On ne la vend pas, on la promène* etc. Régis Michaud in his manual *Vingtième siècle* (1933, Harper) explains (p. 477): "The crier advertises the oysters as just fresh from the boat (barque)." But then one would expect **de la barque!* No. There must be here a renovation of the *à*, which seems today to exhort the public to rush toward the foodstuffs being hawked (*à la verduresse, à la barque*), whereas the *renverdie* summoned people to come to the gathering of cress, of artichokes, of romaine.

[3] The Italians, so adaptable to different milieux and susceptible to *virtuosità*, to *furfanteria*, are rather inclined to introduce pure fancy—if I can judge from a refrain shouted by the ice cream vendors of Baltimore—a refrain derived from the formula of hocus-pocus magicians: The Italian exploits his gift for histrionics and *auto-persiflage*, and the ice cream vendor plays the magician (who can pull anything out of his hat!). Thus the Italian vendors' cry *a uffa!* which was probably accompanied in the beginning by a flourish suggesting the abundance of the merchandise offered to the public, has a rather theatrical tone (cf. REW s.v. *uf*-interjection, in which is accepted an explanation which I had suggested in *Butlletí de dialectologia catalana*, IX, 85). In contradistinction to the Italian crier, with his "free show," the Frenchman allows for the essential realism of his audience.

on that fusion of the aristocracy with the common people, achieved by a France which is no more.

It is the magic charm of the old aristocratic quarters that they are at the same time plebeian. Just as, sometimes, cathedrals used to have them within a stone's throw of their porches (which have even preserved the name, like the porch of Rouen styled the Booksellers', because these latter used to expose their merchandise in the open air against its walls), so various minor trades, but peripatetic, used to pass in front of the noble Hotel de Guermantes, and made one think at times of the ecclesiastical France of long ago. For the appeal which they launched at the little houses on either side had, with rare exceptions, nothing of a song . . . it recalled the psalmody of a priest chanting his office of which these street scenes are but the good-humoured, secular, and yet half liturgical counterpart.

And now we can understand even better how right Proust was to recognize ecclesiastical accents in the music of the cries of Paris, punctuated as they are[4] by mysterious pauses: we know that the secular music of the Middle Ages bespeaks its ecclesiastical origins and M. Gerold in his book, *La Musique au moyen âge,* has pointed out those melismas of troubadour songs and popular songs which betray their debt to the Gregorian chant. When the peripatetic vendors, having become "popular troubadours," transposed the *re(n)verdie* into a street cry, why indeed would they not have imitated the psalmodic tone of declamation mixed with chanting which they heard in church? So that the cries of Paris truly represent an ancient secularized version of that chanting declamation, which no longer exists in our temporal world; they are following a "half liturgical" syntax which is popular and French, but evolved from Latin texts, so that what appears so delightfully secular and open-air to the Parisian tourist was born under the somber arches of the cathedral. Proust, the artist who frames a nascent "social" conflict between two modern lovers, with the centuries-old [5] symphony of Parisian street cries,

[4] This punctuation is most striking in the Parisian tinker's cry, which neither Proust nor Charpentier has utilized, and which seems to destroy intentionally the natural rhythm of the French word in favor of a quite arbitrary scansion, of obviously liturgical origin: *re-é-tameur* (the last two syllables are robbed of any prosodic value, and together with the prolonged *é,* which is chanted on a higher note, they form a sort of dactyl which ends on a caricatural staccato or pizzicato, in which only the syllabic value of these two *brèves* remains).

[5] Are we to recognize in the "singing melancholy," the "pathetic finale" which Proust observes in the cry of the snail vendor (in the words *On les vend six sous la douzaine,* which follow the almost "spoken" words: *Les escargots, ils sont frais, ils sont beaux*) an echo of that air of sadness probably assumed already by the cry of the snail vendor of ancient Rome in the *Cena Trimalchionis* (. . . *tremula teterrimaque voce* . . .), a note of sadness which survives in the cry of the Neapolitan *maruzzaru?* (Cf. M. L. Wagner, *Volkstun und Kultur de Romanen* VI, 6.) If this theory is valid, a continuity would be established with the Pagan tradition.

Intuition and Philology

was well aware of the *basso ostinato* of the enduring Church which follows the believer even into his daily tasks.[6] By going one step further than even he himself realized, Proust performed the work of the historian of civilization.*

[6] We know that Claudel felt even in the binary rhythm of classical verse forms the echo of the Church: "French classical poetry has its canons in the Commandments of God and of the Church and in rustic adages about the weather. Its character is essentially gnomic and mnemotechnic. The same abhorrence of chance, the same need for the absolute, the same distrust of feeling, which are apparent even today in our character and in our social conventions, have molded our grammar and our prosody." The street cry, which in the present instance corresponds to the "rustic adages about the weather," is also modeled on Church canon, and this appropriation of ecclesiastical music and poetry by *le bon sens* confirms Claudel's reflection.

* The final footnote of the original text has been omitted.

The Architecture of Time:
Dialectics and Structure

by Richard Macksey

> Nein: ein Turm soll sein aus meinen Herzen
> und ich selbst an seinen Rand gestellt:
> wo sonst nichts mehr ist, noch einmal Schmerzen
> und Unsäglichkeit, noch einmal Welt.
> R. M. Rilke, *Der Einsame*

As each successive volume of *A la recherche du temps perdu* issued from the cork-lined cell on the Boulevard Haussmann, Marcel Proust anxiously wrote to friends and critics to insist once more on the irreducible unity and symmetry of his life work. As the digressions, characters, and reversals multiplied, from the prismatic variety of the world presented there readers began to select aspects and to make Prousts in their own image: the author as psychologist, memorialist, aesthetician, comedian, martyr of art. And yet the novelist constantly returned in his correspondence to his concern for construction. At times he would analogize his task to that of a composer resolving opposing themes or leitmotivs into a musical structure; more often he would turn to the metaphoric role of architect. It was the master-builder alone who could guarantee that the content would be, in fact, embodied in the shape, that the work of years would preserve the coherence of its original plan. Thus, as early as February 1914, Proust wrote in his first letter to Jacques Rivière with an enthusiasm born of anxiety: "At last I have found a reader who has hit upon [*qui devine*] the fact that my book is a dogmatic work and a construction! . . . In this first volume you have seen the pleasure afforded me by the *madeleine* dipped in tea: I say that I cease to feel mortal etc., and that I do not understand why. I will not explain until the end of the third [i.e., last] volume. The whole is so *constructed*." [1] To Benjamin Crémieux, who was later to defend him as the master of the "composition en rosace," the ordering of episodic losenges into an internally related circle like the great rose windows of the

[1] *Marcel Proust et Jacques Rivière: Correspondence: 1914-1922* (Paris, 1955), pp. 1-2.

The Architecture of Time: Dialectics and Structure

French cathedrals, Proust wrote: "Thank you for comparing my book to a city. . . . People fail only too often to realize that my books form a construction, but drawn to a compass so vast that the structure—a rigorous structure to which I have subordinated everything—takes rather a long time to discern. There will be no denying it when the last page of *Le Temps retrouvé* (written before the rest of the book) closes precisely on the first page of *Swann*." [2] The image of an architectural circle in its simplicity and expansiveness thus encloses the entire work, like the medieval wall which encloses Combray and gives it form.

André Maurois proposes another rich architectural image, that of the gothic arch itself, after he quotes this unpublished letter from Proust to Jean Gaigneron:

> And when you speak to me of cathedrals I cannot fail to be moved by the intuition which lets you guess [*deviner*] what I have never told anyone and am writing here for the first time: that is that I had wanted to give to each part of my book the title: *Porch, Stained glass of the apse*, etc., to answer in advance the stupid criticism which claims that I lack construction in books whose only merit, as I shall show you, is in the adherence of the smallest parts.[3]

Through the design of the builder the opposed piers of the gothic arch were enlisted so as to sustain the whole great mass of the towering edifice. And just as in the medieval cathedral moral directions were embodied in space, so the extremes and the unity of Proust's entire work are suggested in his system of structural oppositions, the piers of his building.

For Proust originality was a quality of "vision," a way of seeing the world whole and unique; he saw his own task as that of enclosing his world in a new structure which, like the parish church of Saint-Hilaire, would include in its unity the "four dimensions of space—the name of the fourth being Time." [4] Although the vocabulary of Proust's extended architectural metaphors frequently recalls his apprenticeship to John Ruskin, two insistent points in such comparisons are peculiarly characteristic of the novelist's own vision: the possibility of creating a dialectic between inside and outside, a living space within which the artist can translate the world; and the possibility, usually represented by the

---

[2] Benjamin Crémieux, *Du Côté de Marcel Proust* (Paris, 1929), p. 80. Proust repeats this argument and description of his method of composition in letters to Paul Souday, Mme Straus, and others.

[3] André Maurois, *A la recherche de Marcel Proust* (Paris, 1949), p. 175. Cf. Ruskin's distinction between architecture and building in the first chapter of *The Seven Lamps of Architecture*.

[4] *A la recherche du temps perdu*, edited by Pierre Clarac and André Ferré, 3 vols. (Paris: Bibliothèque de la Pleiade, 1954), I, 61. All subsequent citations from Proust noted in parentheses are from this edition.

gothic arch or rose window, of bringing into immanent contact two apparently opposed views or ways of life.

The world outside, beyond the walls of the family or of Combray, is always the object of the Proustian character in his moment of dispersion; the mechanism by which he reaches out in a vain attempt to appropriate the shifting surfaces out there for his own may be called love or *snobisme* or even chauvinism, but the trajectory is always the same, a flight from the inside, from the center of the self. Although the Proustian world (the author's vocabulary to the contrary) in no way partakes of the Plotinian world of procession, absolute intelligibility, and eternal essences, yet the novelist's model of the soul with its dialectic of inside and outside, does resemble the neo-platonic sphere on whose outer surface is displayed the cinematic film of the flux of the senses and on whose inner surface is reflected the light from the center, which is Being itself. The first movement in each case is outward toward the flux, the second a turning back on the center. The negative half of Proust's dialectic, the progressive erosion of appearances by change, has led some critics to recognize the Plotinian attempt to abolish everything in reality which is impervious to spiritual penetration. But for Proust the experience of change and the succession of affective states which it brings is absolutely essential to the later, positive phase of the dialectic—the remembering and reconstituting of these experiences. Plotinus, on the other hand, dismisses memory (in the worldly and non-Platonic sense): "The more the Soul strives after the intelligible, the more it forgets. . . . In this sense, therefore, we may say that the good soul is forgetful."[5]

Again, the image of a space within the structure of consciousness suggests the place where Mallarmé's "rose absent from every bouquet" blooms eternally. The quest for an "interior space" of presence and stability is certainly a familiar aspect of the Symbolist program. Yet the element of Proust's revision which must be emphasized here is again the crucial importance, the necessity, of the *outside* in creating a consciousness through its very opposition. The doors of Proust's edifice of consciousness may be sealed against others, but the fantastic windows, like those of the chapel of Gilbert le Mauvais, do admit the very light whereby newly refracted, altered images are composed within.

Existence for Proust is thus defined in terms of an antinomy: a going out toward primitive experience, hopelessly fragmented into sensational instants, and a return toward the interior of oneself to relate these experiences, these instants, to the past: expansion and concentration. There is no existence without content, then, but the Proustian man (like his counterparts described by Kierkegaard and Sartre) crouches within the edifice of his consciousness, removed from the Other. He de-

[5] Plotinus, *Enneads*, IV, 3, 32.

mands this distance between as a requisite of his knowing. In the same way he is, in Augustine's "specious present," at some temporal remove from his own existence; he rather seeks to constitute himself in the very consciousness that he *has existed*. Just as Proust argues that all creation is re-creation, so all cognition is recognition. The precarious present moment is sustained by the presence of the past, "the stalk of recollection" of which he speaks at length. This vital activity of the consciousness can only take place with epistemic and temporal distance; the only possible portrait of the artist is as a young man.

While the image of an historical structure like the cathedral illustrates Proust's dialectic of inside-outside with a temporal dimension, the second implication of Proust's architectural imagery is figured by the arch. This image suggests Proust's need to organize his experience in terms of paired opposites and, where possible, to find some unsuspected similarity as keystone to unite them. This habit of mind is at the very heart of his almost sacerdotal attention to metaphor, to synaesthesia, to puns, to stylistic devices such as syllepsis and oxymoron—all pivots on which to engage opposition. These counterstressed elements of style can be considered monads which reflect the construction of the fictional universe, for the entire work unfolds in terms of oppositions: of point of view, of plot development, and of character. Proust is an author of strenuous dualism. Out of opposites, however, is generated the dynamism toward a dialectic. With Anaximander of Miletus, Proust comprehends life as the paired opposition of basic rhythms: Day and Night, Presence and Absence, Time and Intemporality; with Heraclitus of Ephesus he seeks the possible unity of this dualism in change: "way up, down; one and the same."[6] Plato's captious Elean Stranger of the *Sophist* suggests that Heraclitus' cosmology, along with the system of counterstresses developed a generation later, was the first attempt to reconcile Ephesian Opposition with the Eleatic first principle, the One. Hegel drily glosses the text by remarking that this event was the birth of the dialectics. The attempt to exhaust reality through systems of opposition was, of course, hardly abandoned with the pre-Socratic cosmologies. In fact, Heidegger organizes his *Einführung in der Metaphysik* around four great oppositions which serve to delimit Being: the opposed pairs of Being and Becoming, Being and Appearance, Being and Thought, and Being and Value. In some sense each of these fundamental sets is posed in Proust's novel.

Now to suggest through the image of the arch or circle that extremities can be reconciled in Proust's world in some dialectical manner immediately invokes the name of Hegel. This philosopher's discovery of his own method through a study of the Kantian categories suggests, at least by analogy, the Proustian "general experience." Thus, whereas the

---

[6] Diels fr. B 60. Oddly enough, Proust seems little concerned with the traditional French, that is to say Cartesian, dualism of body and mind; he is much more intimately involved in another sort of opposition, that of inside-outside.

third category, singularity, is for Hegel a synthesis of the preceding two, generality and particularity, Proust seems to discover in the experience of the *extase* a subjective generality mediating between two particular experiences. And yet the word to emphasize in Proust's dialectics is *experience*. Like Kierkegaard and P. J. Proudhon, he is committed to an *affective* and not a rational dialectics; nor does the synthesis destroy the original opposition; Proust is closer to Proudhon's active equilibrium, his "armed union." It is the very isolation of the individual and the Humean discontinuity of time which saves the Proustian man from leaking away dialectically into the Hegelian Absolute. His is not the richly communicable existence of Hegel and Bosanquet, almost nullifying the individual personality in the solemn procession to the whole, the Idea. Heidegger, is much closer to Proust's view of things when he sees the phenomenology of the spirit as the mirror-image of the true itinerarium of the historical destiny; *Dasein* does not create the things-that-are but discovers them and is in some way dependent on them in the foundation of its horizon. Like Kierkegaard or Nietzsche, Proust develops a pathetic (not an intellectual) dialectics, grounded in the moment: from perceptive immediacy to ecstatic immediacy. The Absolute is conceived more as intensity (of suffering or joy) than as totality: more as immediacy than as mediation.

"Je" est un autre

Any investigation of the systems of opposition which are the arches of Proust's construction might well begin with the fictional authority itself. The point of view from which the action is seen is curiously divided betweeen the Marcel of past time who acts and grows old through the course of the narrative, and the Marcel who recollects him from the distant vantage and is at last joined by him to pass, with the final footfall, into time regained. The situation is not unlike that of "Rousseau juge de Jean-Jacques." The division in the narrator underscores the double technique—dramatic and discursive—and the double demonstration—the illusory character of external appearances, minds, and values against the reality and continuity of the self. Thus the action can be likened to an odyssey or pilgrimage where the traveler in time has forgotten the location of the homeland or the significance of the shrine.

The resources available to the narrator in his search are again paired: the voluntary and the involuntary imagination springing from radically different experiences; two kinds of "intelligence," one analytic, rational, dedicated to reducing appearances and behavior to general, axiomatic laws (III, 870-872), the other synthetic and intuitive, devoted to the

The Architecture of Time: Dialectics and Structure

promptings of the involuntary memory or the pure mimetic imagination.

Further, the divided narrator is torn between two conflicting vocations: one, the centrifugal pursuit of the worldly *ignis fatuus*, whether in the guise of a loved object or a social conquest; the other, the centripetal quest for the self and its coherence, which is for Proust the way of art. Before the narrator reaches integration in the last pages, he will pass through the lowest point in his spiritual trajectory when both callings seem to fail him, when disillusionment conspires with acedia.

The Anti-Hero

Through an almost miraculous intervention the narrator does find his course and calling. Yet Proust has installed in his novel a tragic *doppelgänger* who prefigures and parallels the narrator, but who misses the vocation to which he, too, is called. This "anti-hero" has two faces; he is both a spiritual ancestor of Marcel and a glittering contemporary. The technique of displaying successive aspects of essentially the same personality recalls Proust's delight in the Balzacian *retour des personnages:* the successive reincarnations of Vautrin. Paradoxically, in a book where the fiction of stable and coherent characters is constantly being exploded by dramatic reversals and impossible contradictions, the two faces of Marcel's counterpart have in their way a greater consistency than most of the "single" characters. Like the medieval symbol which could be read *in bono* or *in malo*, the novel can be seen as the story of the narrator's salvation through art or the anti-hero's damnation through love. This composite counterpart to Marcel is Charles Swann whose story precedes his, and Palamède de Charlus whose career parallels the narrator's own.

The deflection in time and dramatic focus to the episode of "Un Amour de Swann" has led some readers to argue that the second panel of the first volume is Proust's virtuoso piece, a novel within a novel, and basically irreconcilable with the theme and technique of the grand plan. And yet on this history of Swann Proust rested one pier of the arch which was to be his double investigation of the artist's vocation. Like *King Lear* the entire work is a double plot, a dramatization of two ways of meeting the world (in one case seen from the inside, in the other from without); again, as in *Lear,* the two ways are dialectically opposed. In the play the two aspects of choice are figured by Lear and Gloucester as two errors of the understanding, one active and the other passive. In the novel it is rather a plot of acceptance and refusal; the way of acceptance is art and the way of refusal is, in some guise, love. From the first pages of the book the two imperious callings dispute for the soul of the hero and his counterpart.

Although Swann thinks and feels and loves in a manner which makes him kin to the narrator, this basic similarity of temperaments only emphasizes the radical difference of their two choices. It is Swann who first introduces the narrator to the world of art, just as his daughter introduces him to the world of love. Swann, who cannot profit from his own experience with Odette, is to become for the narrator a kind of *Schwanung*, a presentiment and a warning. Unlike the narrator he cannot see the dialectical corollary to the world of vertiginous change which he discovers behind the moods and appearances of the beloved; the corollary is clearly his own discontinuity. Like the narrator he cherishes some of the same art objects, and like him thinks by vital analogy and similitude. But unlike the narrator at the end of his journey, Swann chooses to enlist the world of art and its message into the service of love. He converts the *petite phrase* of Vinteuil, which calls to him from that world, into the "national anthem" of his love affair with Odette de Crécy. He tries to find in the world of flux the stability of a painting by Botticelli.

In external circumstance or physical appearance the Baron de Charlus bears little similarity to Charles Swann. Yet in their gifts of sensibility and intelligence, more especially in their ways of responding to art and love, they betray an intimate identity. Between them they suggest the range of object and similarity of mechanism which Proust finds in his analysis of the centrifugal force of desire. Both men respond quickly to the stimulus of art, but both pervert its message. Just as Swann demeans the music of Vinteuil by involving it in his affair with Odette (so that eventually the *petite phrase* "says nothing to him"), so Charlus, amateur of Balzac, confuses the events and characters of a fictional world with his own—and disastrously puts his faith in the reality of the latter. He casts himself as Vautrin, as Baron Hulot, even as Diane de Cadignan. In the revealing conversation between Charlus and the members of the clan on the "little train," Balzac becomes the mediator for Charlus' own predilections and obliquities. (II, 1037-1059.) He waxes eloquent on what he calls the "grandes fresques" of Balzac, such as the *Illusions perdues—Splendeurs et misères*:

> "It's magnificent, the moment when Carlos Herrera asks the name of the chateau past which he is driving, and it turns out to be Rastignac, the home of the young man he used to love. And then the Abbé falls into a reverie which Swann once called, very eloquently, the *Tristesse d'Olympio of pederasty*. And the death of Lucien! I no longer remember what man of taste, when he was asked what event in his life had most deeply pained him, replied: 'The death of Lucien de Rubempré in *Splendeurs et misères*.'" (II, 1050.)

M. Charlus' "man of taste" was Oscar Wilde, and the Baron shares with him both the identification with Vautrin and the desire to be an "artist of life." And through the pursuit of the world and its illusions both Charlus and Wilde are ultimately brought to a lover's martyrdom.

During his discussion of Balzac, the Baron further identifies himself with Swann while enlisting him as an authority. Like Charlus and Wilde, Swann has played the artist of life.[7] All three are guilty of the same error for which Proust (in the *Contre Sainte-Beuve*) indicts Balzac himself, the confusion of life and art. Unlike Balzac and Wilde, Swann and Charlus have faith without works. The narrator remarks toward the end of Charlus' discourse:

> But the Baron was an artist to his finger tips! And now that he had begun to identify his own position with that described by Balzac, he took refuge, in a sense, in the tale. . . . He had the consolation of finding in his own anxiety what Swann . . . would have called something "quite Balzacian." The identification with the Princess de Cadignan had been simplified for M. de Charlus by virtue of the mental transposition which was becoming habitual with him and of which he had already furnished several examples. (II, 1058.)

The parallelism of Swann's career and choice with those of Charlus is further reinforced by the skillful articulation of details of plot. The Baron is associated in the narrator's mind with his childhood memories of Tansonville as the "gentleman in twill," friend of Swann and an ambiguous admirer of Odette. The great soirée at the Princess de Guermantes' in *Sodome et Gomorrhe I* marks the point when Charlus inherits Swann's legacy, the point where the former comes to the center of the stage and the latter vanishes into the wings. Even the downfall in love of each, the moment of rejection, is engineered by the same hostess, Mme Verdurin, largely because of her jealousy for the same rival, Mme de Guermantes. Finally, the same musical theme (although radically transformed) orchestrates both events.

A brief consideration of Proust's title and of the first two sections of the novel, *Combray* and *Un Amour de Swann,* will suggest some of the structural circles which enclose his material and more of the arches which support and relate basic oppositions in the narrative.

A la recherche du temps perdu

Much as Erwin Panofsky would turn to the medieval *Sic et non* for a model of the mental habit which animated gothic architecture, the

[7] Cf. the narrator's comment on those who would try to order their experience through the work of someone else, in this case through a *pensée* of La Bruyère: "And as for the pleasure that a perfectly balanced mind . . . finds in the beautiful thought of some master, it is no doubt wholly sound, but however precious may be the men who are capable of enjoying it (how many are there in twenty years?) it nevertheless reduces them to the condition of being merely the full consciousness of someone else." (III, 894.)

reader can find an emblem on the porch of Proust's edifice which suggests the method which was to govern the entire construction. In his title—
A la recherche du temps perdu—the modern architect of the novel telescopes two apparently contradictory titles drawn from his favorite master builder of the preceding century, Balzac. In a passage of his essay "Sainte-Beuve and Balzac" Proust had remarked the evocativeness of the novelist's titles, discussing in some detail *La Recherche de l'absolu* and *Les Illusions perdues*.[8] He notes that whereas for some writers "the title is more or less a symbol, an emblem that must be understood in a more general and more poetic sense than a reading of the book would warrant, with Balzac it is apt to be the other way around." Thus the pursuit of the Absolute in the first title proves to be more of an alchemical investigation than a philosophical affair, while the second title introduces the story of the loss of "quite personal, quite arbitrary illusions." Proust finds in this particularity of application one more symptom of that powerful stamp of reality which he sees as the key to the Balzacian vision. For his own work he would seem to reserve the possibility of having it both ways: a novel intimately particular yet revealing through its very subjectivity a metaphysics. He argues in a letter to the N.R.F. that his own work is a demonstration, not an exposé: "And in the end you can see the metaphysical and moral view point governs everything in the work." [9] *Les Illusions perdues* echoes in the "lost time" of Proust's title as a reminder of the *negative* side of his dialectic: the cumulative assault through peripeties of plot, devices of style, and abortive analyses of the characters' *sentiments*, upon the conventional optic of the reader, upon the naïve belief in the appearance of things and the continuity of personality. *La Recherche de l'absolu* on the other hand suggests the *positive* aspect of Proust's enterprise: a pilgrimage projected backward in time toward what the author found most real, a guarantee of his own continuity. The two activities represented by the telescoped title, the progressive disintegration of external surfaces and the search for a center, thus correspond to the two primitive moments of Proustian man so intimately explored by Georges Poulet: the vertiginous unstable world of the sleeper awakened, and the timeless instant of the "metaphoric translation," experience regained.

Combray

"Combray," the extended overture to the great work, begins and ends in a bedroom: although this room is at a far remove in time from the earliest memories of childhood, the author quickly demonstrates the irreducible identity of every moment of awakening: first the absolute

[8] *Contre Sainte-Beuve* (Paris, 1954), pp. 206-207.
[9] *Les Cahiers de Marcel Proust: VI (Lettres à la NRF)* (Paris, 1932), pp. 103-104.

The Architecture of Time: Dialectics and Structure 113

emptiness and then the thrusting out of the naked consciousness toward what Poulet has called a "vertigo of images," times and places from the past without consecutive relation, much like the flickering world of the magic lantern. Professor Vigneron has felicitously styled the world of Combray "the perfect circle." [10] The narrator's quest is not so much for a beginning (the play of hours and rooms about his mind is itself circular), as for a center which can hold against all this movement. And yet the structure of "Combray" is not precisely circular, for the first moment in the bedroom is one of awakening while the last scene of the overture is one of dawn's breaking; a distance has been traveled in time, the first of Proust's 1001 nights which will hold time in check. The action does indeed describe a circular motion, but paradoxically the descent into time has achieved a certain elevation, suggesting the additional dimension of a spiral.

The circle of past hours and places which emerges in the opening pages (I, 3-9) sketches the affective geography of the entire quest: Tansonville, Combray, Balbec, Paris, Doncières, Venice. In the same way the circle of Combray itself sounds the entire repertoire of themes which Proust is to orchestrate across the length of three thousand pages and a lifetime. These themes are introduced through Proust's characteristic system of oppositions.

There are really *two* Combrays evoked in the overture, one a glimpse of time past and the other an immanent moment of the narrator's life. The first is the fragmentary image captured by the "intellectual" memory, by an act of the will, from the atomized fantasia of the initial Proustian moment of awakening. (I, 9-43.) This voluntary act projects part of a world as a "luminous panel" at a distance from the consciousness of the narrator and alien to him; all that remains of the past is represented by a fragment of the house at Combray. The door which excludes the isolated child from the world of his parents and M. Swann below will recur in many guises as an emblem of the narrator's existential prison cage. Even this "dead" recollection of Combray and the recurring drama of the bedroom is divided into two opposing parts: first the details of the ritual in its generality (I, 9-23), then the particular crisis from which the narrator traces all his long infirmities of will (I, 23-43). The first half of this evocation is keyed to the image of the magic lantern, emblem of the remote world of Geneviève of Brabant and flickering analogue of the entire world of unstable appearances. The sign of the imagination which marks the second, specific evening, the crisis of Swann's visit and the collapse of parental authority, is a book, *François le champi*.

The second Combray rises in all its solidity from the second Proustian

---

[10] Robert Vigneron, "Structure de *Swann*," *Modern Philology*, XLV (1948), 185-207. I am clearly indebted to Prof. Vigneron and MM. Clarac and Ferré for discriminating the major divisions of the "Combray" episode.

moment dialectically opposed to the centrifugal experience of awakening. It is the gratuitous, centripetal miracle of the *madeleine*. (I, 43-48.) Through the intervention of the involuntary memory (which the narrator likens to *gratia naturalis*) and the concerted effort to understand its promptings, the parts of a world cohere and, unlike the distant two-dimensional world of the magic lantern, are intimately *felt;* "so in that very moment all the flowers in our garden and those in M. Swann's park, and the water-lilies on the Vivonne and the good folk of the village and their little homes and the parish church and the whole of Combray and of its surroundings, taking their proper shapes and solidity, sprang into being, town and gardens alike, from my cup of tea." (I, 47-48.)

Like the felt Absolute for Thomas Traherne, the world which emerges from this tea cup is the result of extreme concentration, a movement back to an affective center. Yet it is a world which is itself organized around radical internal oppositions. The first phase in the exploration of this Combray is *temporal,* the recreation of Aunt Léonie's Sundays and the people and events which fill them. At the center of the day and the town is the church of Saint Hilaire. (I, 48-133.) The second phase is presented through a *spatial* metaphor, that of the "two ways." (I, 133-186.) From the viewpoint of the child "le côté de Méséglise" and "le côté de Guermantes" are mutually exclusive, representing complete, discrete days and clusters of experience, *vases clos,* without any communication between them. (I, 135.) Swann's way, "le côté de Méséglise," has as its threshold the street door opening on the rue du Saint-Esprit. The images which define it are intimately linked with two families—Charles Swann's at Tansonville and M. Vinteuil's at Montjouvain. First the names, then the people themselves play on the child's imagination; the experiences prefigure the entire range of the novel's two great themes, art and love. Linked by the privileged imagery of the hawthorn are Gilberte, behind the hedge at Tansonville, and Mlle Vinteuil, who was first evoked in the earlier (Sunday) episode by the color, fragrance, and imagined taste of the blossoms on the altar during the "Month of Mary" devotions. Yet it is at the very moments that these two faces of love are first seen that the narrator, once in the church and again before the white hawthorn of Tansonville, achieves his first acts of the pure imagination, translating the external stimuli of the flowers by a kind of interior mimesis: "In following [the stamens of the flowers] with my eyes, in trying to imitate in the depths of myself the action of their blossoming, I imagined it as a swift and thoughtless movement of the head with a coquetish glance from contracted pupils, of a young girl in white, careless and alive." (I, 112.) Metaphor and memory, the two sovereign activities of the artist, are thus linked with a tapestry of floral images which will illuminate the erotic history of the novel.

The other way, "le côté de Guermantes" (I, 165-186), has for its threshold another door, this time opening on the garden, and an entirely different landscape and affective history. Whereas Swann's way opened on the plain, its counterpart follows the path of the Vivonne and the association of floral images is with its water lilies. The associations revive memories of the magic lantern, of the aristocratic past of France; the inaccessible world of the Guermantes introduces the major theme of desire directed toward society, the agony of the *snob*. But "le côté de Guermantes" holds in suspension, too, the antidote for this temptation. It is along this way that the narrator first senses his vocation as an artist (I, 172), and, in the episode of the spires of Martinville, responds to the immediacy of impression with a metaphor, tastes the first joy of literary creation in Dr. Percepied's carriage. (I, 180-182.) The three trees of Hudimesnil (I, 717), seen under similar circumstances, will cry out across time as an echo not recognized, a part of the self rejected. The last sentence of "le côté de Guermantes" is a masterpiece of the Proustian prose rhythm and respires the odor "invisible and persistent" of lilacs, echoing the perfume of the first sentences of "le côté de Méséglise."

The two evocations are completed and the circle closed by a return to the distant bedroom and the narrator recollecting. (I, 186-187.) But in a real sense the circle of "Combray" forms a pier which will arch the entire work. As Proust remarked, the last chapter was written immediately after the first. The *matinée* at the Princesse de Guermantes' responds to and completes the initial *soirée* of Swann's fateful visit. Even more precisely the last chapter repeats the author's initial experiences and concludes his long education. Like so many of the characters, Golo of the magic lantern and *François le champi* reappear. (III, 924, 1044.) The narrator, at the lowest point in his affective life, is revived and sustained by the intervention of three experiences of the involuntary memory. At last he understands the importance of the first invasion of this sort, the episode of the *madeleine* which resurrected the "solid" Combray. With this sense of a vocation found and confirmed he moves on to the *matinée* itself, which becomes the enormous *fête masquée* of time crowning the book. In an order which reverses that of "Combray," three moments in which the narrator turns back on his profound center, freed from time, are followed by confrontation of a drama where time in all its transformations of appearance, station, and character are most acutely felt. The Marcel who suffered through the novel at last joins the Marcel who evoked him from his memory, when, like *Finnegans Wake*, the fictive novel is about to be born.

Un Amour de Swann

The second large structural circle of the first volume is described by the retrospective story of the narrator's counterpart, Charles Swann. Until the two volumes of Marcel's life with Albertine it will be Proust's most detailed analysis of love, an exemplary tale for the narrator and the reader. As Jacques Rivière observed, the author conceived this episode of love in a pattern analogous to sonata-allegro form, that is to say presenting and developing two opposing themes back to a restatement of the initial opposition. The first theme is the object of Swann's desire, Odette de Crécy; she is an object of desire only by chance, for Swann feels no spontaneous attraction to her. The opposing theme is itself musical, the *petite phrase* from Vinteuil's sonata; unlike Odette, it (*elle* in the French) arouses a spontaneous response in Swann, suggesting like so many aesthetic experiences a hieroglyph which conceals a mystery. Swann's life is hopelessly divided between the music which might lead him back to himself and the woman who is drawing him further and further out into a giddy world of unappeasable desire, jealousy, and boredom. Each stage in his gradual enslavement to Odette is punctuated by a reappearance of the *petite phrase* and its appeal to him.

Through his descent into love Swann learns to suffer and through the music he learns to associate the relationship of suffering and creation in the person of the composer. He remains divided, however, and unable to profit from the lesson of the affair or the music. His predicament is brilliantly recapitulated in his painful nightmare (I, 378-380), anticipating Freud's insight in *Jenseits des Lustprinzips*. Like Freud's dreamer, Swann tries to master a painful failure through a symbolic reenactment. Significantly he finds himself divided into two people, one the suffering lover, the other the artist manqué who would try to understand him. (The split recalls William James's "Sick Soul" experience.)

The sonata closes neatly on its beginning; Swann is out of love with Odette and about to embark on the cycle of another affair, indistinguishable from its predecessors. Swann is thus unable to emerge from his circular trap, is unable to translate the message of the music into a new life. The *petite phrase* has, however, a life of its own; in new incarnations it will orchestrate the career of the narrator and help him to the self-knowledge which eluded Swann.

Visages de l'amour

After the complementary cycles of "Combray" and "Swann," the third panel (the beginning of the *jeunes filles* plot) returns to the narrator's life and chronology. Odette has become Mme Swann and her daughter Gilberte, first seen in all her ambiguity beside the hawthorn at Combray, at once links Marcel to the spiritual inheritance of her father, and figures the intimately opposed claims of love and art. Proust recognized the paradoxical similarity of love and art as solitary activities of the imagination; yet he saw in the centrifugal motion of life toward a series of identical desired objects a servitude to change, and in the centripetal return of creation the only real freedom. Remarking in *Jean Santeuil* on Stendhal's attempt to reduce all human activities to aspects of love, Proust admits similarities between love and poetry, but adds: "Another individual, however remarkable he may be—and in love there is usually nothing remarkable about him—has no right thus to limit our interior life. . . . And yet our whole interior life does become thus systemized, so that the world is a sort of two-horse rig." [11] This double, the Other, is always multiple, opaque, and beyond possession; it is rooted in exclusion and thrives only in absence. Marcel's love for Gilberte is itself a paradox, grounded in a misunderstanding and springing up only after she is no longer present. As with that other erotic prefiguration from childhood, the encounter with the Mme de Guermantes in the chapel of Gilbert le Mauvais, it is only at the other side of the arch, in the last pages of the novel, that the narrator realizes that his initial, his primitive impression, uncolored by the analytic intelligence, may have been the only accurate one (cf. III, 693-695; 1023). The narrator, always the solitary outsider seeking admission, tries in vain to enter the charmed circle of love—at first the circle of children at play in the Champs Elysées, later the personality of the beloved itself. Each circle penetrated reveals only another exclusion and draws the lover further from his own center.

In addition to the initiation rites of love, the *"actions sacrées"* of another cult are suggested by Marcel's encounter with Gilberte. Since the days at Combray her name has been linked for the narrator with the name and works of Bergotte. This Bergotte is not the "man in society" but the man seen through his works, his love of Racine and the cathedrals of France. His faith in metaphoric expression, the ritual action of his art, is to become the key to the narrator's own vocation. The two Proustian emotions turn on the axes of love and art: intense suffering and total joy. Both can serve the narrator in his search for his vocation. Thus, the dialectical opposition of the way of love and the way of art, already foreshadowed in the career of Swann, is first revealed to the narrator in the paradoxes and associations of his first love affair. Although love is here and in the future a failure as a means of appropriating reality, it does provide a valuable by-product—the *feelings*—which can be translated through a very different process into the material of art. (The aesthetic experience is not for Proust a way out of process, as it was for Schopenhauer, but a consecrated process itself which feeds on and transforms the polarities of desire.)

In his relations with Gilberte the narrator discovers the first lesson of what might be called his apprenticeship in love: the paradoxical reality of love in absence. In his long courtship of Oriane de Guer-

[11] *Jean Santeuil* (Paris, 1952), pp. 121-122.

mantes and the society she crowns, the narrator discovers the corollary of this lesson: the absence of love in reality. Marcel thus can love Mme de Guermantes *before* he knows her, but in her presence he is unable to sustain this emotion born of the imagination and the magic of names. Just as his attraction to Gilberte was dialectically related through Bergotte to the initiation into the "other way" of art, so his first view of the world of Mme de Guermantes finds its own artistic foil in the Opéra-Comique. The dazzling spectacle on the Guermantes side of the footlights dissolves in a cascade of aquatic images; but through the mediation of la Berma the narrator is reminded of the paradoxical reality of the actors' world on the other side, an "absolute space." The dizzying manifestations of love and desire in the Faubourg Saint-Germain are successively counterpoised by the attraction to the security of art represented here by the great performing artists. While Marcel learns from his discovery of a great actress or violinist, Charlus, his counterpart, characteristically continues to pervert the message of art to the service of life in his pursuit of Morel not as interpreter but as loved object. The first way points to the eventual recognition of the narrator's vocation, while the second leads to the degradations of the first part of *Le Temps retrouvé.*

Finally, as the narrator's life with Albertine is alternately dramatized and analyzed, all the paradoxes implicit in the earlier initiation into love and art are again revealed, this time in depth. The object of love is, in her insignificance, identical with her predecessors, constant in her inconstancy. This return of the beloved is one more structural reminder of Marcel's inescapable solitude (and stands as one more implicit tribute to Proust's admiration of Balzac and Hardy). Albertine, pretext for the fullest treatment of the Other in the novel, has *two* worlds for her realms, the beach at Balbec and the bedroom at Paris, and is intimately related to the message of *two* artists, Elstir and Vinteuil. In the marine world of Elstir's paintings, the elusive and fragmentary images of reality, so like the successive aspects of Marcel's sea goddess, are mastered through the temporal perspective of "metaphor." In the enclosed world of the Parisian apartment the ocean has been translated through dream and reverie into an image of the private sea of Albertine's unfathomable mind. The paradox of the Other who guarantees the isolation of Self is played out in the image of the jailor who has become himself the prisoner. From this labyrinth of mirrors, of lies and illusions, it is again an artist who suggests an escape through the "other way" of art. This time it is the artist Vinteuil, resurrected and transfigured in the septet which his daughter's perverse friend had deciphered after his death. The reappearance of the music of Vinteuil thus punctuates the careers of all the novel's great lovers; for Swann the *petite phrase* signals the beginning and the end of his love for Odette; for Charlus the performance of the septet at the Verdurins' is the moment of his betrayal and crushing reversal; but for the narrator the music which, as the *petite phrase,* had once seemed to promise something withheld, now suggests not the end of an affair but the beginning of a vocation, a release from the tyranny of time and a promise of the seven-volume septet to come. The enduring genius of Vinteuil, "his profound originality and his power of making us see the universe with other eyes," recalls the narrator at long last to "a lost homeland," the only true paradise. (III, 252-259.)

L'Espace et le temps rendus sensibles au coeur

Proust's enterprise is twofold, both a negative demonstration and a positive experience. By a profoundly "doubtful" path, an extended Cartesian meditation, the narrator arrives at an immanent belief. The polymorphic dualities of the novelist's technique reveal his content. To build is to exclude: the reversals of plot and the transformations of imagery expose the instability of the world beyond the film of consciousness. The characters, like the two ways of Combray, are discovered to be *vases clos,* discrete and hermetic. This discontinuity without is mirrored within the narrator by his *intermittences du coeur;* he is unable to live fully in the instant and unable, save at crucial turnings, to recover the instant in its uniqueness. His psychology lacks a dimension.

With Husserl, Proust ultimately rejects "psychologism" as a means to certainty. Like the philosopher, he insists that an experience cannot be objectfied as *things* can be; thus knowledge of the consciousness must be entirely different from knowledge of the physical. Husserl argues that the psychical can only be grasped by a special kind of reflective experience, an *Erlebnis;* a temporal depth is demanded. But true reflection is inseparable from what is reflected upon: I cannot know *what* a flower is until I live reflexively my own consciousness of the flower.

There is for Proust a similar reflective character in his *prise de conscience,* which suggests the final dimension of his edifice: Time. This destroyer of all external objects of desire becomes, in turn, a creative force: it allows recollection. Value resides only in past experience possessed and translated in the present. The artist's two means to achieve this vital simultaneity are memory and metaphor. Both require for Proust, as for Coleridge, "the reconcilement of opposite or discordant qualities: of sameness with difference."

The great danger in Proust's affective psychology is that all past moments will remain discrete and yet indistinguishable from one another—like the shattered images of the world outside. The task is to compose them like the minute pieces of glass in the rose window of his cathedral into felt relationships. In the Proustian dialectic of the temporal and the intemporal, even the very intermittency of time has a vital role to play. As moments are separated from each other like the successive spatial planes of Cézanne's landscapes, a new law of perspective is possible, unexpectedly combining (like the dancing spires) instants which could not be contiguous in any sort of continuous time. This new law of *temporal* perspective was beautifully perceived by Georges Poulet in the emblem which crowns Combray, the spire of Saint Hilaire. From the vantage of this point surmounting the work of centuries, the opposition of the mutually exclusive ways of Méséglise and Guermantes was resolved, the arch was closed. A genealogical emblem illustrating the same phenomenon appears near the end of the novel in the person of Mlle Saint-Loup, so like both her parents and yet so enigmatically herself; she, too, closes the two ways as a living keystone to the arch.

For Proust, even what appears to be the purely temporal experience of music demands this perspective in order to be comprehended. The notes of Vinteuil's sonata as they are heard by Swann in successive instants are primitive impressions, delicious sensations, promises of an unknown love. But there must be a dialectic between the flux of becoming and the patterns of form before he can recapture, can understand his experience:

> And so, hardly had the delicious sensation which Swann had experienced died away, before his memory had furnished him with an immediate transcript, summary, it is true, and provisional, but one on which he had kept his eyes fixed while the playing continued, so effectively that, when the same impression suddenly returned, it was no longer uncapturable. He was able to picture to himself its extent, its symmetrical arrangement, its notation, the strength of its expression; he had before him that definite object which was no longer pure music, but rather design, *architecture* . . . which allowed the music to be recalled. (I, 209.)

In this final architectural image—the imposition of spatial relations on time—Proust at once suggests the character of his own creative act, a kind of achievement of simultaneity through analogy, and he offers directions to the readers who will visit the edifice after him. His ideal reader would come not once but *again* in order to comprehend the original experiences and their network of associations. As early as the *Contre Sainte-Beuve,* Proust argued that to be nourished by art is "to distinguish a subtle harmony . . . between two impressions or two ideas," one past and one present.[12] Thereby the viewer of two pictures by the same artist "perceives something which is in neither the first nor the second but in some way exists between them, a sort of ideal picture which he sees projecting itself in spiritual substantiality outside of the picture; he has been nourished, and begins to live and be happy again."

---

[12] *Contre Sainte-Beuve,* p. 302; cf. III, 890.

The narrator first discovers the dimensions of this "solid psychology" (*psychologie dans l'espace*, III, 1031) within the intimacy of his own conscious life, which is for him the first and authentic book. Walter Strauss has justly concluded that Proust's cathedral has at its center— where all lines converge—an altar dedicated to literature. On the high altar there is indeed a book, one which shares the temporal dimension of the building—in Dante's image the *libro de la mia memoria*. The image of a subjective, an interior *totum simul* where all dualities meet, epitomizes the duty and the task of the writer. Proust the man furnishes, in his own words, a "grimoire compliqué et fleuri"; Proust the artist translates this into his life's work:

> To read the subjective book of those strange signs (signs standing out boldly, it seemed, which my conscious mind, as it explored my unconscious self, went searching for, stumbled against and passed around, like a diver groping his way), no one could help me with any rule, for the reading of that book is a creative act in which no one can stand in our stead, or even collaborate with us. . . . This book, the most difficult of all to decipher, is also the only one dictated to us by reality, the only one the "imprinting" of which on our consciousness was done by reality itself. (III, 879-880.)

Proust, Bergson
and Other Philosophers

by Robert Champigny

The first part of this essay will be devoted to a comparison between Proust and Bergson. The maze of opinions on this familiar topic is such that an attempt at a clarification does not appear superfluous.

In the last chapter of *Creative Evolution,* Bergson stresses his opposition to the Classical view according to which becoming is ontologically inferior to being, conceived as eternity, immutability. To improve the ontological prestige of becoming, Bergson presents it as creation: "Time is invention or it is nothing."[1] Being is based on doing: "What does nothing is nothing."[2] Bergson does not distinguish self from duration, that is to say, creative becoming. The Bergsonian psyche functions in and for an organism. Duration covers the biological as well as the psychological perspective. In this way it can be conceived as heterogeneous, yet continuous.

Proust, on the other hand, stresses the destructive aspect of becoming rather than its constructive aspect.[3] The crystallization of a love is not lived by the Proustian lover as being his creation. He does not identify himself with the process. The man of Proust is "in time." He does not attempt to coincide with becoming, but to abstract himself from it. Lacking the context of the organism, mental becoming appears discontinuous: moods, attitudes, roles, selves.[4]

"Proust, Bergson and Other Philosophers" (Original title: "Temps et reconnaissance chez Proust et quelques philosophes"). From *Publications of the Modern Language Association of America* LXXIII (1958). Reprinted by the gracious permission of the author and publisher.

[1] *L'Evolution créatrice,* 62nd ed. (Paris: PUF, 1946), p. 341.
[2] *La Pensée et le mouvant,* 22nd ed. (Paris: PUF, 1946), p. 102.
[3] Cf. *A la recherche du temps perdu,* edited by Pierre Clarac and André Ferré, 3 vols. (Paris: Bibliothèque de la Pleiade, 1954), I, 427, 482, 671; III, 930, 1038. The numbers in parentheses in my text refer to the volumes and pages of this edition.
[4] Jacques Rivière noted that Proust "unwittingly achieved the contrary of what Bergson advocated: his psychology is based on distrust toward the self, that of Bergson on trust in the self." Cf. Frédéric Lefèvre, *Une Heure avec,* 2nd series (Paris: NRF, 1924), p. 98.

The choice of Proust is not so clearly drawn as the choice of Bergson. Bergson sets out to magnify certain words such as *duration, intuition, élan vital,* at the expense of some others. His terminology is tighter, less inconsistent than that of Proust. On the other hand, Proust shows more respect for the variety of experience, which can say yes and no to any style of painting, to any philosophical selection and system. It would be possible to find passages in the *Quest of Time Lost* [referred to elsewhere as *In Search of Lost Time*] whose content would be at variance with an anti-Bergsonian characterization of Proust. Thus: "My dreams of travel and love were only moments—which I separate artificially today as if I were cutting sections at various heights of an iridescent and apparently immobile jet of water—in one inflexible surge of all the powers of my life." (I, 87.) Despite the banality of the image, this assertion of continuity and this suggestion of coincidence between self and vital drive might be construed as Bergsonian. Still, the weight of evidence appears to be on the other side. This partiality contributes to the coherence, or at least cohesion, of the *Quest.*

Bergson ventures the hypothesis that the continuity of a duration may not be broken by death. He suggests another life, which would not be an eternal rest: "I picture this life as a life of struggle again, as a call for invention, as a creative evolution." [5] Proust alludes to this hypothesis. (II, 984-5.) He voices his own skepticism, basing his argument on the fragility of consciousness: "Each cerebral tremor alters it; a fainting fit annihilates it. How could I believe that it will continue after death?" Proust was probably unaware that Bergson had discussed this type of objection (the date of the relevant lecture of Bergson is 1912). The novelist, at any rate, adopts a cautious approach: a "Norwegian philosopher" is supposed to report Bergson's views.

The existence of the Bergsonian self consists in doing, intending. The man of Bergson is what he does, what he makes of himself through his action.[6] The man of Proust needs a more static, reflective, identity. The man of Proust is what he has. He hopes to secure himself and the world through memory, in a way which may be called "mystic." The work of Proust is concerned with a quest for a spontaneous possession.

Proust is surprised at recovering himself when he wakes up. He is struck by the miraculous aspect of memory. According to him, the possibility of a survival should rest on the bridge of memory, not on

[5] *L'Energie spirituelle,* 42nd ed. (Paris: PUF, 1946), p. 27.
[6] On this point, the opposition between Proust and Bergson would also be an opposition between Proust and Sartre. The emphasis which Sartre places on choice rather than duration suggests a certain psychological discontinuity. But here again he could be contrasted with Proust: if there is a privileged experience for the man of Sartre, it is the experience of breaking with the past.

the flow of duration: "The resurrection of the soul after death might be conceived as a phenomenon of memory." (II, 88.)

By memory, he means clear remembering, not the implicit and total memory which is involved in the Bergsonian concept of duration: "We possess all our memories, says after Bergson the great Norwegian philosopher. . . . But what is a memory without a remembrance?" (II, 985.) This non-reflective memory suggests the possibility of a survival to Bergson, but can I picture this survival as being mine? "Is the being which I shall be after death likely to remember the man I have been since my birth? Does the latter remember what I was before birth?" (II, 985.)

The model experience for Bergson must have been his own as a creative thinker. He assumes optimistically that such experiences can serve as a basis for generalization: "If, in every domain, the triumph of life is creation, should it not be assumed that human life has its raison d'être in a creation which, unlike that of the artist or scientist, can proceed ceaselessly in every man: the creation of oneself by oneself, the development of personality through an effort which produces much out of little, something out of nothing, and adds constantly to the wealth of the world?" [7]

A sick man, a *mondain*, Proust does not offer a promising field of application for this theory. It may be objected that he was also, or became, an artist and that the artistic enterprise was for him a conversion, a tenacious reaction against sickness and the frittering away of existence. In a passage which deals with Balzac and Wagner, we encounter "the joy of the producer." (III, 161.) Is it not possible to apply the phrase to Proust himself and to interpret it in a Bergsonian perspective?

Unfortunately Proust intimates that he does not value this creative joy very highly: the word *fabricateur*, which he uses, has a derogatory tinge. The activity of composing does not appear to have altered his vision radically. He does not write in order to invent; he writes in order to discover and recover: reflective possession, not constructive action, is the ultimate purpose. A Bergsonian would be interested in the process of creation and self-creation. As a mystic, as an aesthete, Proust prefers to be enchanted with the origin and with the result. Besides, he is far from sharing Bergson's ethical optimism: the man of Proust can create, but cannot create himself. So it is that "art" and "life" are for him the terms of an opposition, whereas a Bergsonian would point out that art is an activity and that to be active is to be alive. Proust is inclined to value the static over the dynamic, abstraction from becoming over sublimation of becoming.

According to Bergson's terminology, it is "intelligence," as opposed

[7] *L'Energie spirituelle*, p. 24.

to "intuition," which abstracts the static out of the dynamic in order to establish reliable conditions for action. The method of Proust has been called intellectualistic. It might be in a Bergsonian sense: he has to fix and abstract the object in order to describe and analyze it. But his "intellectualism" concerns the form rather than the content, which is "intuitive." This opposition cannot be likened to the Bergsonian opposition between intelligence and intuition. According to Bergson, "to think intuitively is to think in the perspective of duration," [8] that is to say, in the perspective of creative becoming. Proustian intuition, if the term is to be used, consists rather in isolating for analysis stable entities which "intelligence" cannot apprehend directly.

As I read Proust, I sometimes have the impression of reading the prose commentary of a poem which has not been written. In view of the subject-matter, a Bergsonian might think of a Romantic, reflective epic, like Wordsworth's *Prelude*. But the prose of Proust appears here and there to be the companion of an unborn sonnet, not of an epic: sonnet of the *madeleine,* sonnet of the paving-stones. A sonnet is a moment's monument.

Speaking of the "joy of the producer," Proust regrets that this joy "has destroyed a little" "the sadness of the poet." The dynamic, creating poet has betrayed the static, experiencing poet. Action has transformed the waterfall into a power-station. The reader is meant to understand that Proust intends to avoid this alteration. Instead of creating from inspiration (or experience), Proust tries to place himself beside it. He wants to respect "inner reality" (III, 882), as if what is thought and felt could be kept apart from what is said about it. Hence my impression, at times, to be reading the commentary of an unborn poem. Proust sees the creator as a "translator." (III, 890.)

The man of Proust is wont to turn the experienced into an imaginative essence abstracted from the common spatio-temporal field. The child takes regular walks toward, only toward, Méséglise or Guermantes, which are thus established as stable, transcendent domains. Swann transfers people to the metaphysical space of paintings. Marcel places the duchess of Guermantes in a stained-glass window or a tapestry and petrifies Albertine on a church portal. He uses philological information to give a legendary aura to the places where he has been. The names of places where he has not been are the kernels of imaginative essences. Let us also note the fascination which the theatre exerts on Proust. The stage, to quote Mallarmé, is an absolute place. The actor is in the common space-time, not the character. And yet we see one as we see the other.

What is to be possessed needs the stability, the aloofness of an imaginative essence and the concreteness, the accessibility of the per-

[8] *La Pensée et le mouvant,* p. 30.

ceived. The desire of possession may thus be thwarted in various ways. Human beings are wont to step out of the picture frame: "These charming blends which a girl composes with a beach, with the plaited hair of a statue on a church, with a print . . . these blends are not very stable." (II, 352.) The aesthete lacks the power of the Platonic artificer who could force form upon matter and achieve "beautiful mixtures," stable blends. On the other hand, the work of art (someone else's work), if it has stability and aloofness, if it creates its own metaphysical field, lacks the accessibility of the perceived. A character in a novel is only imagined; a character in a performed play is perceived, but only the actor or actress can be reached in this our space-time.

A privileged phenomenon of memory provides Proust with a model experience. Proustian recognition, or recurrence, abstracts both subject and object from becoming: "A minute liberated from the order of time has recreated in us, to enjoy it, man liberated from the order of time." (III, 873.) In the self-contained sphere of the moment, the conditions of contemplation are met. Furthermore, the imaginative essence penetrates the common spatio-temporal field in theory (in the past) and in actuality (in the present). The multiple location of the same experience in space and time suggests its transcendent status (like a scientific law based on recurrence). What is especially important is that perception is involved as well as memory: the power of actualization is verified. Perception complements "the dreams of imagination with what they usually lack, the idea of existence." (III, 872.) Finally, we are dealing with an experience rather than with an object: the epistemological dichotomy between subject and object, or self and not-self, does not occur. My use of the word "mystic" alludes to this characteristic. Proust notes: "This essence was not in me, it was myself." (I, 45.) The identification of the remembered and the actual and the identification of self and not-self make for a privileged satisfaction of the desire of possession. Relying on this support, the narrator of *Time Recovered* dispatches his characters into decrepitude and death. These characters are the puppets of becoming, on which Proust wants to take an artistic revenge.

The trinity of author, narrator and character within and without the *Quest* can be interpreted as emulating the modalities of the model experience. The division of roles is designed to assert the given, rather than created, status of what is signified. This is the contemplative aspect, the aspect of discovery. But the division is also an identity: this is the possessive aspect, the aspect of recovery. The identity of past and present in the experience becomes the identity of character and narrator in the book. The identity between subject and object becomes the identity between author and character-narrator.

Proust draws a distinction between "involuntary" and "deliberate" memory. (I, 441; II, 11-2; III, 689.) This distinction, which is so important to him, cannot be found in Bergson.[9] The emphasis on spontaneous memory is in accord with Proust's preference for the given over the created. The "celestial food" of the model experience (III, 873) has to be "given as it is" (III, 879). The fact that this experience owes nothing to deliberation and effort guarantees its authenticity. It has come by chance, a chance which deserves to be called grace. This is an illustration of Proust's opposition to Bergson's activism.

In *Matter and Memory*, Bergson draws a distinction between "contemplative" and "motive" memory.[10] In his article on the experience of déjà vu, he characterizes the phenomenon as a "momentary pause in the drive of our consciousness." [11] In this case as in the case of contemplative memory, consciousness relaxes its "attention to life"; we are dealing with memories, or false memories, *"de luxe."* Proustian recurrence can be considered as a special case of contemplative memory; and it includes the impression of déjà vu, though it is not reducible to it. What Bergson says regarding contemplative memory and déjà vu could partly apply to Proust's model experience. But what is "luxury" to Bergson is essential to Proust. The values of Bergson are at odds with the values of Proust.[12]

Proust's opposition to Bergson does not make him a Platonist. Here and there, the word "essence" appears in the vocabulary of Proust. The model experience is supposed to reveal "the essence of things." To define the object of Proustian longing, I have myself used the word "essence," but I have specified that this essence was imaginative, so as to prevent a Platonic misinterpretation. Two false analogies between Proust and Plato may be pointed out: one concerns abstraction, the other reminiscence.

As an aesthete, as a mystic, and also as an artist, Proust seeks and treasures what can be abstracted from becoming: the permanent, or recurrent. At the same time, what is abstracted must retain a perceptive, or imaginative, aspect. Proustian essences can thus be of three kinds: model experiences of the type described above; ideas of individual objects: "the identity of the Verdurin *salon* in various times and places" (III, 718); ideas of qualities (Baudelaire's correspondences): the writer must bring out the quality "common to two sensations," unite these sensations in a metaphor, thus "saving them from the contingencies of time" (III, 889).

[9] Cf. Robert Dreyfus, *Souvenirs sur Marcel Proust* (Paris: Grasset, 1926), pp. 287-92.
[10] *Matière et mémoire*, 46th ed. (Paris: PUF, 1946), p. 173.
[11] *L'Energie spirituelle*, p. 149.
[12] This opposition finds an echo in a comment of Bergson reported by Floris Delattre: "In his opinion, the author of the *Quest of Time lost* had failed to understand that there can be no real greatness in a work of art which does not exalt and stimulate the soul and which does not leave the door open to hope." [*Bergson et Proust: accords et dissonances* (Paris: Albin Michel, 1948), p. 126.] Needless to say, Bergson is thinking of a naturally Bergsonian type of soul.

Let us now turn toward Platonic essences, or Ideas, or Forms. In the *Parmenides*, the young Socrates grants the status of Idea to mathematical relations and to ideal values. He is more hesitant concerning concepts of species (such as Man) and other physical concepts (such as Fire). He rejects with horror the suggestion that there might be an Idea of mud: Mud in itself. As for Plato himself, his growing distrust of common language and his desire to eliminate the sensual from the Forms make it clear, despite the absence of a definite commitment, that he tends to consider the mathematician as the proper discoverer of Ideas: a notion would belong to the arsenal of Ideas in so far as its expression could be reduced to a mathematical formulation.

This divergence between Proust and Plato, or Socrates, concerning essences can be illustrated with the example of Swann who "held musical themes to be authentic ideas, belonging to another world . . . impervious to intelligence, yet perfectly distinct, unequal in value and significance." (I, 349.) A possible Platonic Form in this case would not be a musical theme, but something which could be grasped by mathematical intelligence: a scale of frequencies for instance. Students who were not geometers were supposed to be barred from the school of Plato. Proust compares himself to a geometer (III, 718); but the contrast appears to me more striking than the analogy. The analyses of Proust show great insight ("intuition") and a gift for metaphor; but they are lacking in "geometry," that is to say, in rigor, distinctness, coherence. Proust is wont to treat concepts as if they were moods or smells; he flits and drifts like a butterfly. The label of intellectualism can be used to refer to a tendency of Proust, to his taste for analytic prose, not to an achievement.

The disparity between Proustian repetition and Platonic reminiscence follows from what has been said about essences. Proust recognizes a past experience and asserts its identity with the present sensual experience. In the *Meno*, the object of reminiscence is not an experience in this life (we are dealing with a myth) and there is no identification between this object (the Form) and the sensual object (a triangle, for instance) in which it manifests itself.

Bergson and Plato are not the only philosophers with whom literary criticism has associated Proust. Thus, Proust has been presented as a Spinozist.[13] Spinoza distinguishes three kinds of knowledge. The third kind, also called "intuition," is the apprehension of objects under the species of eternity; it is supposed to bring perfect intellectual satisfaction. But it is enough to quote one sentence of Spinoza to realize how far we have strayed from the world of Proust: "To conceive things under the species of eternity is to conceive them in so far as they are conceived through the essence of God as real entities, or in so far as they

[13] Cf. Henri Bonnet, *Le Progrès spirituel dans l'oeuvre de Marcel Proust* (Paris: Vrin, 1949), II, 242-55.

involve existence through the essence of God." [14] This kind of knowledge would not be concerned with entities such as the Verdurin salon, a musical theme, or Proust's model experience. In the case of Spinoza, Plato, or any Classical philosopher, the emancipation from becoming is meant to satisfy the desire of contemplation and thus concerns only the intellect, the epistemological subject. Proust, on the other hand, is interested in possession as well as contemplation, hence in a less theoretical type of emancipation: the emancipation of subjectivity as total; of the object, or experience, as unique.

Schopenhauer, who has also been mentioned in connection with Proust, is a more likely choice than Bergson, Plato or Spinoza. Unlike Plato or Spinoza, he belongs to the Romantic era. Unlike Bergson, he belongs to the "pessimistic" branch of Romanticism: he stresses life and becoming, but the will-to-live is painted in darker colors than the élan vital. Bergson tends to be lyrical concerning individual life and epic about creative evolution (with other Romantic thinkers, it would be History). Schopenhauer sees the individual as a victim of the will-to-live of the species and considers individual life as a comedy in detail and a tragedy as a whole. This is more in keeping with Proust's outlook. The privileged role which Schopenhauer grants to art is also to be noted. Works of art, rather than social progress, can realize the idea of man toward which the vital drive strives blindly. The artistic genius is able to emerge from the Will, to encompass it and bring it to rest in a representation. The artistic analysis, in the etymological sense, brings about an adequation of subject and object.

Let us note, however, that, concerning life, Schopenhauerian Will evokes in Proust only the partial echo of the desire of possession. This desire is individual: the perspective of the species is lacking in Proust. Not unrelated to this difference is the fact that Proust stresses chance (and grace), whereas Schopenhauer stresses causality, that is to say, a relation which transcends individual life. Besides, concerning art, Schopenhauer considers that genius consists in eliminating individual things, so as to apprehend the Ideas and to stand opposite as their correlative, "no longer as an individual, but as the pure subject of knowledge." [15] Now it must be admitted that there is an intellectualistic tendency in Proust. It must also be recognized that, as a Romantic theorist, he presents art as a kind of knowledge, as the expression of a kind of "truth," so as not to concede the ownership of this impressive word to the fanatics of a triumphant science. Still, in spite of Schopenhauer's unusual interest in art, we encounter once again, between philosopher and artist, the disparity which has been noted. Proust's desire of possession is not likely to be satisfied by epistemological adequacy. Artistic composition is for him an attempt at recovering what

[14] *Ethica*, part V, proposition 30.
[15] *Die Welt als Wille und Vorstellung*, book II, section 37.

has been lived. The model experience is a privileged phenomenon of memory. There is no analogue for this basic revelation in Schopenhauer. Regarding this model experience which functions as a sun in the world of Proust, I see only one philosopher who can provide the material for a significant relationship: Kierkegaard, the philosopher of uniqueness and repetition. By repetition, Kierkegaard does not mean the type of recurrence with which scientific laws are concerned. Like Proust, he considers repetition in the perspective of personal history. It cannot be technically produced in application of causality: it occurs through grace. Kierkegaard compares repetition and recollection: "Repetition and recollection are the same movement, only in opposite directions; for what is recollected has been, is repeated backwards, whereas repetition properly so called is recollected forwards." [16] Proust is not "carried back" to the past instances of the experience. Rather, the experience comes up spontaneously to repeat itself in the present. Except for the word *category*, the following sentence of Kierkegaard could serve as a fitting epigraph to the work of Proust: "When one does not possess the categories of recollection or of repetition, the whole of life is resolved into a void and empty noise." [17]

The fact that repetition is conceived by the two authors in the perspective of individual existence and holds a paramount importance for both, allows for a significant relationship. But it also prevents the relationship from being a close analogy. For the temperaments and destinies of the two men are quite different. Kierkegaard's concern with repetition stems from his awkward dealings with Regina Olsen, whereas the model experience of Proust does not involve a human being. Besides, Proust starts from experienced repetition, whereas Kierkegaard thinks about its possibility and does not even make clear what is supposed to be repeated. For Proust, repetition is a fact on record; for Kierkegaard, it is a matter of speculation and indistinct faith.

Kierkegaard distinguishes between an aesthetic sphere of existence and a religious sphere. He tries to "leap" from one to the other; and he places the possibility of authentic repetition in the religious sphere. One might say that Proust effects the opposite move: he is an aesthetic mystic. The formula of Kierkegaard: "True repetition is eternity" thus finds an ambiguous echo in Proust. But even this analogy in contrast may be misleading. For the word *aesthetic* cannot be applied to Proust in quite a Kierkegaardian sense; and the word *religious* can be used to label the starting-point of Proust only if its meaning is kept very hazy.

Kierkegaard, like Proust, is a Romantic, post-Christian, author. He is not resigned to this situation and he tries sedulously, or complacently,

[16] *Repetition*, tr. Walter Lowrie (Princeton, N. J.: Princeton University Press, 1941), pp. 3-4.
[17] *Ibid.*, p. 34.

"to become a Christian." Proust, on the other hand, transfers religiosity to a non-religious frame of thinking. The mythical past (the lost paradise) becomes a personal past. Mystic experience is not interpreted in the language of a theistic myth. Religious belief, ethical striving, are superseded by an artistic task. Experiences are to be "saved," not souls. In the Christian paradise, no redemption, no repetition, is scheduled for the Vinteuil sonata or the steeples of Martinville.

The Profundity of Proust

by Charles Du Bos

"Profundity" according to Littré's dictionary is "the extent of anything measured from the surface or point of entry to its depth,"— and this is the word that comes to mind every time I think of Marcel Proust. His eye encompasses the whole: installed in front of things like an organist before his keyboard, he pulls his stops as he pleases and transports us from one level to another. He does not just happen upon things, he knows them: others conquer truth by force of arms, he has an air of taking it out of his pocket like an article of common use. The labor of conception has taken place in the recesses of the mind so that, at the moment of expression, speaker and truth confront each other in perfect mutual independence. No doubt at the beginning truth seemed to him "that ideal which we can attain only through the inner growth of thought and with the heart straining every effort," [1] but growth and effort have been carried to such a pitch of success that Proust reigns over what he sought only to reach, and transcends it. Thus, some of his pages are like the topographical maps in our schoolbooks; and the way in which this geologist of relatively unknown lands eases our passage from one stratum to another suggests a distinctive quality of Proust's genius, agility in depth.

No one, I think, can deny this agility, if he possesses the only quality Proust demands of his reader, namely, that he must not be short of wind. Watch the movement of his sentences as they go up and then

"The Profundity of Proust" (Original title: "Points of View on Proust"). Translated by Angelo P. Bertocci. From *From the NRF,* edited by Justin O'Brien. Copyright 1958 by Justin O'Brien. Reprinted by permission of Justin O'Brien and Meridian Books, Inc.

[1] "The role of reading can become dangerous when, instead of awakening us to an independent life of the spirit, reading tends to take its place; when truth seems no longer an ideal to be realized by the inner growth of thought and with the heart straining every effort, but like a material thing, deposited between the pages of books like a honey ready-made by others and that we need only take the trouble to reach for on the shelves of libraries and to digest and enjoy passively with perfect repose of body and spirit." *Pastiches et mélanges,* p. 254.

come down the flexible but tightly-knotted rope-ladder of his narrative. As they make their crossing, they define: they never camp on the field of victory. Nothing stops their movement, neither the dependent clauses nor the parentheses which the author adds to their burden; just as in certain Louis XV panels, the torrent imprisoned in its channels still bounds along its way, so do clauses and parentheses here deepen all the more as they complicate the course of the original motif.

Every artist who attaches major importance to reality in his art reaches his goal when he has succeeded in building a three-dimensional world. But his aim obliges him, in no small measure, to take the world of external perception at face value, and to act as if he believed in the properties of solidity and resistance that it presents to naïve sensation. Up to Proust's time this was the last stage of make-believe inherent in any art transcending the merely decorative which therefore sets up limits, generous but definite, to the mind's activity. Nor need we remind readers of *Swann in Love,* and members of the inner circle of the salon of Mme de Villeparisis, or guests of the Duchess de Guermantes, that Proust's mastery of the three-dimensional world is second to none; but though that world seems the settled abode of our normal existence, it is for Proust only one—and certainly not "the best"—"of all possible worlds." "Perhaps the immobility of things around us is imposed upon them by our dogmatic assumption that things are what they are and not otherwise and by the very immobility of our thought in their regard." [2] The man who wrote these lines and whose mind, moreover, is endowed with an unbelievable capacity for disintegration, will not and cannot admit either of the two forms of immobility. Here the special nature of his genius drives him to a position the very opposite of our own. We ordinary people find ourselves almost adrift before we are willing to suspend, in our own cases, the fiction of immobility: Proust, on the other hand, from a vantage point removed from the flux, looks down as from an observatory upon its inexhaustible flow. (His debt to Bergson in this matter and his differences from Bergson will no doubt provide material for a long time to come for some of us, but the subject could hardly be scratched in an article of a few pages.) Such is the power of emission of this spirit that its ray penetrates every zone; and its course, revealing in its very zig-zags the "possible worlds" of the philosopher, illuminates impersonally—and with a light almost grown cold—all the contingencies written into the constitution of our own world.

For this sense of the contingent is what Proust's books communicate to the highest degree. Just as to reduce everything to a single cause would achieve nothing but a deceptive show of appearances, so would the knowledge of every single cause and even of each separate field of operation disclose the fundamental absurdity of those compounds is-

---

[2] *A la recherche du temps perdu,* I, 6.

suing from a small number of 'simple bodies and irreducible elements,'[3] and all the more amusing for their rigorous determinism. In fact, if the laws of nature, applied to natural phenomena, manage to maintain an air of dignity, with respect to human phenomena these same laws lose all gravity not only because of man's laughable efforts to evade them, but even more because of the success he imagines he achieves with every effort.

If the novel as a literary genre could not satisfy Marcel Proust, neither could art for its own sake; or rather, having understood and assimilated the earlier forms of art, he inaugurated an entirely new one, the only kind thoroughly suited to the conditions of our time in its novelty. Between the disintegrating pressure his mind could exert and that disaggregation of the primary data characterizing our age there was a singular accord. In this sense the completion of the search for a vanished past in *A la recherche du temps perdu* could never in the least make up for what is irreparable in his disappearance. His work conceived and executed—and with singular foresight—within the freest and most flexible of frameworks could not only absorb an infinite wealth of additions; but, whenever he should be ready once and for all to write *finis* and detach himself from the characters and the society with which he had lived so long, the very form of his genius fitted him especially to depict the form of our own time. Without prejudice of any kind or—what amounts in practice to the same thing—recognizing as such those prejudices from which death alone can deliver us, with a unique capacity for distinguishing between a prejudice and a real thought, he had reached the heights of that scientific impartiality which today constitutes perhaps the only possible position of the artist who wants to render contemporary humanity. Here Proust's kind of vision is irreplaceable.

Other writers, sometimes very talented ones, seek to establish a sense of community with these new conditions by incorporating them, so to speak, into expression itself. But Proust's community with them was above all a matter of vision: it proceeds from his position, from the point of intersection from which he writes. The very hyperaesthesia of his vision is only the most subtle instrument of an insatiable love of truth. Although his manner of speech is inimitably his, he never entrusts to the mimicry of a manner the task of transmitting the message: the Proustian style is a docile servant, diligent and capable of more than one turn of phrase; but never the mistress.

Since Proust's originality was a matter of depth, with its guarantee of

[3] "If one knew how to analyze the soul as if it were matter, one would see that under the apparent diversity of minds and personalities, just as in the case of things, there are only a few simple bodies and irreducible elements and that what we call our own personality is made up of very ordinary substances to be found almost anywhere in the Universe." *Pastiches et mélanges*, p. 103.

The Profundity of Proust

a certain reserve force in the background, he could allow himself free play on the surface and with all surfaces. Where others would have been left stranded in hopeless eccentricity, he had a unique way of getting back to the center through depth-analysis of the eccentricity itself. French literature alone, perhaps, is distinguished by a rendering of surfaces so completely expressive and perfect as to shine with a depth of its own, though to be sure it also boasts of writers who establish themselves once and for all in the profundities. But between surface and depth there lies a certain ill-defined intermediate plane which makes itself felt right away through a kind of uneasy vacillation; a rather forbidding section but overpopulated, and where so many writers, not necessarily the least gifted, make their quarters throughout their entire existence. (An instinct of self-preservation guides them, for this is the only level on which they can be productive, since they lack the gift both for surface and depth.)

Many were the planes over which Marcel Proust extended his domain, but with this intermediate plane his genius never signed a pact.

In Search of the Self

by Ramon Fernandez

Mais ils savaient d'instinct ou par expérience que les élans de notre sensibilité ont peu d'empire sur la suite de nos actes et la conduite de notre vie, et que le respect des obligations morales, la fidélité aux amis, l'exécution d'une œuvre, l'observance d'un régime, ont un fondement plus sûr dans des habitudes aveugles que dans ces transports momentanés, ardents et stériles.
(Marcel Proust.)

[But they knew by instinct or by experience that the flights of our sensibility have little dominion over the continuity of our acts and the conduct of our life, and that the respect of moral obligations, faithfulness to friends, the achievement of a work, the observance of a system, have a surer foundation in blind habits than in these momentary, ardent and fruitless transports.]

I

The objections that are aroused by the work of Proust, considered as an integral analysis of the heart, as revealing the depths of our nature, may, in my opinion, be reduced to two essentials: it does not erect a hierarchy of values, and it does not manifest, from its opening to its conclusion, any spiritual progress.[1] This double lacuna puts it into

"In Search of the Self" (Original title: "The Guaranteeing of Sentiments and the Intermittences of the Heart"). From *Messages* by Ramon Fernandez, translated by Montgomery Belgion. Copyright 1927 by Harcourt, Brace & World, Inc. Reprinted by permission.

[1] It is extremely difficult for me to define, in a study not addressed to professional philosophers, what I understand here by spiritual. What for me is essentially spiritual is what Mr. Brunschwieg calls, in connection with the Cartesians, "the internal unification of which the contrary is multiplicity outspread *partes per partes.*" (See the discussion of the word *spiritualism* in the *Bulletin de la Société française de Philosophie,* January-February, 1917.) But adopting a strictly psychological point of view, I am considering here only the internal unification of each one's concrete experience, the act, the psychic contraction which enables the individual to attune his

In Search of the Self

an equivocal situation, which enables some people to greet in it the corner stone of a positive literature, free of hypocrisies, an architecture of the intelligence which would perform the task of reducing fancies and sublimations to real movements of the sensibility, and which leaves others, more ambitious or more cowardly, with a bitter bouquet of disenchantment. I shall reduce my criticism to a single example: by his masterly analysis of the "intermittences of the heart," Proust raises a problem of extreme gravity, for upon its solution depends our conception of the value of man and of the orientation of the future. It seems to me that it is altogether urgent, before the echoes respond on all sides to the master's voice, to pick up carefully the problems which he set without solving, or which he solved with hasty and often illegitimate generalizations. The Proustian analysis of the intermittences of the heart has this in particular about it that it reveals at one and the same time, and in a same movement of the mind, the mechanism of Proust's thought and its limitations.

The famous text, the first phrases of which make one think of the breathless and fiery notes of a fresh convert, is familiar:

> *My whole person overwhelmed.* Already on the first night, while I was suffering from an attack of cardiac fatigue, trying to master my sufferings, I bent down carefully and slowly to take off my boots. But hardly had I touched the first button of my boot than my chest swelled, filled with an unknown, a divine *presence,* sobs shook me, tears coursed from my eyes. The being coming to my rescue, *saving me from the drought of the soul,* was the one who, several years earlier, at a moment of identical distress and solitude, at a moment in which I no longer had any of myself, had entered, and had returned me to myself, for it was myself and more than myself (the container that is more than the contained and that was bringing it to me). I had just *perceived,* in my memory, bending over my fatigue, the tender features, preoccupied and disappointed, of my grandmother, as she had been on that first evening of arrival, the features of my grandmother, not of her whom I had been surprised at, and self-reproachful for, regretting so little, and who had of her only the name, but of my veritable grandmother whose . . . *living reality I met in an involuntary and complete recollection* . . . and thus, in a wild desire to throw myself into her arms, it was only at this instant, more than a year after her funeral, because of that anachronism which so often prevents the calendar of facts from coinciding with that of the feelings,—that I had come to learn that she was dead.

---

living activity to his intellectual activity, to make the synthesis of the two, and thereafter to progress, to grow *in so far as he is a living man.* It is this power of synthesis which, according to me, Marcel Proust lacked. His analysis ends in an "outspread multiplicity" and the only progress in him is that of the intelligence. [*The reader must always bear in mind that this essay was written before the publication of* The Past Regained. *Ed.'s note.*]

Then come some general reflections, highly significant, but before quoting their essence I should like to distinguish them from the preceding passage a little more precisely than has been done hitherto.

The eminent critics who have quoted these reflections seem to see in them the natural continuation of the affective overwhelming felt by Proust, as if this experience could be logically translated only by the law of the intermittences of the heart. But, in fact, this sudden reversal of values, this unexpected vision of reality, this passing without transition from the purely intellectual idea of the being to the shock provoked by its miraculous "presence" in us, does not in the least imply the dissociation of personality which Proust deduces from it. What occurs here, on the contrary, is a normal stage of the spiritual progress towards more consistence and unity, the latter consisting essentially,— as Newman has established in definitive terms—in a passing from intellectual comprehension to *real* comprehension of a thing, a feeling, or an act. The law of the intermittences, of which you are going to reread the subtle enunciation, is only the restrained, and in a way the pathological, version of a human phenomenon of which it would falsify the sense if one did not hasten to put it at its level in the hierarchy of spiritual laws.

At whatever moment we consider it [Proust writes], our *total* soul has only an *almost fictitious* value, in spite of the numerous tally of its riches, for now some, then others, *are* unavailable, and this, by the way, just as much whether they be actual riches or those of the imagination, and for me, for example, quite as much for the ancient name of Guermantes, as for those how much graver, of the true recollection of my grandmother. *For to the cloudiness of memory are linked the intermittences of the heart.* It is doubtless through the existence of our body, similar for us to a vase in which our spirituality might be enclosed, that we are induced to suppose that all our internal goods, our past joys, all our sufferings, are *perpetually in our possession.* Perhaps it is just as incorrect to belive that they get away or come back. Anyhow if they remain in us, most of the time they do so *in an unknown domain* where *they are of no service to us,* and where even the most usual ones are pushed back by recollections of a different order *which exclude all simultaneity with them in consciousness. But if the frame of sensations in which they are preserved is caught again,* they in their turn are endowed with that same power of expelling all that is incompatible with them, *of installing solely in us the ego which lived them.* Now as he whom I had suddenly rebecome had not existed since that distant evening on which my grandmother undressed me upon my arrival at Balbec, it was quite naturally, not after the present day which that ego was unaware of, but—*as if there were, in time, different and parallel series*—without any solution of continuity, at once after the first evening of yesteryear, that I was adhering to the minute in which my grandmother had leaned towards me.[2]

[2] *A la recherche du temps perdu*, II, 755-757.

In Search of the Self

It can be seen what Proust adds and what he subtracts by his analysis to and from the phenomenon of *realization* which he has so powerfully described. The real recollection—as opposed to the intellectual, fictitious recollection—is inscribed in a frame of sensations, and indeed, to imagine powerfully one must feel powerfully; but nothing guarantees the effectiveness and duration of the hold on the real afforded to him by the live recollection, because the new ego thus created is bound up with the actual and sensorial frame out of which it was born. This ego does not react on its own account, does not seek to take advantage of the experience to reinforce the unity of Proust's moral person: as well say that it does not try to become a veritable ego. For there must be no mistake: whatever may be the bearing of his analysis, Proust creates confusion here by an improper use of the word soul and of the word *ego*, or, more exactly, he implicitly gives for one and the other definitions which would have to be accepted before being affirmed, either because he is mistaken or because he has renovated the psychology of the human heart. It appears in this passage that he understands by soul the *collection* of our sensible and affective experiences scattered in time, and by *ego* the passive subject of one of these experiences brought back into consciousness by memory thanks to an affective association. These definitions may correctly express reality, but in that case the only thing to do would be frankly to strike the two words from our vocabulary. We should then be composed of independent and transitory waves of which our consciousness would register the as rapid as unexpected passages. They would have exactly the same value as those purely physical waves of pain or pleasure traversing us, which compress or open up our sensibility, and which we can prolong only by provisional and hasty reveries or pacify by drugs and the mechanical re-education of our will. In this multiplicity of relived experiences the only real link would be ensured by memory and the only possible principle of unity would be the intelligence which would co-ordinate these states by *comprehending* them. The only effective progress would be that of the intelligence, the only non-illusory perfecting would be the perfecting of our intellectual consciousness.

Accepting these judgments, and turning man towards practice and throwing him among his fellows, forthwith we must revise our ideas of moral guarantee and responsibility. Proust himself invites us to do so by the typical remark which serves as an epigraph for this study. I willingly believe it: if the flights of our sensibility are dependent upon a phenomenon of reminiscence, if to be aware of a sentiment we must await the affective spark which will enable us to relive integrally an anterior experience, if to understand, and feel, and desire, and will, we must first undergo an inverted metempsychosis, whereby the useless forms of our past lives, imperious and exclusive, are returned to us, we are no better than those little South American republics which each month change their programmes and their promises with a change of dictators.

The problem is grave. If Proust is to be believed, not only can man not guarantee his sentiments, and consequently his acts, and consequently man must be an eternal failure, but also he must renounce the consolation of feeling that he progresses despite this discontinuity and this intermittent blindness and will be able to reduce and surpass both. A real progress is a growth, and a growth of the whole being. To understand better and better that one is not progressing is not progress: progress consists, on the contrary, in understanding better and better that one is feeling more and more vanely and that one wills with more and more effectiveness. All spiritual evolution must be accomplished, not in the interior of the intelligence, but in the interior of the individual. Therefore it is the problem of spirituality, of the value of the ideal, of the future and of human progress, that is set by the Proustian analysis of the intermittences of the heart. It may be formulated in these terms: all that seems to us to be good and just, the internal forces guaranteeing our future words and acts, the aspiration towards the better state called the ideal, the sentiment of surpassing oneself called spiritual progress—all this is a discontinuous illusion of our senses, or, at least, in all this we can guarantee only the apparent results, thanks to various subterfuges: moral gymnastics, mechanization of our acts by habit. If the intermittences of the heart and their corollaries represent the depths of human nature, the supreme experience of our *ego,* then the spiritual life must be ranged in its entirety in the category of imagination, and the intelligence is the highest point of human development to which we may pretend. Then we must demand from the intelligence that sentiment of elevation, of dignity, of beatitude, that tradition demanded from the spiritual life. The victory of the intelligence would mark the defeat of the mind, and man's highest task would be to deny the millenary effort of man.

II

Before concluding with Proust in vital renunciation and in the exclusive cult of the intelligence, it is necessary to do for him what he failed to do, to situate him in a hierarchy. For there is another manner than his of understanding oneself without surpassing oneself, that of Montaigne, which consists in ranking oneself in an order at the same time as putting oneself in order. I imagine a reader of Montaigne discovering himself to be, in the light of his intelligence, equal to him on almost all points except one or two, and seeing that these few distinctive traits are discerned by Montaigne himself in the figure of a hero, a saint, or simply of a man exhibited: thereupon this reader is naturally led to raise himself one degree, to try his luck in the superior regions; he does not know whether he will be able to live in them, but he knows that they exist and that others breathe in them easily. The more we advance in the reading of the *Essais*, the more we draw away from the rather rhetorical exercises at the outset, then the more we see Montaigne anxious not only to define himself, but further to *classify* himself: his ego does not fill the frame, there is space around him in that noble picture containing Epaminondas. The great weakness of Proust's work, so splendid in many respects, is that everything is brought back in it to the lowest common denominator of a passive sensibility which manifests no index of maturity, that the field of our vision is obstructed in it by an *ego* larger than life-size which the most lucid analysis fails to render transparent.

To remedy this defect one must cross to the other side of the barricade and question the men who have seen in individual sensibility and imagination the guarantee of our sentiments and of the continuity of human effort. It is remarkable indeed that the more thought ripens, the more it conceives the necessity, so as to touch reality and plough its furrow, of being supported by the most concrete reactions of the individual which it opposes to the abstract undertakings of reason—notably, by that real comprehension of things which Proust has described in terms of dramatic lucidity. The most profound analyst of this thought, of this concrete logic so typically modern, Cardinal Newman, has given of it an interpretation well worth comparing with Proust's analysis.

Newman distinguishes two ways of understanding things: they may be understood *abstractly*, by inferences bearing on notions, and they may be understood *really*, by an act of assent bearing on concrete representation through our imagination of an experience, of a feeling, of a particular act. For example, before the "overwhelming of his being," Proust understood abstractly the death of his grandmother[3] and the affection which he bore her, he did not have a real comprehension of it. Newman sees in *real* assent (which he distinguishes from abstract assent, the conclusion of an inference) the strongest and most perfect hold that the mind may have on reality, veritable knowledge in the order of sentiment and in the order of action, and even in the order of ideas in so far as they are susceptible of enlisting all the forces of

[3] Certainly the narrator had had the concrete experience of his grandmother's death, but some accident to his sensibility—no doubt the presence in him at that period of a different and exclusive ego—had prevented him from realizing this experience and of it he had retained only the idea. The knowledge which he had of the event belonged therefore, in a sense, to deduction. There is nothing in that that is not rather normal, especially if one remembers that in rethinking his experience Proust deepened it, augmented it by all the relief which the intelligence that pushes adds to reality. One must always in Proust take into account this magnifying-glass which he applies to himself, which produced a deformation exactly the opposite of imaginative deformation, but did not always differ in its effects.

our being, and it is in that sense that Proust remarks, with a great aptness, that he had just "learned" of his grandmother's death one year after the event. As far as this very point Newman and Proust are perfectly in agreement. The former even goes so far as to recognize, like the latter, the hazardous, unexpected and accidental character of the conditions of real assent. We cannot, he says, make sure for ourselves of real apprehension and assent, "because we have to secure first the images which are their objects, and these are often peculiar and special. They depend on personal experience; and the experience of one man is not the experience of another. Real assent, then, as the experience which it presupposes, is proper to the individual, and, as such, *thwarts rather than promotes the intercourse of man with man.*" [4] And further on, still in connection with real assent: "It cannot be reckoned on, anticipated, accounted for, *inasmuch as it is the accident of this man or that.*" The coincidence of thoughts is significant: there can be no doubt that Proust must have known and experimented with the first phase of the maturation of thought encrusted in us by images, which enables us to fix our sentiments and to give weight and consistence to our personality.

But it is clear also that he knew only the first phase: his birth into spiritual life soon shows the characteristics of an abortion. Newman is as explicit as can be: for him the fixation of thought by concrete representations marks a considerable progress, a deepening of the spiritual life, and, as it were, a taking root of human values. "They [real assents] are sometimes called beliefs, convictions, certitudes; and, as given to moral objects, they are perhaps as rare as they are powerful. Till we have them, in spite of a full apprehension and assent in the field of notions, we have no intellectual moorings, and are at the mercy of impulses, fancies, and wandering lights, whether as regards personal conduct, social and political action, or religion. These beliefs, *be they true or false in the particular case,* form the mind out of which they grow, and impart to it a seriousness and manliness which inspires in other minds a confidence in its views, and is one secret of persuasiveness and influence in the public stage of the world." [5] Thus Newman discovers the roots of spiritual life in the very experience which according to Proust renders it impossible: he guarantees our sentiments and our acts through the operation which for the author of Swann involves the failure of our personality. And yet Newman's point of view is here clearly pragmatic, his conclusions are independent of any metaphysical postulate. Therefore, either Newman must not have known how properly to decipher his own experience, or there must have been in Proust's

---

[4] The quotations of Newman are taken from his *Grammar of Assent.*
[5] *Ibid.* And elsewhere: "Great truths, practical or ethical, *float on the surface of society,* admitted by all, valued by few . . . *until changed circumstances, accident* . . . force them upon its attention."

a principle of corruption which prevented it from unfolding normally. Newman's opinion is singularly reinforced by that of Meredith, who, very hostile to the Cardinal's mysticism, not in the least anxious to ensure rigorous relations to speculative thought, and preoccupied only with attaining and following the individual through intuition and analysis, returns from his man-chase with experiences which confirm Newman's judgment. "Wilfred," [6] he says, "was a gallant fellow. . . . But, he was young. Ponder on that pregnant word, *for you are about to see him grow*. One may also be a gallant fellow, and harsh, exacting, double-dealing,[7] and I know not what besides, in youth. The question asked by nature is, *Has he the heart to take and keep an impression?* For, if he has, *circumstances will force him on and carve the figure of a brave man out of that mass of contradictions.*"

Take and *keep:* Proust takes but does not keep, or rather he keeps in a very peculiar fashion, and it would be perhaps more correct to say *that he is kept by the object of his impression*. For this impression, in being filtered through his consciousness, is not purified nor is it schematized so as to form both a kernel of sentimental resistance and a sheaf of tendencies oriented in a certain direction: instead of representing his experience by simplifying it, it projects his ego out of himself and fixes it in that experience. The process described by Newman and Meredith is accomplished in Proust in reverse order: to keep an impression is for them to transpose into the key of the mind a particular concrete experience, to cast off the spatial and temporal moorings of that experience, and to confer upon it the infinite plasticity of a living personality in perpetual growth; for Proust it is to fuse one's ego entirely in the experience, to deposit this ego at the points of time and space where the experience has taken place, and thereby *to cut it up into pieces each of which is identified with a particular experience and lodged in a corner of time which thus acquires a fixity and an externality which are characters proper to space*. The importance of time in the work of Proust has been much stressed: it has not been remarked enough perhaps that he gives to time the value and characters of space (as is shown notably by the expression, "parallel series," which he uses on its behalf), by affirming that the different parts of time are

---

[6] Wilfred Pole in *Sandra Belloni*. According to Meredith, the type of "sentimentalist" who feels his love diminished because a slight smell of tobacco is floating in his beloved's hair.

[7] Cf. Proust: ". . . my words and my thoughts as a young man ungrateful, selfish and cruel." It is very remarkable that these psychological traits which Proust attributes to himself, and which he attributes in general to human nature, are seen by Meredith as provisional characteristics of youth to be modified by the natural experience and development of the man. Could there have been in Proust a premature fixation of sensibility, an arrest of growth which he remedied later on through the bias of intelligence? This would explain perhaps the absence, in his work, of a properly spiritual progress.

reciprocally exclusive and remain external to one another, whereas spiritual experience leads us to think, on the contrary, that we bring together all the moments of time in the actual moments of our duration.[8]

III

One cannot compare Proust to the great analysts of concrete thought without perceiving in his work a veritable reversal of thought. Newman and Meredith think in progressive schemes and tendencies, Proust thinks through the integral reconstruction of past experiences. It is thus seen how the form of Proust's experience prevents the intelligence from fostering the least vital and spiritual progress, since this intelligence, incessantly invited to rethink an experience in its integrality to give to Proust that self-intuition without which we cannot live, works automatically in the past. It is also seen that this peculiarity of his thought incites him to exaggerate, to stress in relief, a sensible disposition which another method and some other hygiene would perhaps have modified. In Newman and Meredith, on the contrary, the permanence of the impression, because the latter is spiritualized, accumulates in the mind a strong force which enables the intelligence to fulfil its proper function, which is to surpass present experience, to create future. And note that I have chosen purposely two men who are not pure speculators, who consolidate their feeling with their thought and prove their thought through their living. Is it therefore not allowable to believe that Proust did not discover the germ of the unity and consistence of personality, that he did not catch in the net of his analysis the principle of a real sentiment?

It seems, indeed, that it is very dangerous to begin with the analysis of the sensible and affective manifestations of feeling, these being only one aspect of it and not the most significant one; and as one meets with these manifestations in many mental disorders, in nearly all disorders of the sensibility, and in what one may in general call crises of faltering, it follows that they serve as snares far more often than as guides in the study of feeling. In listening to them we hear only the mechanical voice of the body. In this connection Descartes pronounced some eternal words, picked up and meditated by the profound Alain.[9]

[8] Proust, who never gave to his thought a rigorous form, is at one moment Bergsonian, at another clearly anti-Bergsonian. Generally he has quite a Bergsonian manner of getting into contact with his duration (see the episode of the *madeleine*.), but by the reactions of his intelligence upon his sensibility, which reactions determine the curve of his work, he rather tends to be oriented towards a *spatialization* of time and memory.

[9] Professor Émile Chartier (b. 1876), the author of *Mars, ou la guerre jugée* (Paris: 1921); he obtained the pen name Alain from his namesake, Maistre Alain Chartier, the fifteenth century writer who for his "golden words" was kissed by Mary Queen of Scots. This Chartier's *Crurial* was translated into English by William Caxton.—*Translator's Note*.

In Search of the Self

Marcel Proust suffered from a hypertrophied affectivity: now, pleasure and pain felt too strongly destroy the order of things and draw back to themselves the sentimental values through an easily conceivable subterfuge. Through the disproportionate resonances which they are able to ring from the body, they give a false voice to the soul, in the same way as ventriloquists surprise dumb spectators by making them speak. The victim of these strong discharges, misled by his intimate sense, and yielding to this imperious orchestration, ends by believing that he lives, whereas he is lived by the things of which these spasms are only the transient waves; nothing turns him aside from the supreme error consisting in mistaking sensations for sentiments; and when the affective wave ebbs, or some accident interferes with its breaking, suddenly he feels himself naked, useless, and emptied, until another wave uplifts him and creates for an instant the phantom of his ego. Most serious of all is that the preponderance of affective discharges prevents him from distinguishing things from one another through their value, and consequently from distributing wisely the effort of his intelligence, since the scent of a rose and the scent of a soul alike create for him an ego and equally justify his aversion or his desire.

The absence of the moral element in Proust has been noticed,[10] but always as if it would have needed only some revelation or some mystical anxiety to bring about in him a recovery. I see the question for my part from an entirely other point of view. Mystical reactions mean no more in my eyes than sensible reactions, so long as I am not convinced of a man's power of creating sentiments with his impressions. For the whole problem is in that. One may form sentiments for oneself and obey them without mystical help—so long as one does not call mystical everything that is sentimental—and mysticism may be applied on to incurable sensuality. This is not the place to enter upon details of an analysis of feeling, but it will perhaps not be idle to indicate briefly the essential points of such an analysis.

In a recent study I defined a sentiment as "a perpetual possibility of *correct copies* by the action of a certain pretension, a possibility guaranteed by the intuition of an internal resistance." [11] If this definition is correct, the quite secondary value of sensible testimonies becomes at once perceptible: the two essential elements of a sentiment are the in-

---

[10] I am thinking especially of the pages devoted to Proust by François Mauriac and Henri Ghéon. The former (*Revue hebdomadaire,* Dec. 2, 1922) remarks very finely that Proust's characters manifest no moral progress, the moral value of some of them being as spontaneous and involuntary as the weakness or vice of others. The latter notes the Proustian reduction of spiritual life to the sensible life. But there may be moral progress within the limits of a radical atheism and these critics make such a progress dependent upon a religious inspiration. Proust's defect for me is of a psychological order, it is a flaw in the machine; hence it may be observed independently of any metaphysical assumption.

[11] *The Message of Meredith,* p. 187.

ternal resistance and the pretension, or intention of the mind, both of which are confirmed, and especially *may at any moment be confirmed, by our acts*. Now, what is the cause of this internal resistance if not the image, the living representation which Newman makes the object of real assent, the impression which one must "keep," according to Meredith, if one wants to get out of the nebula of contradictions enveloping the origin of our being? And where may the pretension of the mind be sought if not in an understanding between the latter and the impression, in the faculty which we have of thinking this sentiment, *of according with the proper laws of the intelligence the impression with which an experience leaves us?* Thereupon, if on the one hand we have an impression fixed by the images which represent in us what is outside us, and if on the other hand we have an intelligence which tends to combine, analyze, judge, progress in conformity with its own activity, *a sentiment must be born of a sort of psychic contraction which operates the synthesis of one with the other,* in such fashion that the activity of judgment be always regulated and guaranteed by the impression, and that the impression acquire the mobility, the transparence, and the certainty of judgment. Sentiment is therefore situated on a plane of consciousness intermediate between intellectual activity and sensible impression. One cannot say that it is a truth, since it is based upon an ineffable intuition which can be proved only by action; but neither can one say that it is a state of purely passive receptivity, since it participates in the activity of the mind and enables the latter to accomplish its most eminent function, which is to conceive with certainty the future. A man who has a deep sentiment *knows* how he would act in such and such circumstances because he has intimate knowledge of the immutable principle of his future actions. Sentiment therefore is much rather a response by all our being which cannot be translated indifferently either into the language of the intelligence or into that of sensibility, but of which our acts are the veritable signs, the only ones which make possible the exact measurement of its value. It is easy to verify this by a counter-test: observe the conduct of an individual who is "losing his head": you will remark that he applies himself unconsciously to enlarging into caricature the traits which we have noticed; but, as he is deprived of that centre of resistance and certitude which makes the whole reality of sentiment, he puts the cart before the horse and obstinately, by multiplied and memorable gestures, and in continually accelerating his delirium, mimics what he cannot attain. In order to demonstrate he is reduced to demonstrations. Such a man condemns himself to living with uplifted arm, and that is why we see him fumbling feverishly in all the recesses of sensibility to extract from them fresh proofs, and advancing, if necessary, right as far as death. On the contrary, the immediate expression of the true sentiment is silence, the religious silence of certitude, and it does not occur without a certain immobility, although it may produce violent movements. If it leads sometimes to the most extreme resolutions, it never describes the foreseen curve of passion, and these resolutions always bear the mark of the suppleness and presence of mind, like a happy gesture, like a well conducted thought. For a true sentiment teaches how to think well as it teaches how to act well. Far from moderating the audacity of the imagination, it warms it up in the heat of an ineffable presence accompanying it in all its twistings; nothing material guarantees it, but it is able to guarantee itself by that I know not what which is eternal and appears in its slightest testimonies; and one may say that the true sentiment, whatever it may be, imprints the seal of justice upon the most terrible actions.

Here we perceive that the problem has turned: it is no longer a question of knowing if man can guarantee his sentiments in spite of the intermittences of the *heart,* but if he can do so in spite of the intermittences of *sensibility* and *affectivity.* We have seen that Proust reduced the heart to the state of sensible and affective receptivity, which contradicts the results of the complete analysis of sentiment practiced upon themselves by men absolutely trustworthy. To simplify, let us call *psychic contraction* the formation of sentiment such as we have described roughly, and *spiritualization* the sentimental elaboration of the sensible experience. I am saying that in Proust this contraction does not take place, that this spiritualization miscarries originally, and that the ego, at one moment tense, at once relaxes and spreads out alongside the object, then with the help of the intelligence, is stabilized and localized in the affective zone surrounding it. And his technique is at the same time rigorously symmetrical with his mental mechanism. When he makes his characters live, he proceeds exactly as when he organizes his experience: he never seizes what one may call the center of radiance in a being, he does not integrate such a being, he sews recollections together and leaves the seams showing. The dynamism of his recollections may have created an illusion, but cannot be confused with creative dynamism. I shall be answered that it is because of this that he is truer than most novelists and analysts. But if it is true that the human mind is able to produce sentiments, Proust is not truer than those who have described their durable effects; if it is true that there have been artists who were able to place their characters, so to speak, at the free disposal of their imagination without deforming them, Proust is not truer than such novelists. It is precisely because it is always marvellously true without ever being quite true that Proust's work raises such a grave problem.

—But, you will object, a sentiment such as you have just described, being extremely rare, concerns only a minute part of humanity, and we are admiring in Proust his incomparable manner of establishing the average in hearts.

—Let us understand each other: to Proust the symphonist of his affectivity I bear the homage of a total admiration. I joyfully greet his "unhoped for" achievement, to borrow Charles du Bos's apt expression: it is with Proust the constructor of human nature that I am quarrelling, it is he that I believe it is all the more urgent to refute, since he has armed us with an irreplaceable method for fathoming ourselves. It is just because his machine is admirably conceived that the part missing must quickly be added in order that such a machine may work normally. Let us admit that true sentiment is an ideal: tradition teaches us that this ideal has been realized, and as everything that is real for one single man is possible for all others, it is this possible never attained which magnetizes human nature and gives it a form in giving it a sense. It is not at the moment when we no longer depend upon anything but ourselves, when our figure must be cut entirely out of our stuff, that we should allow ourselves to be deprived of any one of our means. Now, this is what Proust does by suppressing, between the impression and the intelligence, the synthetic intermediary of sentiment, by rendering impossible the progressive spiritualization of our experience, and thereby by condemning the intelligence to understand in the past, to construct what has disappeared, to progress backwards. His work is not content with transforming the ascent towards the mind into an ascent towards the intelligence: it breaks a spring of our nature which we must repair as quickly as we can, it raises around us artificial barriers that we must first resolutely demolish. We shall then understand far better his true beauty, the marvellous effectiveness of his method, and the masterless energy of an intelligence which sticks to things and lets go of them only after having espoused every contour.

The intermittences of the *heart* therefore merely set a problem of hierarchy: they have their place, and it is a legitimate place, below sentiment which they disturb and which gives us the strength, if not to reduce them, at least to dominate them. In this sense it is true that a real sentiment is never more evident for us than when it does not awaken echoes in our body, since then it is an ideal, but an ideal which gives to us the same sort of certitude as a successful experiment or a true judgment. Certitude, the sensible impulse: these are the two ends of the chain which modern man must hold on to firmly, at the same time connecting them progressively with intermediate links. Unless one is to bid farewell all of a sudden, and by decision, to spirituality. But, I ask, is it possible to consider man in his reality, in his whole reality, without taking into account his spiritual tendencies, and is it not obvious that, far from being added to him from the outside, like a strange body which would not alter anything in his constitution, they develop, try, and modify, the most hidden parts of his nature, that his least aspiration is a sign of which a graphology subtle enough would take advantage, and that finally we know indeed what he is only when we

In Search of the Self

know what he wants to be? So that in reading Proust and admiring him, I can nevertheless draw no conclusions concerning human nature, because I have before my eyes only a restricted, fixed, and outspread, part of this nature. And let it not be said that it is thus at bottom, and that the rest is illusion, an artificial superstructure: as well pretend that all that is real in the statue is the material with which it is made.

Proust and Human Time

by Georges Poulet

I

And when I awoke in the middle of the night, not knowing where I was, I did not even know at first who I was; I had only in its primal simplicity a sense of existing, such as may flicker in the depths of an animal's consciousness; I was more destitute than the cave-dweller.[1]

At the beginning of the Proustian novel there is, then, an instant which is not preceded by any other, just as with Descartes or Condillac, just as with Valéry. But if this instant is of a "primal simplicity," that is because it is about to become the starting point of the immense development that follows it; but it is oriented not toward this "becoming" but toward the nothingness which precedes it. Here, this first moment is neither a moment of fullness nor of birth. It is pregnant neither with its future possibilities nor with its present realities. And if it reveals a fundamental emptiness, that is not because it needs anything from "ahead" but because it lacks something from "behind": something which *is no longer;* not something which *is not yet.* One might call it the first moment of a being that has lost everything, that has lost itself, because it is dead: "We have slept too long, we no longer exist. Our waking is barely felt, mechanically and without consciousness. . . ."[2]

The sleeper awakes from sleep more naked than a cave man. His nakedness is the nakedness of a lack of knowledge. If he is reduced to the state in which he is, that is because he does not know who he is. And he does not know who he is because he does not know who he has

---

"Proust and Human Time." Translated by Elliott Coleman. From *Studies in Human Time* by Georges Poulet. Copyright 1956 by the Johns Hopkins University Press. Reprinted by the gracious permission of the publisher and the author. *Studies in Human Time* was originally published in French as *Etudes sur le temps human* by the Edinburgh University Press.

[1] I, 5. The translated passages from *A la recherche du temps perdu* are those of C. K. Scott-Moncrieff, *Remembrance of Things Past* (2 vols.; New York: Random House, 1927-32), with a few changes.

[2] *Ibid.*, II, 464.

been. He knows *no longer*. He is a being who has lost his being because memory and the past have been lost:

> Then from those profound slumbers we awake in a dawn, not knowing who we are, being nobody, newly born, ready for anything, our brain being emptied of that past which was previously our life. And perhaps it is more wonderful still when our landing at the waking-point is abrupt and the thoughts of our sleep, hidden by a cloak of oblivion, have no time to return to us progessively, before sleep ceases. Then, from the black tempest through which we seem to have passed (but we do not even say *we*) we emerge, prostrate, without a thought, a "we" that is without content. What hammer-blow has the being or the thing that is lying there received to make it unconscious of anything . . . ?[3]

He who surges now into existence seems less a being than one emptied of his being. He is a being *in vacuo*, in emptiness; a being "without consciousness," since consciousness can only be consciousness of something. He is "without content," "more lifeless than a jelly-fish," returned to "the most elementary kingdoms of nature"; a being that cannot be described otherwise than by calling it "the being or the thing that is there."

But how is this thing which is there, in a moment "outside of time and all measures," how is it going to be able to leave this moment which isolates it before and behind? How shall it repair its monstrous ignorance of time, place, and its own person? Doubtless, to the animal feeling of its own existence there corresponds the feeling of the existence of a world in which it seems confusedly immersed. Awakened, and at the very instant when it awakes, this sleeper discovers himself and discovers at the same time that he *is there*—there, that is to say somewhere: at a certain time; in a place; among things. But suppose he awakens in the middle of the night, in darkness: in what room is he? in what place? in what time? Certain images of places and times come and go, excluding each other and superimposing themselves upon him:

> Perhaps the immobility of the things that surround us is forced upon them by our conviction that they are themselves, and not anything else, and by the immobility of our conceptions of them. For it always happened that when I awoke like this, and my mind struggled in an unsuccessful attempt to discover where I was, everything would be moving round me through the darkness: things, places, years.[4]

Vertigo of images. The world, as the awakened sleeper discovers it, is indeed a world of things, but of interchangeable things, in which nothing is attached to one particular point of space or duration; a world

[3] *Ibid.*, p. 271.   [4] *Ibid.*, I, 5.

of things doubtful rather than certain; possible rather than necessary; a world similar to the legendary images of Golo and of Geneviève de Brabant which the play of the magic lantern substituted for the walls of the room of the child Proust, to make "a stained glass window, flickering and momentary."

The being that is uncertain of himself wants to lean upon the stability of things. But what stability can be offered by things which are "even more unreal than the projections of the magic lantern"? Unreal as the forms he has just encountered in the world of sleep:

> . . . deep slumber in which are opened to us a return to childhood, the recapture of past years, of lost feelings, the disincarnation, the transmigration of the soul, the evoking of the dead, the illusions of madness, retrogression towards the most elementary of the natural kingdoms (for we say that we often see animals in our dreams, but we forget almost always that we are ourself then an animal deprived of that reasoning power which projects upon things the light of certainty; we present on the contrary to the spectacle of life only a *dubious vision, destroyed afresh every moment by oblivion,* the former reality fading before that which follows it as one projection of a magic lantern fades before the next as we change the slide).[5]

The awakened sleeper, Proust, is never entirely able to detach himself from this first figuration of the world. One would say that, if Goethe taught himself to represent the universe as a theater of marionettes, Proust learned to represent existence as the "flickering and momentary" play of the light of a magic lantern. The Proustian world is always to be an intermittent world. A world in which things project themselves before the eyes in instantaneous images which in turn are replaced by other images belonging to other moments and other places; a world in which the apparition of any one image does not necessarily entail the apparition of the one following; where one may find oneself going backward as well as forward; where "the magic chair may carry us at all speed in time and space"; a world of "doubtful visions," whose lacunae the mind will have to fill up by its conjectures, whose vacillations it will have to remedy by its beliefs. The Proustian world is a world anachronistic in itself, without a home, wandering in duration as well as in extent, a world to which the mind must precisely assign a certain place in duration and space, by imposing its own certitude upon it, by realizing oneself in the face of it.

But in order to impose our certainties upon the world, we must first find them in ourselves. Now what certainties can a consciousness without content find in itself? What can it offer, denuded of all, beggar that it is? The human being on the threshold of awakening, the child at

[5] *Ibid.,* p. 617.

the onset of the night, finds itself face to face with "doubtful visions destroyed every minute," and confronted by things of which it is impossible to know "whether they are themselves and not others." Thus the child Proust, in the room that the projection of the magic lantern metamorphosized: "The mere change of lighting destroyed the customary impression I had formed of my room, thanks to which the room itself, but for the torture of having to go to bed in it, had become quite endurable. For now I no longer recognized it, and I became uneasy, as though I were in a room in some hotel or "chalet," in a place where I had just arrived for the first time. . . ."[6] It is a place one no longer recognizes, which therefore can be any other place, a place which has become doubtful, strange, anonymous; a place disconnected from its occupant, because nothing in it responds to the demand of his thought. Then, in the consciousness of the hostile refusal of things to put themselves in touch with the mind, the child Proust takes account of the depth of his solitude, and the anguish begins:

> Having no world, no room, no body now that was not menaced by the enemies thronging round, invaded to the very bones by fever, I was alone, I wanted to die.[7]

For the anguish of solitude is not only that of being detached from things and beings; it is being detached from fixity, from the permanence one would like to have beings and things possess and give us by return; it is to feel oneself betrayed, without any help from them, to the indeterminate power of thought, which ceaselessly imposes upon us metamorphoses, which perpetually changes us into another "self," and which every instant makes of us, and for us, a stranger.

Thence proceed those contractions and rebellions of the threatened parts of our whole selves "which we must recognize to be a secret, partial, tangible and true aspect of our resistance to death, of the long resistance, desperate and daily renewed, to a fragmentary and reiterated death such as interpolates itself through the whole course of our life . . . ."[8] successive deaths, more imminent, more reiterated, more total in proportion as a thought without content finds in itself no resource for establishing fixity and consistence.

The human being, for Proust, therefore, is a being who tries to find justification for his existence. Not knowing who he is, either he is like someone stricken with amnesia who goes from door to door asking people to tell him his name, or he feels himself to be what things indifferently become in him: a bundle of anonymous images that obliterate themselves and reform, like the iridescent spray from fountains of water. He is nothing or anything by turns, anything which is still

[6] *Ibid.*, p. 8.   [7] *Ibid.*, p. 506.   [8] *Ibid.*, p. 510.

nothing. Now this being who is nothing finds himself thrown into a moment lost in the midst of others, that is to say, a moment which resembles nothing and rests on nothing. And since this instant is inevitably going to be annihilated by another, he sees in this instant his own death, and he does not know whether he will be born again, or into what sort of being he will be reborn.

> I think each day is the last day of my existence.[9]

> All my effort has tended in the opposite way [from Maeterlinck's], not to consider death as a negation, for this is meaningless and contrary to all death makes us feel. It manifests itself in a terribly positive way.[10]

For to be dead, for Proust, is not simply to be no more; it is to be *another being*. Such is a man who after an illness is shocked to see that his hair has turned white.

> And when I realized that I felt no joy at the thought of her being alive, that I no longer loved her, I ought to have been more astounded than a person who, looking at his reflexion in the glass, after months of travel, or of sickness discovers that he has white hair and a different face, that of a middle aged or an old man. This appalls us because its message is: "the man that I was, the fair young man, no longer exists, I am another person." And yet, was not the impression that I now felt, the proof of as profound a change, as total a death of my former self and of the no less complete substitution of a new self for that former self, as is proved by the sight of a wrinkled face capped with a snowy poll instead of the face of long ago?[11]

What is death but to be different from oneself? The fear of death is not so much the fear of no longer feeling and no longer being conscious; it is the fear of no longer feeling that which one feels, and of no longer being conscious of that of which one is conscious. Yet such a death seems an ineluctable reality, not only at the end of total existence, but at the end of each of these tiny closed existences, of these "drops of time" which are each one of the moments of our life:

> . . . truly a death of ourselves, a death followed, it is true, by resurrection, but in a different ego, the life, the love of which are beyond the reach of those elements of the existing ego that are doomed to die.[12]

Condemned, then, to a fragmentary and successive death, not knowing whether he will come to life again or in whom he will come to life,

---

[9] *Lettre à Nathalie Clifford Barney*, N. C. Barney *Adventures de l'esprit*, p. 65.
[10] *Lettre à G. de Lauris, Revue de Paris*, June 15, 1938.
[11] *Remembrance of Things Past*, II, 833.   [12] *Ibid.*, I, 510.

Proust and Human Time   155

the human being such as Proust depicts is haunted by the anguish of this substitution of self for self which for him is death. Against this anguish he has only one recourse: to give himself the assurance of this survival; to believe that, beyond all this, one will be able to find *oneself again*. But it is impossible for this faith to assure him as to the future, since one cannot find there anything imaginable; since this future is the present of the monstrously inconceivable being into which death will have changed us. From this side, *from the side of the death to come*, the grave is insuperable. The future is closed by death; confronting the closed future, we are in anguish.

Free-floating anguish, indeterminate, "at the service one day of one feeling, the next day of another." But whether it presents itself under the form of the indefinable dejection into which the spectacle of a strange room throws us, or under the form of the anxiety of the child who waits in vain for the kiss of his mother before going to sleep, fundamentally this anguish is of a being who, finding himself in an existence which nothing, it seems, can justify, incapable of discovering for himself a reason for being, incapable at the same time of finding anything which guarantees the continuation of his being, experiences simultaneously horror of a future which changes him, contempt for a present which seems powerless to establish him, and the exclusive need of saving himself, come what may, from his cruel contingency by discovering in the past the basis of this being that he is, and yet that *he no longer is*.

For if it is impossible beforehand to burst open the precincts of death, is it not possible to do so, one might say, behindhand? If we are always *on this side* of our death to come, are we not always *on that side* of a death *already come*, a death beyond which lies our past life? Is there not then an act by which one might be able to rediscover himself and the basis of his existence?

This question is answered in the strange beginning of Proust's novel, where, with hardly an initial moment admitted, the thought gets underway and begins to march, but in reverse. A journey backwards, as if at the very moment the being discovers his existence, he experiences as well the need of sustaining rather than fulfilling it, of giving himself reasons for being rather than reasons for acting.

Proust's novel is the history of a search: that is to say a series of efforts to *find again* something that one has lost. It is the novel of an existence in search of its essence.

> One is no longer a person. How then, seeking for one's mind, one's personality, as one seeks for a thing that is lost, does one recover one's own self rather than any other? . . . What is it that guides us, when there has been an actual interruption . . . ? There has indeed been death, as when the heart has ceased to beat and a rhythmical friction of the tongue

revives us. . . . The resurrection at our awakening—after that healing attack of mental alienation which is sleep—must after all be similar to what occurs when we recapture a name, a line, a refrain that we had forgotten. And perhaps the resurrection of the soul after death is to be conceived as a phenomenon of memory.[13]

II

In Proustian thought memory plays the same supernatural role as grace in Christian thought. It is this inexplicable phenomenon that comes to apply itself to a fallen nature, irremediably separated from its origins, not to restore it integrally and at once to its first condition, but to give it the efficacy to find the highway of its salvation. Remembrance is a "succour from on high" which comes to the being in order "to draw him from the nothingness out of which, by himself, he would not have been able to emerge." Also it appears continually in the work of Proust under a form at once human and superhuman. It is at one and the same time an unforeseeable, "involuntary" thing that is added to the being, and the very act of this being, the most personal act because constitutive of the person. And, as there are some graces which fall on rich soil, and others on barren ground, some graces to which one responds and others which one ignores, so it is with memories. There are numerous examples in the work of Proust of these mysterious solicitations which a spirit distraught by its own ends fails to heed. More numerous still are those in which a debased memory finds itself reduced to being only a vassal of the intelligence or a sort of habit: grace corrupted, which then loses its efficacy and becomes a "frozen memory," a "memory of facts":

> . . . the memory of facts, which tells us: "You were such," without allowing us to become such again, which avers the reality of a lost paradise, instead of giving it back to us through remembrance.[14]

A memory no longer supernatural, a fallen memory by the will of which it is vain to hope to "re-establish ourselves in that state we were in," for we can do nothing by our own strength and our own will, and all depends from the first on supernatural chance.

But if it all depends from the first on this miraculous contingency, if it is this originally which is the first cause, it is not a unique cause; it calls for our collaboration; it exacts the maximum effort from us. The Proustian memory has often been identified with the affective memory of the psychologists. And—psychologically speaking—it is that without doubt: that is to say, a revival in us of a forgotten state of mind. Furthermore the very term *involuntary*, by which Proust qualifies

[13] *Ibid.*, p. 776.   [14] *Pastiches et mélanges*, p. 197.

it, seems to confirm this identification, since for the psychologist the affective memory is in the final analysis spontaneous and unforeseeable, the simple raising of old emotions up into the mind; a raising up in which the mind assists less as an actor than as a patient. But for Proust profound remembrance is not only that, something involuntarily undergone, but at its point of arrival in us something which is or which ought to be the point of departure for our spiritual action. It is an invitation, an appeal, which is addressed to all our being, and to which all our being ought to respond. It opens to us a road through the depths, but it is up to us to advance on that road. Paradise lost is returned to us if we wish it, but only if we wish it.

It is for that reason that there are in the Proustian novel so many examples of abortive memories and portions of the past ultimately lost. For that reason also there are many more memories which, brought to light, leave only, after the spectacle of their brief resurrection, the regret for a "paradise lost," lost for the second time. Just as for the Scholastics there was an infinity of degrees in the "perfection" of grace, so for Proust there is an infinity of degrees in the "perfection" of memory. But in his case each of these degrees is like that of one descending scale, and sometimes the being seems stopped at one level, sometimes a little lower, when what he seeks is away below. But most of the time "we lack the strength to penetrate to the very depths where truth lies, the real universe, our authentic impression."

Nothing could be more false than to consider Proust's novel a simple novel of the affective memory. That would be to confound it with the novels of Loti, each one of which—and from beginning to end—is a journal of such emotional encounters, mysterious wells, by which the soul should be able to penetrate to the depths of itself, but into which it is more often content simply to peer. And nothing could be more inexact than to make Proust the author of a purely psychological novel, in which everything is explained in the final analysis, as with Taine or Ribot, by the law of association of ideas. This would be to confound him with a writer of fiction like Bourget, who, moreover, wrote novels whose entire plots are articulated about a central phenomenon of affective memory.

From this point of view the most famous of all the passages of Proust, the episode of the *madeleine,* ought not at all to seem to us to have exhausted the meaning of the novel. It contains it without doubt, but it does not reveal it. Or rather, if it reveals something of it, it is precisely that the whole mystery lies beyond the psychological explanation of it: "I still did not know and must long postpone the discovery of *why* the memory made me happy."

The real significance of the episode of the *madeleine* resides entirely in precisely this: that it gives us a moment of happiness. To the unhappy instant with which the book began there now succeeds a happy instant, as if the grace of memory consisted in exchanging the one for the other. In the moment of awakening one sees the hero discover a nocturnal world, anguished, in which he knows neither who he is nor whether things are as they seem; in the moment of remembrance we watch him find himself in diurnal life, in the broad daylight of a Sunday morning of his childhood, surrounded by customary things, in a familiar time and place: "Everything that took *form and solidity* had sprung, town and gardens, from my cup of tea."

Form and solidity. If it is true then that remembrance is an exchange, it is also true that the moment exchanged has no longer the tragic inconsistency of what it replaces. It is a moment in which things have a form, in which they are solid, in which one knows what they are as well as one knows who one is. And it is such a moment because it represents this daily face of the life of childhood, his *face of the sun*, in which things in full light offer their form and solidity to a being who addresses toward them his desire and his faith. Deep remembrance is only the return of a deep impression. Now if it appears to us so beautiful, if its return makes us so happy, that is because it expresses between the being who feels and the object felt a spontaneous accord in which the desire of the one meets with the solidity of the other; as if the external world were now precisely what we would desire it to be:

> For a desire seems to us more beautiful, we repose on it with more confidence, when we know that outside ourselves there is a reality which conforms to it, even if, for us, it is not to be realized.[15]

If reality conforms to it, then and only then, we can *believe in it* and not simply feel it. Thus the deep impressions are not merely impressions we are content to submit to, even in a repetitive fashion, but experiences in which we add something to what they bring us, namely the adherence of our *complete being*, that is to say, our love. Such a desire is experienced by Marcel for the milk-seller who passes along the length of the train:

> She passed down the line of windows, offering coffee and milk to a few awakened passengers. Reddened with the glow of morning, her face was rosier than the sky. I felt in her presence that desire to live which is reborn in us whenever we become conscious anew of beauty and happiness. . . . Alien to the models of beauty which my fancy was wont to sketch when I was by myself, this strapping girl gave me at once the sensation of a certain happiness (the sole form, always individual, in which we may learn the sensation of happiness), of a happiness that would be realized by my staying by her side. . . . I was giving the milk-girl the benefit of what was really my own entire being, ready to taste the keenest joys . . . .[16]

[15] *Remembrance of Things Past,* I, 539.   [16] *Ibid.*, p. 498.

When we are young, at the age I had reached at the period of my walks along the Méséglise way, our desires, our faith bestow on a woman's clothing an individual personality, an irreducible essence.[17]

Desire and belief: terms almost interchangeable which express the two aspects of the same activity, an activity of all one's being. For just as the perfection of memory demands the conjunction of a given object and an effort of the mind, so that which is discovered deeper than memory, the primitive impression, contains for us a given object and a movement on our part to seize it. A movement which, insofar as it issues from the being, is called *desire,* and which insofar as it applies itself to and rests in the object is called *faith.*

In the depths of being, then, what comes to light is a moment of the past which is exactly the inverse of the present moment of awakening: a moment when, instead of being separated from things, and of not being sure whether they are themselves or other things, one is sure they are different from all others; and that because one now has the power to bind oneself to them, to confer upon them an individual particularity, an irreducible essence:

> Moreover—just as in moments of musing contemplation of nature, the normal actions of the mind being suspended, and our abstract ideas of things set on one side, we believe with profound faith in the originality, in the individual existence of the place in which we may happen to be—the passing figure which my desire evoked seemed to be not any one example of the general type of "woman," but a necessary and natural product of the soil. For at that time everything which was not myself, the earth and the creatures upon it, seemed to me more precious, more important, endowed with a more real existence than they appear to full-grown men. And between the earth and its creatures I made no distinction.[18]

If the primitive impression, then, is worthy of *faith,* that is because it involves a *moment* and a *place;* and not, as with the being of awakening, a moment which can be any moment, a place that can be any place; but a moment so well defined in time and space that it cannot be confounded with any other, and of so great an authenticity that we cannot doubt it. Extreme depth where truth lies, little universe having its own particular time and place in which our *authentic impression* rediscovers itself in its lost reality, thanks to memory:

> What I had long lost, the feeling which makes us not merely regard a thing as a spectacle, but believe in it as in a creature without parallel . . . .[19]

[17] *Ibid.,* p. 994.   [18] *Ibid.,* p. 146.   [19] *Ibid.,* p. 50.

What was lost and what is found is not just time, but a fragment of time to which clings a fragment of space; and in the interior of this small universe, the self, the individual is indivisibly bound by its faith and its desire to this moment of time and to this point in space. From a feeling of existence detached from times and places, the being finds himself brought back by deep remembrance to a first feeling, truly original, constituent of himself and of the world, the act of faith by which the sentient being adheres instantaneously, locally, to sensible reality.

In bringing us back thus, across the past, to a primitive impression, Proust reminds us of Condillac: "The only means of acquiring knowledge," Condillac says, "is to go back to the origin of our ideas, to follow the generation of them, and to compare them . . . ." But if Proust goes back to the origin, it is not by analysis and a taking of things apart, but by a synthetic intuition—remembrance—because it is not for him a question of arriving at a simple entity, but at a primitive complex which analysis would irremediably lose.

It is rather to Rousseau that he must be compared. For the one, as for the other, at bottom, at the origin, there is a natural identity between the feeling self and the thing felt. But with Rousseau identity is posed simply as such; with Proust, on the contrary, it appears as proposed rather than given; it must be achieved in a movement of the self toward the object and culminate in belief:

> For this is the point to which we must always return, to these beliefs with which most of the time we are quite unconsciously filled, but which for all that are of more importance to our happiness than is the average person whom we see, for it is through them that we see him, it is they that impart his transitory grandeur to the person seen.[20]

Only a transitory grandeur, to be sure, as happens with all correspondences between him who regards and that which is regarded; but an imperishable grandeur as well, because the object thus transfigured by belief, detached by the very fact of the general motion of things and the flux of duration, leaves upon the mind of him who *believed in it* an indelible image. The image *will be found again*. In the midst of a magic-lantern world, a vacillating unreal world made of "doubtful visions" in which one cannot believe, the awakened sleeper, if he remembers, will find once more in the depths of his memory, in his first impressions, this *passing grandeur* which an act of childlike faith has fixed in him forever.

[20] *Ibid.*, p. 708.

III

The scent of hawthorn which strays plundering along the hedge from which, in a little while, the dog-roses will have banished it, a sound of footsteps followed by no echo, upon the gravel path, a bubble formed at the side of a waterplant by the current, and formed only to burst—my exaltation of mind has borne them with it, and has succeeded in making them traverse all these successive years, while all around them the once-trodden ways have vanished, while those who trod them, and even the memory of those who trod them, are dead. Sometimes the fragment of landscape thus transported into the present will detach itself in such isolation from all associations that it floats uncertainly upon my mind, like a flowering isle of Delos, and I am unable to say from what place, from what time—perhaps, quite simply, from which of my dreams—it comes. But it is pre-eminently as the deepest layer of my mental soil, as firm sites on which I still may build, that I regard the Méséglise and Guermantes "ways." It is because I used to think of certain things, of certain people, while I was roaming along them, that the things, the people which they taught me to know, and these alone, I still take seriously, still give me joy. Whether it be that the faith which creates has ceased to exist in me, or that reality will take shape in memory alone, the flowers that people show nowadays for the first time never seem to me to be true flowers.[21]

In this sort of nothingness or of night, which extends behind him, deep down within him, and which is called the past, the being in search of himself has now discovered certain luminous points isolated; pieces of landscape, fragments of his former life which survive the destruction of all the rest. Behind him is no longer total nothingness but a starlighted nothingness. Doubtless because of their isolation, their remoteness, these vestiges of the past appear today to be without force. Nevertheless, as in the astrology of the Middle Ages, it is owing to them alone and to their influence that the living being can hope for the support of his own personality and for the power to confer some reality upon the world which offers itself to his eyes today. For he no longer possesses the efficacy of belief and desire to adhere strongly to things. He has "ceased to believe in the truth of the desires directed outside of himself" which he continues to form.

Without renouncing these desires, he has ceased to think them realizable. He has no more hope in the future, and he no longer enjoys the present. From the time of his youth, Proust verified this detachment from desire and this drying up of faith:

> Even the disinterested joys of hope are not left any more to us. Hope is an act of faith. We have undeceived its credulousness; it is dead.

[21] *Ibid.*, p. 141.

> After having renounced enjoyment, we cannot any more be enchanted with hope. To hope without hope, which would be wise, is impossible.[22]

And later, in a letter to Princess Bibesco:

> Alexander is right when he says that to cease hoping is despair itself. But though I never cease to desire, I never hope. Perhaps also the great austerity of my life, without journeys, without walks, without company, without sunlight, is a contingency which renews in me the perenniality of desire.[23]

Perennial desire, but without hope in the future as without faith in the present. Proustian desire, then, can *hope,* hope to find an object of faith, only in looking backwards. He comes to "hope without hope," wisdom of the impossible. As in the Kierkegaardian repetition, Proust ends by no longer placing hope in anything except the past. And what can he hope from the past except to be re-established in his faith?

This restoration of faith is memory—ephemeral faith, doubtless, and one which lasts for him only for the instant in which he remembers; *but* for as long as it does last, the being who remembers finds he has become once more a being who once had faith. The immense force, the living force of these small luminous fires he has rediscovered, rises from the depths of an obscure firmament where their rays reside and lengthen, extending their splendor and warmth into the present moment. It is in them alone that he can hope for a reality and a resting place. The being is sustained, from underneath, by a faith he no longer possesses. There is a sort of continued creation of himself, of the being one is by the being one has been, of the moment in which one recollects by the moment that one recollects; the Proustian existence is an existence which always risks destruction or decay, unless it be supported and ravished by the grace of memory.

> ... We do not believe in the beauty of life because we do not remember it, but if perchance we smell an old fragrance, we feel elated; likewise we think we no longer love the dead, but this is because we do not remember them; if once again we see an old glove, we dissolve in tears, upheld by a grace or a flower stalk of remembrance.[24]

Like Christian grace, Proustian reminiscence is truly represented under the form of a *flower stalk,* but the essential point is that here the action of this support is exerted not from top to bottom but from bottom to top. That is the reason Proust employs the expression *basement (soubassement)* and *deep layer (gisement profond),* and also

[22] *Les Plaisirs et les jours,* p. 232.
[23] *Cahiers Marcel Proust,* No. 4, p. 119.
[24] *Lettres à René Blum, Bernard Grasset, Louis Brun,* p. 61.

supporting terrains on which one has to lean (terrains résistants sur lesquels on s'appuie). In the Proustian world, it is not God, it is simply the past which confers on the present its authentic existence. It is *the already lived* that saves *the living;* otherwise it would fall into the insignificance of oblivion, even before being *lived.*

But in order for this past to be indeed the continuer of the self and the founder of an authentic present, in order for it to be the source of our restored faith, will it not seem necessary that *in its time* it had been invested by us with the power which it now exerts over us? It seems that only the memory of a moment of faith can create a new moment of faith. Or should, then, the being who remembers find himself forced to go back from memory to memory in search of a creative moment, as philosophy strove to proceed from cause to cause until it reached a creative cause?

Let us recall, however, the alternative formulated by Proust in the citation which opens this chapter: "Whether it be that the faith which creates dries up in me, or whether it be that reality forms itself only in memory . . . ." Alongside the moment of primal faith there would be then another source of present reality, a source that cannot be assigned either to the single original moment or to the single actual moment, but that would be found *between the two,* in the memory:

> We make little use of our experience, we leave unachieved in the summer dusk or the precocious nights of winter the hours in which it had seemed to us that there might nevertheless be contained some element of tranquility or pleasure. But those hours are not altogether lost. When, in their turn, come and sing to us fresh moments of pleasure which by themselves would pass by equally slender and linear, the others bring to them the groundwork, the solid consistency of a rich orchestration.[25]

Moments unachieved in their time, slender and linear, which seemed, however, to give the present a consistence, a reality that they themselves did not possess.

But if this is so—and it is so throughout the Proustian novel—the preceding theory becomes, if not false, at least insufficient. It is not necessarily in a moment of early faith that the being finds his creative foundation, since memory can join to a slender present an unachieved past, and their conjunction can bring to birth something that is achieved and that is consistent.

On the other hand, there would no longer be only certain privileged moments of the past which could have the chance of being saved from oblivion. Any moment could be regained, or better, brought to significance. There is no sensation, puny as it may be, which has not a chance to see the light again and find its completion in the present;

---

[25] *Remembrance of Things Past,* I, 1002.

as if, the interval of years being nothing, or equal simply to a brief distraction of the mind, this could, almost without solution of continuity, reassume the impression it had formerly left and bring to it now the complement it lacked.

But what is the nature of the complement? Assuredly it is not at all a question here of affective memory, but of an act authentically new by which the mind operates upon remembrance, as earlier, in infancy, it operated upon the first impression. One might call it an act of faith indefinitely retarded, then tardily accomplished; as if the reality regained in memory appeared richer in import, worthier of faith than it was lately in sensation. This is the invariable experience the Proustian novel gives us. For the adult being, there is something incurably imperfect in the present, something impure in exterior perception, which leaves the perceiver indifferent and incapable of believing in it; but let this present become past, let this perception become memory, and immediately, with the same energy as the child in its act of faith, the adult adheres to this memory.

Faith centers in an impression that is immediate, or regained, or completed. Proustian thought always inevitably returns to the mystery of the relation between an object and a consciousness. It all comes finally to this question: how can an exterior object be transmuted into this interior and immaterial thing, as intimate to us as ourselves, in which the mind freely plunges, moves, takes delight and life?

But in immediate impression we know how rare and difficult this spiritualization of the object can be. The object is the thing which is there. Flower, tree, or church, steeples of Martinville or bushes of hawthorn, the thing is there, outside, in its existence as thing. To look at it is to feel oneself joined to it only by a sensation which attests less its reality than its absolute otherness. How shall we penetrate it or draw it into ourselves when we have no affinity with it other than a sensation which we are well enough able to intensify and to repeat but not to transcend? And yet already this very sensation invites us to do so. It gives us the further presentiment of something it does not communicate to us, but of which it makes us divine the existence. It prompts our desire. We feel confusedly called to discover in a prolongation of sensation we know not what secret:

> . . . Suddenly a roof, a gleam of sunlight reflected from a stone, the smell of a road would make me stop still, to enjoy the special pleasure that each of them gave me, and also because they appeared to be concealing, beneath what my eyes could see, something which they invited me to approach and seize from them, but which, despite all my efforts, I never managed to discover.[26]

[26] *Ibid.*, p. 137.

Proust and Human Time

It is the same in one of the most famous passages of the novel, the episode of the hawthorns. Before the flowering hawthorns the child on his walk experiences in the contact of the sensation the same feeling of pleasure and expectation. But this time, twice over, and in two quite distinct fashions, the sentient being leaps over the frontier of what is felt, and, going on beyond the sensation, penetrates into the mysterious intimacy of the object. The first occasion is when, in the exaltation into which the beauty of the flowering bush throws him, he is no longer content to feel this beauty; he tries unconsciously to reproduce it in himself:

> Higher up their corollas were opening, keeping around them so negligently, like a last vaporous garment, the nosegay of stamens which so entirely enveloped them with the mist, that when I tried to mime in the depths of my mind the gesture of their efflorescence, I fancied it, without being aware of the process, the flighty motions of a thoughtless and vivacious young girl.[27]

Marvelous image, and so significant that Proust takes and uses it for the title of one part of his novel: *A l'ombre des jeunes filles en fleur*. For the meaning of this image does not consist simply in its exactitude, in the felicity with which it translates what it describes; but also in the visible motion of the mind which brings it to its existence and its perfection of image. It seems here that one comes upon the spiritual operation ordinarily the most hidden, even from the eyes of him who performs it: the operation by which, *in miming within his own depths the exterior gesture of the sensible object*, one *imagines*, one creates something which is still the object of sense, but this time no longer outside: rather, it is on the inside, no longer strange and impenetrable, but recognizable, identifiable: for this thing comes of us; it is us.

It seems that here we are assisting at the very genesis of an image: an image so perfect that surely the mind has, in this moment, accomplished the task incumbent upon it, even without clearly perceiving its nature. It has accomplished it, not without effort, but without realization, almost inadvertently; and not having recognized that it has found what it sought, it continues to search.

It is then that the second spiritual operation is accomplished. While the child remains in contemplation before the flowers, someone calls him and shows him a little farther on some other hawthorns, but this time of a different color, no longer white but pink:

> Then, inspiring me with that rapture which we feel on seeing a work by our favorite painter quite different from those that we already know, or,

---
[27] *Chroniques*, p. 93.

better still, when someone has taken us and set us down in front of a picture of which we have hitherto seen no more than a pencilled sketch, or when a piece of music which we have heard played over on the piano bursts out again in our ears with all the splendour and fullness of an orchestra, my grandfather called me to him, and, pointing to the hedge of Tansonville, said: "You are fond of hawthorns; just look at this pink one; isn't it pretty!" And it was indeed a hawthorn, but one whose flowers were pink, and lovelier even than the white.[28]

Between the instant in which the child sees the white flowers and the one in which he catches sight of the pink, there is, so to speak, no transition; nevertheless, the first is the moment of a past sensation, and the other of a present sensation. The one achieves and crowns the other; it is not the repetition but the transfiguration of it. Hence the child's joy, a joy of a very particular kind, and one which the Proustian character experiences continually in the course of the novel. It is the joy of Swann, finding again in the visage of a servant the traits of a person contemplated some time before; that of Marcel in discovering in the Septuor of Vinteuil the little phrase of the Sonata. It is the joy that one always feels when one perceives under the variations of a "common type" a "same palpable quality," when one *recognizes* in what he feels something he recalls having felt before. To recognize is to identify; and to identify is to find an equivalent between what is there, outside, and on the other hand what is here, inside, within ourselves, since it is *our* memory.

In the passage on the hawthorns Proust indicated the two ways of going beyond the external object: sometimes by a direct effort which in making us mime interiorly the motion of the object gives us the "spiritual equivalent" of it—and it is an act of pure imagination; and sometimes by finding and recognizing this same equivalence in the depths of ourselves—and this is the peculiar act of memory.

"All impression," says Proust, "is double: half enveloped in the object, and half produced in ourself . . . ." But usually we pay attention only to the exterior part of the impression, which teaches us nothing of its nature or of ourselves. But when by an act of the imagination or of memory we extricate this interior part which is truly ours, then this "pure and disincarnate" essence withdraws from the exterior object, and also then from the ensemble of temporal contingencies in which its place is assigned as in a series; it no longer appears a determination of things, but as a free production of our mind. For the act of imagination or of memory is nothing other than that: to oppose to the exterior perception an image which might be our own creation; to raise up the impression into an expression; to find the *metaphor*. Such is the spiritual effort every tangible object demands of us.

[28] *Remembrance of Things Past*, I, 107.

We hear this immediate and urgent demand every moment of our lives, but nearly always we prefer easier tasks. It now and then happens, however, that in renouncing for some banal occupation this duty which present sensation incessantly proposes to us, we experience a kind of remorse, the remorse of having at the same time renounced ourselves, of having failed to bring to the light of day this being which is us, and which only exists and is recognized in the creative act of the making of images. Thus, when, on a road near Balbec, Proust withdraws from the three trees that have addressed him in vain with one of those mysterious solicitations, he seems to hear them say:

> "If you allow us to drop back into the hollow of this road from which we sought to raise ourselves up to you, a whole part of yourself which we were bringing to you, will fall forever into the abyss." [29]

Again, when in *Les Plaisirs et les jours* a poet who was giving a banquet refuses to extend hospitality to a stranger passing by because this wayfarer enjoined the dismissal of all the other guests, he sees the stranger withdraw saying:

> "You will see me no more. Yet you owed me more than you owed to the others who presently will desert you. I am in you, yet forever I am far from you, I am almost no more. I am your soul, I am you." [30]

Thus, almost always we allow a part of ourselves to be removed or to fall into nothingness: precisely that part of us which should have been created or recreated in the present moment. It is *given* us that we may make of it our substance. But we almost never do so, and for not having done so we lose our present existence.

On the other hand, we may also happen to lose it for the contrary reason: not because we have neglected sensation, but because we have allowed ourselves to be absorbed by it. So it is in the state of drunkenness:

> ... The alcohol that I had drunk, by unduly straining my nerves, gave to the minutes as they came a quality, a charm which did not have the result of leaving me more ready, or indeed more resolute to defend them; for while it made me prefer them a thousand times to anything else in my life, my exaltation made me isolate them from everything else; I was confined to the present, as heroes are, or drunkards; eclipsed for the moment, my past no longer projected before me that shadow of itself which we call our future; placing the goal of my life no longer in the realization of the dreams of that past, but in the felicity of the present

[29] *Ibid.*, p. 545.
[30] *Les Plaisirs et les jours*, p. 210.

moment, I could see nothing now of what lay beyond it. . . . I was glued to my immediate sensation . . . .[31]

Glued, that is to say, making a lump with the thing felt. Then it alone exists without possibility of equivalence. Its presence abolishes all the rest. There is no longer any past, no longer any future, no longer even that sort of distance which in the interior of the moment the mind tries to establish between the sensation it experiences and the act by which it is conscious. The sentient subject has become what he feels. He has excluded himself from himself. Outward, in the object, he lives an intense, euphoric, but entirely passive life. Instead of transcending the object, he is engulfed in it.

State of pure passion, of brute sensation, which is the very opposite of the creative activity by which the imagination re-invents the object in the self.

Whether it adheres too closely to the tangible object, or whether on the contrary it neglects it, Proustian thought succeeds very rarely in finding at once the metaphoric equivalent. In contrast to Hugo or Rimbaud, Proust hardly ever finds, on the spot, a corresponding image. Or, let us say, the image does not seem chosen by him with this characteristic of sovereign liberty which is precisely the property of invention. It sometimes happens, however, that, in a certain state of mind, confronted by such and such a sensation, the Proustian being somehow spontaneously forms the equivalent image. Thus Swann, in love with Odette, hears the Little Phrase of Vinteuil's sonata, and as this little phrase has the effect of effacing his anxiety over material interests and so of creating in his soul a sort of margin, he finds himself *free* to inscribe upon it the name of his love.

Now this margin is precisely what time and forgetfulness produce in us. Between the reborn memory and the being we now are, before recognition, before the identification of the one by the other which memory achieves, there is this: the consciousness of a margin, a distance; and this margin appears in the interior region where one has ordinarily the feeling of being determined by causes or series of causes, of being the prisoner of time:

> . . . Between our present state and the memory that suddenly comes back to us . . . there is such a wide distance that that fact alone, regardless even of any specific individuality, would suffice to make comparison between them impossible. Yet, if, thanks to our ability to forget, a past recollection has been able to avoid any tie, any link with the present moment, if it has kept its distance, its isolation in the depths of a valley or on the tip of a mountain peak, it suddenly brings us a breath of fresh air—refreshing just because we have breathed it once before—of that

[31] *Remembrance of Things Past*, I, 614.

purer air . . . which could not convey that profound sensation of renewal if it had not already been breathed; for the only true paradise is always the paradise we have lost.[32]

A single minute released from the chronological order of time has recreated in us the human being similarly released, in order that he may sense that minute.[33]

Because the sensation which comes back to us, and from so great a distance, is not bound to the temporal motion which actually sweeps us along, we find ourselves for an instant detached from this current. We cease "to feel mediocre, contingent, mortal"; we feel *free:* free to determine ourselves; free to recognize ourselves in what we were; free to establish the metaphoric relationship between our past and our present.

Sometimes, however, this relationship remains merely an outline within us. Memory, then, appears to be no more than a kind of negative; beyond the feeling of this margin which is created within us, we simply know that there is something we are unable to read. Of past and present only the latter shows itself clearly upon the field of consciousness, and yet between the two one still feels there is already an invisible affinity formed which one would like to be able to identify. Such is the phenomenon of the *already seen* that one finds in every degree in the work of Proust. Sometimes the mind experiences it in the vaguest degree, and then it wonders and worries, searching vainly within itself for a corresponding image.

Sometimes the mind, in approaching from a new angle a world once upon a time familiar, discovers the known in the unknown, and, after a moment of hesitation, sees surge unexpected and assuaging from the depths of memory the sensory equivalent. And then sometimes at the call of the present object it seems to spring complete, without effort, as if the silent work of memory had been precisely to prepare for this meeting, and then the sole duty of the mind is to *recognize* this identity of the past and the actual, and to recognize itself within it:

> The concert began. I did not know what they were playing, I found myself in a strange land. Where was I to locate it? Into what composer's country had I come? I should have been glad to know, and seeing nobody near me whom I might question, I should have liked to be a character in those *Arabian Nights* which I never tired of reading and in which, in moments of uncertainty, there arose a genie or a maiden of ravishing beauty, invisible to every one else but not to the embarrassed hero to whom she reveals exactly what he wishes to learn. Well, at this very moment, I was favoured with precisely such a magical apparition. As, in a stretch of country which we suppose to be strange to us and which as a matter of fact we have approached from a new angle, when after

[32] *Ibid.*, II, 994.   [33] *Ibid.*, p. 996.

turning out of one road we find ourselves emerging suddenly upon another every inch of which is familiar . . . so, all of a sudden, I found myself in the midst of this music that was novel to me, right in the heart of Vinteuil's sonata.[34]

Now to recognize oneself in a place, in a piece of music, in a sensation, is more than to regain this sensation; it is to rediscover there one's own being. A passive memory has no more meaning than a brute sensation for Proust. Neither the one nor the other has anything to communicate except its obscure sensible reality. Neither the one nor the other by itself can raise the being to the expression of what it really is. The thought in search of itself glides over the sensation as over a smooth and impenetrable surface. It cannot rest there any more than it can found itself on an abstract memory of what it once was. For what has one been except what one has felt, and how shall there be any recognition unless one feels it anew? Perhaps the greatest difficulty of the Proustian enterprise consists in the fact that for him knowledge can never cease to remain impression. It is possible to know only that which can once more become immediately contemporaneous to the heart. Now "knowledge in these matters being intermittent and incapable of surviving the effective presence of feeling," the result is that for Proustian thought the *knowing* as well as the *being* finds itself bound to a world essentially ephemeral and intermittent, the very affective or emotional world in which Maine de Biran had given up trying to find permanence and identities. It seems that the mind is caught in a dilemma: either of knowing nothing but what it feels, or of recalling it has felt without recalling how it has felt. In both cases it is condemned never to attain its being.

The only cognition of self that is possible, then, is re-cognition. When at the call of present sensation past sensation resurges, the relationship established lays the foundation of the self because it lays the foundation of its own cognition. The being one recognizes as having lived becomes the basis of the being one feels to be alive. The veritable being, the essential being, is he whom one recognizes, not in the past, nor in the present, but in the rapport which binds past and present together, that is to say *between the two:*

> . . . The person within me who was at that moment enjoying this impression enjoyed in it the qualities it possessed which were common to both an earlier day and the present moment, qualities which were independent of all considerations of time; and this person came into play only when, by this process of identifying the past with the present, he could find himself in the only environment in which he could live and enjoy the essence of things, that is to say, outside time.[35]

[34] *Ibid.,* p. 553.   [35] *Ibid.,* p. 995.

At this point the dialectic of being ends in Proust. One sees the whole length of the road it has traveled. Emerging from sleep, the awakened sleeper was first discovered empty of his past, without content, without connection with vacillating sensations, himself metamorphosable, unknowable, plaything of time and death. Then, by the grace of profound remembrance, certain impressions of a totally different species surged up within him. These seemed to affirm the existence of a world of specific things, and to each of these things there was attached the action of a being who put his faith in them, and who found his reality in this act. But this being was infinitely remote; he re-found himself only after an intermittent and fortuitous fashion. His strength of faith, the source of his true existence, was exhausted. He was the being that had been; he was also the being that was no longer.

Now besides these rare reviviscences of a being forever vanished, others are discovered, less total but more numerous, more frequent, each one bringing to light a former sensation. Between this regained sensation and the present sensation there is established a relationship of the same nature as that between the faith of the child and the object of his belief; and from this metaphoric relationship between two impressions there has finally surged up the self; not a present self, without content, at the disposal of time and death; and not a past self, lost, and hardly retrievable; but an essential self, liberated from time and contingency, a primal and perpetual being, the creator of itself, the author of an "eternal song immediately recognized":

> ... that peculiar strain, the monotony of which—for whatever its subject it remains identical in itself—proves the permanence of the elements that compose his soul.[36]

It is thus that, leaving the moment and having made an immense voyage across lost time, the existence traveling in search of its essence finds it in timelessness.

IV

The Proustian novel began with a moment *empty of all content*. It completes itself in a series of other moments as different from the first as can be, since they contain "certain impressions veritably *full*, those which are outside of time." Nevertheless the quest of the novel is still not entirely accomplished. Embarked upon the search for lost time, the Proustian being has found two things: certain moments; and a kind of eternity. But he has not regained time itself. Doubtless in a certain measure he has conquered time:

[36] *Ibid.*, II, 559.

... A profound idea which succeeded in enclosing within itself space and time, is not any more submitted to their tyranny and cannot perish.[37]

But if, thanks to the metaphoric operation of memory, the mind has escaped the tyranny of time as well as of space, the time and space that it has enclosed in this profound idea are only the time and space of a moment recaptured. A moment, it is true, of an extraordinary profusion and one which, as in Baudelaire, seems to be due to a power of infinite expansion: "An hour is not merely an hour. It is a vase filled with perfumes, sounds, plans and climates." [38] But this vase is similar to those spoken of in the *Thousand and One Nights,* which Proust made one of his favorite reading: when one uncorks them, a genie floats out capable of condensing or dilating itself indefinitely. Each moment is one of these vases, and each moment has its distinct genie:

... The most insignificant gesture, the simplest act remains enclosed, as it were, in a thousand sealed jars, each filled with things of an absolutely different colour, odour and temperature. Furthermore, these jars, ranged along all levels of our bygone years—years during which we have been constantly changing, if only in our dreams and thoughts—stand at different altitudes and give us the impression of strangely varied atmospheres.[39]

Closed vases, walling in their particular and mutually exclusive qualities, the diverse moments of time are like places in space which cannot be simultaneously traveled:

... The habit we had of never going both ways on the same day, or in the course of the same walk, but the "Méséglise way" one time and the "Guermantes way" another, shut them up, so to speak, far apart and unaware of each other's existence, in the sealed vessels—between which there could be no communication—of separate afternoons.[40]

"Imprisoned in the cell of distinct days," regained moments are then not a true duration but, so to speak, atoms of full time, swimming far from each other in a sort of open, empty time, a nothingness of oblivion. From there, intermittently, their fires flash upon us.

Thus nothing is more false than to compare Proustian duration to Bergsonian duration. The latter is full, the former empty; the latter is a continuity, the former a discontinuity:

... We live over our past years not in their continuous sequence, day by day, but in a memory that fastens upon the coolness or sun-parched heat of some morning or afternoon, receiving the shadow of some solitary place, enclosed, immovable, arrested, lost, remote from all others ....[41]

[37] *Chroniques,* p. 186.   [38] *Remembrance of Things Past,* II, 1108.
[39] *Ibid.,* p. 994.   [40] *Ibid.,* I, 104.   [41] *Ibid.,* p. 1003.

What we suppose to be our love, our jealousy, are, neither of them, single, continuous and individual passions. They are composed of an infinity of successive loves, of different jealousies, each of which is ephemeral, although by their uninterrupted multitude they give us the impression of continuity, the illusion of unity.[42]

Nothing could be less Bergsonian than these passages. Far from being as Bergson wished it, a *"continuité mélodique,"* human duration in Proust's eyes is a simple plurality of isolated moments, remote from each other. But, as Proust himself remarked, the difference in nature between these two durations necessarily entails an equal difference in the ways by which the mind must proceed to explore them. It is as an easy and gentle gliding backwards that Bergson conceives the search for lost time. Loosening itself in the course of a reverie, the mind allows itself insensibly to be merged into a past whose liquid and dense substance never stops pressing in gently from all sides. For Proust, on the contrary, the exploration of the past seems at the outset so tremendously difficult of achievement that it requires nothing less than the intervention of a special grace and the maximum effort on the part of him who is the subject. Thus aided, thought must first pierce or dissipate that whole zone of deceitful appearances which is the time of the intelligence and of the habits, chronological time, in which conventional memory disposes all that it thinks to conserve, in a rectilinear order that masks in each case its nonentity; then, having dispersed these phantoms, it must face the true nothingness, that of oblivion:

Memory . . . nothingness out of which, from time to time, a similitude lets us draw, resuscitated, dead remembrances.

"Immense patches of oblivion," negative time, pure absence, place of nonbeing, whose sight brings vertigo, and across whose emptiness, in order to land upon some lost island, one must leap.

Time vertiginously traveled, time of a fall. With no intermediary stage, the being fallen from the present moment is in time past. Nevertheless, the being that has traveled these spaces with such lightning speed has felt the depths of them:

I can measure the resistance, I can hear the echo of great spaces traversed . . . .[43]

. . . resisting softness of this interposed atmosphere which has the same expanse as our life and which is the whole poetry of memory.[44]

In discovering the strange time-mutation which in a flash it has achieved, the mind measures "the abyss of the difference in altitude." And

[42] *Ibid.*, p. 285.   [43] *Ibid.*, p. 35.   [44] *Pastiches et mélanges*, p. 108.

the consciousness of this temporal distance, the contrast of epochs at once linked and separated from each other by all this emptiness, finally and especially the feeling that between them there is established something analogous to spatial perspective, all that ends by transforming this negative time, this pure nonbeing, into a palpable appearance, and into a dimension:

> This dimension of Time . . . I would try to make continually perceptible in a transcription of human life necessarily very different from that conveyed by our deceptive senses.[45]

Thus, little by little, Proustian time is constructed into an entity at once spiritual and tangible, made of relations of moments which are infinitely remote from each other but which, nevertheless, in spite of their isolation and their fragmentary character, stud with their presences the depth of temporal space and render it visible by their shining multiplicity.

Already more concrete than vacant time, another form of time now appears which is constituted by the incoherent and diverse ensemble of all the moments the mind remembers. For the being who recollects himself does not discover his life in the form of a continuous thread along which one passes insensibly from the similar to the dissimilar; but on the contrary one discovers it under the aspect of a perpetual and radical dissimilarity of all the elements composing it. Life which is not a life, time which is hardly a time: "simple collection of moments," each of which occupies a particular and variable position with respect to all the others, in such a way that in this time of plurality the problem consists in constantly trying to reunite these universes, these modes of feeling, and of living so mutually exclusive. Moreover, like the stars in the sky, these universes do not remain immobile, fixed in a static order, by aid of which one could construct a chronology. They disappear and reappear. Sometimes they seem monstrously remote, sometimes miraculously near. A vast, essentially erratic motion, the activity of memory, guides them along paths it is impossible for the mind to determine.

Thus time appears to the eyes of Proust as a thing of exclusions and resurrections, of fragments and spaces between fragments, of eclipses and anachronisms; a time fundamentally anarchic and, since to regain it at one point is not to regain it at another, a time *unregainable,* perhaps permanently lost to the mind.

As early as the period of *Les Plaisirs et les jours* Proust had already given an expression to this feeling of spiritual powerlessness which among all our thoughts that of time makes us most painfully experience:

---

[45] *Remembrance of Things Past,* II, 1121.

His only sorrow was not to be able to reach immediately all the sites which were disposed here and there, far from him, in the infinity of his own perspective.[46]

And yet is it not with concrete time as with concrete places? If space also, at first—just as erroneously as time—is taken for a continuum whose simultaneous spread seems to be easily understandable, does it not reveal itself later on as a plurality of *aspects* which are mutually exclusive? Space then would be really only an ensemble of points of view each of which could be discovered only in its turn amidst successive perspectives. And yet does not its real signification consist in the totality of these perspectives, as in those cubist paintings in which the painter tries to give at one and the same time all those aspects of an object which one could ordinarily discover in it only by viewing it turn by turn from different angles? And is it not properly the role of time to surmount this reciprocal exclusiveness of points of view which is the property of space? The spires of Martinville, for example, appearing first in front of an immobile spectator, in the depth of an immutable perspective, grant an aspect only "episodic and momentary"; but when they find themselves engaged by the displacement of the spectator in an inverse motion, they enter, by the simple, successive changing of their lines, into an entirely different universe; a universe that is no longer one in which the three dimensions of space compose an episodic and momentary totality, but a universe in which the fourth dimension, that of time, divests the object of all that is episodic and momentary in order to bestow *all* of its aspects upon a spectator moving at once in space and in time. Thus this sunrise perceived through the windows of a moving train:

> . . . I was lamenting the loss of my strip of pink sky when I caught sight of it afresh, but red this time, in the opposite window which it left at a second bend in the line, so that I spent my time running from one window to the other to reassemble, to collect on a single canvas the intermittent antipodean fragments of my fine scarlet, ever-changing morning, and to obtain a comprehensive view of it and a continuous picture.[47]

Time, then, is like a fourth dimension which in combining with the other three perfects space, assembling together and providing a new canvas for those opposed fragments, enclosing in a veritable continuity a totality which otherwise would remain irremediably dispersed. Seen through the perspective of time, space is set free, transcended.

But can anything do for time what time can do for space? Is time in itself a place of nonsimultaneities, of reciprocal exclusions, incapable of

[46] *Les Plaisirs et les jours*, p. 171.
[47] *Remembrance of Things Past*, I, 497.

unification by a supra-temporal action which would allow us to possess all its successive aspects simultaneously? Are the Méséglise Way and the Guermantes Way consigned irremediably to be forever sealed in the closed vases of different afternoons?

But, as we have seen, there is such a supra-temporal action: it is the metaphoric action of memory. Between times, between "intermittent and opposite qualities," the mind is found capable of establishing those rapports which are now no longer negative rapports. Between the regained moments of its existence the mind discovers identities; it finds in each of them a common root, its own essence. Applying this timeless presence, by means of art, to the entirety of existence, it is transported to a high place where all the temporal horizon is seen to rise tier on tier. Thus at the beginning of the novel, when the Méséglise Way and the Guermantes Way seem entirely and forever separated, a phrase of the parish priest of Combray gives presage of a day when they will be united. For from the top of the steeple, he says, "one encompasses at once things he can habitually see only one by one." This is the characteristic of metaphoric memory. It is the steeple which surmounts temporal extension, but which, in dominating it, far from abolishing it, gives it its completion. Time is truly achieved only if it is crowned by eternity. This human eternity, seized by the being in the possession of his essence, permits him retrospectively to contemplate beneath him that very time, his temporal being, formed of different levels of which each constitutes a stratum. A time which now seems to him singularly positive, an architecture. This musical architecture brings him sounds emanating from different parts of the edifice. As in the thought of Joubert, Proustian time expresses a music made of a spray of themes, each one of which remains distinct and constitutes a being, the ensemble of which is a *sum total:* "a plenitude of music, made complete, in effect, by so many various musics, each one a being."

Time regained is time transcended.

On the one hand, then, the Proustian novel seems to be a novel without duration. A being awakens in a moment of dearth which is replaced by a moment of plenitude—such plenitude that an immense meditation cannot suffice to exhaust its meaning. But within it, in the instant when it is accomplished, as in the *Cogito* of Descartes, everything is contained. Everything proceeds from one instant, from one cup of tea.

On the other hand, the novel of Proust seems, in the manner of other novels, to embrace the duration of an existence. But this existence is a retrospective existence. It is not a unity advancing into the future. It is an "ulterior unity found between fragments which are simply to be joined." It is from a preliminary plurality that it gently disengages itself and always under the form of a retrograde perspective which is found behind one, when one advances in the work, so to speak, backwards. For there is not a line in the book which does not purposely "provide the reader with an improvised memory" and produce in him the repeated and tardily meaningful memory of what he has already read. Everything is disposed under the form of recalls, so that the entire book is one immense "resonance box."

Resonance box in which are perceived not only the *times* of an individual existence and the *timeless* traits of a particular spirit; but where retrospectively are found also all the *times* of French thought, to its origins. For this being which awakens in a naked moment, like the being in Valéry, is going to immerse itself in the past, in the temporal depth of which Baudelaire sang, and for which Romanticism has had such a deep longing. If in the depths it regains the primitive impression, it is, like eighteenth-century thought, in order to grasp hold of itself in sensation and in the instantaneous. But it cannot equate itself with sensation, and, in spite of all, its being affirms itself essentially, not as an impression, but as a consciousness perpetually creating its moments of thought. A being always recreated, always re-found and always re-lost, as the human being is in all thought since Descartes, depending also on a precarious grace, as does the human being in all religious thought whether of the Reformation or of the Counter-Reformation, the Proustian being in the final count attains to this total structure of iself which human existence had lost after the Middle Ages. Like the vast *Summae* which were erected then, all is simultaneously discovered here on the different levels which are the tiers of time. And so the work of Proust appears as a retrospective view of all French thought on time, unfolding in time, like the church of Combray, its nave.

To the Reader

Marcel Proust

Happy the man who could write such a book, I thought to myself; what a mighty task before him! To give some idea of it, one would have to turn to the noblest and most diverse arts for comparisons; for this writer, who, moreover, would have to display the most contradictory sides of each of his characters in order to give his book the feel of solidity, would need to prepare it with minute care, constantly regrouping his forces as if for an attack, endure it like a trial, accept it like a rule of life, build it like a church, follow it like a regimen, overcome it like an obstacle, win it like a friendship, spoon-feed it like a child, create it like a world—without neglecting those mysteries whose key is probably to be found only in other worlds, the presentiment of which is the experience which moves us most deeply in life or art. And in those great books there are sections which there has been time only to sketch in and which will no doubt never be completed precisely because of the very magnitude of the architect's plan. How many great cathedrals remain unfinished! Such a work one nourishes over a long period of time, fortifies its weaker parts, cherishes it; but later it is the book itself which grows, marks our grave, protects it against false report and for a time against oblivion. But to return to myself, I had a more modest view of my book and it would be incorrect to say even that I was thinking of those who might read it as "my readers." For, to my mind, they would not be *my* readers but the very readers of themselves, my book serving only as a sort of magnifying glass, such as the optician of Combray used to offer to a customer; my book might supply the means by which they could read themselves. So that I would not ask them to praise me or to speak ill of me, but only to tell me that it is as I say, if the words which they read within themselves are, indeed, those which I have written.

A la recherche du temps perdu, III, 1032-1033. Selected and translated by Richard Macksey.

Chronology of Important Dates

1870	Dr. Adrien Proust marries Mlle Jeanne Weil.
1871, July 10	Birth of Marcel Proust at Auteuil, near Paris.
1880	Marcel Proust has his first attack of asthma.
1882-1889	Secondary education at the Lycée Condorcet.
1889	Receives his baccalaureate; military service in Orléans.
1888-1895	Begins to frequent the salons of Mme Emile Strauss, Madeleine Lemaire, Mme Armand de Caillavet as well as the Faubourg St. Germain; he becomes a friend of Count Robert de Montesquiou.
1890-1893	Studies at the Ecole des Sciences politiques and at the Sorbonne where he attends Henri Bergson's courses.
1892-1895	Summer stays at Trouville, on the Channel; articles on literature, art, and society life.
1896	Publishes *Les Plaisirs et les jours*. [English translation by Louise Varèse under the title *Pleasures and Regrets* (New York: Crown Publishers, 1948).]
1896-1901	Writes his unfinished novel posthumously published as *Jean Santeuil* in 1954. [English translation by Gerard Hopkins under the same title (New York: Simon and Schuster, Inc., 1956).]
1897	Duel with Jean Lorrain, a Paris journalist who had criticized *Les Plaisirs et les jours*.
1894-1900	Marcel Proust follows the famous *Affaire* with a good deal of pro-Dreyfus passion.
1900-1904	Articles on aesthetic subjects and society life.
1904	Translation of *The Bible of Amiens* by John Ruskin (*La Bible d'Amiens*), followed in 1906 by *Sesame and Lilies* (*Sésame et les lys*).
1905, September 26	Marcel Proust loses his mother; after a month in a sanatorium, he moves, early in 1906, to the famous cork-lined bedroom at 102 Boulevard Haussman, where he writes most of *Remembrance of Things Past*.

1913	*Swann's Way* (*Du Côté de chez Swann*), first volume of *Remembrance of Things Past* is published by Bernard Grasset, at the author's expense, after being rejected by several publishers.
1914	Albert Agostinelli, chauffeur and friend of Marcel Proust, is killed in an airplane accident.
1918	Publication by Librairie Gallimard of *Within a Budding Grove* (*A l'Ombre des jeunes filles en fleur*), which receives the Prix Goncourt in 1919.
1919	*Pastiches et Mélanges*.
1920	*Guermantes' Way* (*Du Côté de Guermantes*); *Cities of the Plain* (*Sodome et Gomorrhe*, I).
1922	*Sodome et Gomorrhe*, II.
1922, November 18	Marcel Proust dies.
1923-1927	Posthumous publication of the last volumes of *Remembrance of Things Past*.

Bibliography

A la recherche du temps perdu, edited by Pierre Clarac and André Ferré. 3 vols. Paris: Gallimard, Bibliothéque de la Pléiade, 1954. This excellent edition completes and supersedes all the earlier ones.
Remembrance of Things Past, translated by C. K. Scott-Moncrieff and Frederick A. Blossom. 2 vols. New York: Random House, 1932. This translation, which has been acclaimed as a model, is, of itself, a work of art. (Available in *Modern Library* editions.)
Blondel, C. A. *La Psychographie de Marcel Proust.* Paris: Vrin, 1932. One of the outstanding studies of Proustian psychology.
Cattaui, Georges. *Marcel Proust: documents iconographiques.* Geneva: Caïller, 1956. Photographs of Proust, his family and friends; the world of *Remembrance of Things Past* in pictures.
Curtiss, Mina. *Letters of Marcel Proust.* New York: Random House, 1949. An English translation of selected letters with notes and explanations.
Curtius, Ernst-Robert. *Französischer Geist im zwanzigen Jahrhundert.* Bern: Francke Verlag, 1952. (Previously published in *Französischer Geist im neun Europa.* Stuttgart: Deutsche Verlag-Anstalt, 1925.) There is a French translation of this important essay on Proust's style by Armand Pierhal. Paris: Editions de la Revue nouvelle, 1928.
Kolb, Philip. *La Correspondance de Marcel Proust: Chronologie et Commentaire critique.* Urbana, Ill.: The University of Illinois Press, 1949. A scholarly exposition of the problems posed by Proust's correspondence.
March, Harold. *The Two Worlds of Marcel Proust.* Philadelphia: University of Pennsylvania Press, 1948. A good introduction to the life and works of Proust, even though written before the publication of *Jean Santeuil.*
Martin-Chauffier, Louis. "Proust and the Double 'I'," *Partisan Review* (October 1949), pp. 1011-1026. An interesting article on the multiple role of Marcel, in the Proustian novel.
Maurois, André. *Proust: Portrait of a Genius.* Transalted by Gerard Hopkins. New York: Harper & Brothers, 1950. A good biography which makes use of unpublished documents.
O'Brien, Justin. "Albertine the Ambiguous: Notes on Proust's Transposition of Sexes," *Publications of the Modern Language Association* (December, 1949). For a discussion of this article, see: Harry Levin and Justin O'Brien, "Proust, Gide and the Sexes," *Publications of the Modern Language Association* (June, 1950). An interesting controversy on Proust's fictional transposition.
Painter, George D. *Proust: The Early Years.* Boston: Little Brown & Co., 1959. The first of a projected two-volume biography.
Wilson, Edmund. *Axel's Castle.* New York: Charles Scribner's Sons, 1931. Contains an interesting essay on Proust.